A Descriptive Catalogue

of the

Bibliographies of

20th Century British Writers

IN MEMORIAM S. L. M.

OBIIT MCMLXXI

A Descriptive Catalogue
of the
Bibliographies of
20th Century British Writers

by
Elgin W. Mellown

The Whitston Publishing Company
Incorporated
Troy, New York
1972

PREFACE

I have compiled this *Descriptive Catalogue* in order to assist the student and the general reader of twentieth-century British literature, in finding the most reliable bibliographical information for the authors of the period. The information located and described in the *Catalogue* makes possible a thorough, disciplined study of twentieth-century literature; and hopefully the *Catalogue* will also be of value to librarians and others who are seeking to establish reference holdings in an area which remains largely uncharted.

In the *Catalogue* I have listed (in alphabetical order and with birth and death years and pseudonyms) all the British writers who, born after 1840, published the larger part of their work in England or Ireland after 1890 or thereabouts and who have been the subject of bibliographical study. I have included authors less by judging the nature and quality of their work than by considering which ones the users of this *Catalogue* might expect to find here. Thus I list only the better-known writers in the social sciences and the sciences, but I include all the imaginative writers and writers in the humanities whom I have been able to name and for whom I have located bibliographies. It is probable that, if one does not find the name of such a writer here, there is no readily available, published bibliography of his work.

The bibliographical information is given in two forms. For those writers who have only been included in one or more of the General Bibliographies which are listed and described below (pp. viii-xii), the author-entries contain the appropriate abbreviations of these general bibliographies. For those writers who have been the subjects of more intensive bibliographical study, the author-entry is subdivided into three main sections. Under PRIMARY are

v

bibliographies of writings *by* the author, while under SECONDARY are lists of writings, either critical or biographical, *about* the author. Under GENERAL are those bibliographies listed below. The entries within these three sections are chronologically arranged, the aim being to list the most inclusive, informative, and authoritative bibliographies, and the inclusion of several seemingly similar items indicating that each one provides information not found in the others. I have also tried to find both a British and an American publication for each category. These PRIMARY and SECONDARY bibliographies are subsequently described in reference to four main areas:

I.   The scope of the work in question.

   Primary signifies that all writings and all editions are included. *Primary first editions* shows that all first editions or first publications are included, but not reprints or later editions. *Primary books* indicates that no other form is included. *Secondary* means that the compiler has attempted to list all writings about the author, while *secondary selected* shows that the compiler has consciously omitted some writings.

II.   The arrangement of each bibliography.

   The arrangement is described as either *Chronological*, indicating one year-by-year list; or *Form*, meaning that it is divided according to the form of publication--book,periodical, part of a book, etc.--and is generally chronological within each section; or *Genre*, indicating a division according to literary genre--poetry, drama, fiction, etc.--and generally a chronological arrangement within each section; or some special arrangement which is described.

III.   The details provided by each bibliography.

   The description may include:

      Transcribed title page;

Full collation: information concerning the format (the binder's term--quarto, octavo, etc.--is given), the signatures, the total number of pages, and the size of the volume in inches or centimetres;

Partial collation: information about two of the points listed above;

Pagination: description of each page;

Binding: description of physical appearance of volume;

Date of publication;

Price;

Number of copies;

Variants: an account of textual variants;

Reprints;

Contents: a list of titles or parts within the volume;

Notes: either bibliographical or textual.

IV. Evaluation of the bibliography.

When possible, I quote some authority; if the bibliography is the only one available, or if one should consult all of the bibliographies listed, there is generally no comment.

Since the GENERAL bibliographies give the same type of information for each author, the descriptions of them are given here, along with the abbreviations which refer to them in the *Catalogue.*

GENERAL BIBLIOGRAPHIES

Adelman & Dworkin.

Irving Adelman and Rita Dworkin. *Modern Drama. A Checklist of Critical Literature on 20th Century Plays.* Metuchen, N. J.: Scarecrow Press, 1967. Pp. 370.
> Alphabetical list of authors with titles of plays under each name; relevant studies under each title. Books: place, publisher, date. Periodicals: volume, date, pages.

Batho & Dobrée.

Edith Clara Batho and Bonamy Dobrée. *The Victorians and After, 1830-1914.* Volume IV, *Introductions to English Literature,* General Editor, Bonamy Dobrée. New York: R. M. McBride and Co.; London: Cresset Press, 1938. Pp. 370.
> Authors arranged by genre and chronology; for each author, titles and dates of primary books arranged by genre; selected secondary books. A British guide for the beginning student.

Bufkin.

E. C. Bufkin. *The Twentieth-Century Novel in English: A Checklist.* Athens: University of Georgia Press, 1967. Pp. vi, 138.
> Alphabetical list of authors with titles of their novels (no other genre included). Title, place, publisher, date, of first English edition.

CBEL.

F. W. Bateson and George Watson, editors. *Cambridge Bibliography of English Literature.* Cambridge University Press, 1941,

1957. Four volumes with supplementary volume five.
Authors arranged by genre of work. For each author, primary
books with date, sub-divided by genre. Selected secondary
bibliography. Authoritative lists of primary writings. For
most authors the NCBEL (below) replaces the CBEL.

Coleman & Tyler.

Arthur Coleman and Gary R. Tyler. *Drama Criticism. Volume
One. A Checklist of Interpretation since 1940 of English and
American Plays*. Denver: Alan Swallow, 1966. Pp. 457.
Alphabetical list of authors with titles of plays under each
name; relevant studies under each title. Includes criticism
written between 1940 and 1964. Books: place, publisher,
date. Periodicals: volume, date, pages.

Daiches.

David Daiches. *The Present Age. After 1920*. Volume V, *Introductions to English Literature*, General Editor, Bonamy Dobrée.
London: Cresset Press; Bloomington: Indiana University Press,
1958. Pp. x, 376.
Authors arranged by genre and chronology; for each author,
titles and dates of primary books arranged by genre; selected
secondary books. A British guide for the beginning student.

Hagen.

Ordean A. Hagen. *Who Done It? A Guide to Detective, Mystery
and Suspense Fiction*. New York and London: R. R. Bowker Co.,
1969. Pp. xx, 834.
Alphabetical list of authors with titles of their "detective,
mystery, or suspense" books only. English and American
titles (if different), publisher, date. Various appendices and
indices. Since this is the obvious source for bibliographical
information concerning such writers, I have not included
authors who are listed only in Hagen.

Hetherington.

John [Aikman] Hetherington. *Forty-Two Faces.* London: Angus and Robertson; Melbourne: F. W. Cheshire Pty Ltd., 1963. Pp. [xiv] , 250.
> Chronological list of authors. For each, short biographical essay and list of primary books: place, publisher, date. Essay usually suggests titles of other primary writings.

Longaker & Bolles.

Mark Longaker and Edwin C. Bolles. *Contemporary English Literature.* New York: Appleton-Century Crofts, Inc., 1953. Pp. [xviii] 526.
> Information as in Millett (below); in addition short discussions of each author, the whole arranged under headings determined by genre and chronology. For the beginning student.

Millett.

Fred B. Millett. *Contemporary British Literature. A Critical Survey and 232 Author Bibliographies.* Third revised and enlarged edition, based on the second revised and enlarged edition by John M. Manly and Edith Rickert. New York: Harcourt, Brace and Co., 1935, 1950. Pp. [xii] , 556.
> One alphabetical list of authors. For each author, titles and dates of primary books arranged by genre; short secondary selected bibliography of books (author, title, date) and periodicals (volume, date, pages). Ends at 1934. Obviously restricted in scope but very useful for the beginning student.

NCBEL.

George Watson, ed. *New Cambridge Bibliography of English Literature. Volume III. 1800-1900.* Cambridge University Press, 1969. Pp. xxiv; columns 1-1948; Index, pp. 1949-[1956] .
> Information as in CBEL (above). Authoritative primary checklists of book titles, with place and date.

Palmer & Dyson.

Helen H. Palmer and Anne Jane Dyson. *European Drama Criticism*. Hamden, Conn.: Shoe String Press, Inc., 1968. Pp. [viii], 460.
> Alphabetical list of authors with titles of plays and date of performance under each name; relevant studies under each title. Books: publisher, date, pages. Periodicals: volume, date, pages.

Salem.

James M. Salem. *A Guide to Critical Reviews. Part III. British and Continental Drama from Ibsen to Pinter.* Metuchen, N. J.: Scarecrow Press, Inc., 1968. Pp. 309.
> Alphabetical list of authors with titles of plays under each name; date of first American performance (1909-1966) of each play and reviews of this performance. Periodicals: volume, pages, date. Various appendices and Index.

Temple & Tucker.

Ruth Z. Temple and Martin Tucker. *Twentieth Century British Literature: A Reference Guide and Bibliography.* New York: Frederick Ungar Publishing Co., 1968. Pp. x, 261.
> Alphabetical list of authors; for each author, titles, dates, and genre of primary books; title of one or two critical or bibliographical studies. The American contender for the audience of the not-yet-published NCBEL, 1900-1950. Various appendices and indices, and useful checklists of primary books.

WW or WWW.

Who's Who or Who Was Who. London: A. and C. Black; New York: St. Martin's Press.
> Information supplied by the subject of the entry (and hence sometimes erroneous or incomplete): usually titles and dates of books. Since the information varies so much from one entry to another, I have referred to *Who's Who* only for those authors whose entries provide a list of books which appears to be almost complete or which supplements existing bibliographies. Periodicals to which the author contributed are sometimes referred to, but details of specific contributions are never listed.

ABBREVIATIONS

AWTW. *Australian Writers and Their Work*

TEAS. *Twayne's English Authors Series*

TUSAS. *Twayne's United States Authors Series*

WTW. *Writers and Their Work*

Periods. Periodicals

During the four and a half years that I have worked on the *Catalogue*, I have been assisted by various persons, and it gives me pleasure to thank them here. I am grateful to the Duke Research Council for financial assistance that enabled me to spend the summer, 1967, at the British Museum Reading Room, and to the Duke Endowment for subsequent financial assistance. I appreciate both the personal and professional kindnesses shown to me by Ian R. Willison, Assistant Keeper and Superintendent of the North Library of the British Museum Reading Room; but indeed I am indebted to the entire staff of the Reading Room for assistance over a number of years: my work on this particular project confirmed once again what all students privileged to use the Reading Room know: that helpfulness, courtesy, and efficiency are unfailing at the British Museum. I have also been greatly helped by the Acquisitions Department of the William R. Perkins Library, Duke University, and by members of the Reference Department, especially Miss Florence Blakely and Miss Mary Canada; and also by the staff of the Woman's College Library, particularly the Librarian, Miss Evelyn Harrison. And to my family and colleagues, especially Professors Grover Smith and Ronald Butters, who have all patiently listened to "some little talk awhile"--of collations and paginations--, I give my thanks for indulgent forbearance.

December, 1971.   Elgin W. Mellown
                                                   Duke University

A DESCRIPTIVE CATALOGUE

A. E. or Æ: see RUSSELL, GEORGE WILLIAM

ABERCROMBIE, LASCELLES   (1881-1938)

PRIMARY

Jeffrey Cooper. *A Bibliography and Notes on the Works of Lascelles Abercrombie.* London: Kaye and Ward, Ltd., 1968; Hamden, Conn.: Archon Books, 1969. Pp. 166.

Primary complete. Form arrangement. Books: transcribed TP, full collation, pagination, binding, date, price, contents, extensive notes on textual history and bibliography of each piece of writing. Periods (arranged alphabetically by title of periodical): volume, pages, date, extensive notes on Abercrombie's association with each periodical. Reviews by Abercrombie include author and title of book reviewed. Each section begins with list of books or periodical titles described in the section. Pp. 150-152, Table of Item Numbers in Chronological Order. Pp. 155-166, Index. An authoritative and extremely helpful work.

GENERAL

Millett; Longaker & Bolles; Daiches; Batho and Dobrée; Temple & Tucker.

ACKERLEY, JOE RANDOLPH   (1896-1967)

PRIMARY

J. R. Ackerley. *My Father and Myself.* London: Bodley Head, 1968. Pp. 219.

Although there is no bibliography in this autobiography, there are many references to Ackerley's writings, with his books being listed on p. [2].

GENERAL

Bufkin.

ACKLAND, RODNEY   (1908-   )

WW 71.

ACTON, HAROLD MARIO   (1904-   )

WW 71.

ADCOCK, ARTHUR ST. JOHN   (1864-1930)

WWW 29-40.

AGATE, JAMES EVERSHED   (1877-1947)

PRIMARY

James Agate. *An Anthology*. Herbert Van Thal, ed. Introduction by Alan Dent. London: Rupert Hart-Davis, 1961. Pp. [xxiv], 288.

P. ii, list of primary books, 1917-1949. Chronological arrangement. Date. Pp. ix-xxiii, bibliographical information, *passim*.

Additional information can be gained from Agate's autobiography, *Ego* (Vols. 1-9), London, 1935-1948.

GENERAL

Temple & Tucker.

ALDINGTON, RICHARD   (1892-1962)

PRIMARY

Alistair Kershaw. *A Bibliography of the Works of Richard Aldington from 1915 to 1948.* London: Quadrant Press, 1950. Pp. [xii] , 57.

Primary books. Genre arrangement. Transcribed TP, part collation, date, occasionally contents, printer. Includes translations by Aldington.

Kershaw modestly describes his work as "an extended checklist," but it is quite complete.

-- and Frédéric-Jacques Temple, eds. *Richard Aldington An Intimate Portrait.* Carbondale: Southern Illinois University Press, 1965. Pp. [xxii] , 186.

Pp. 175-186, "A Chronological Checklist of the Books of Richard Aldington," by Paul Schlueter. Primary British and American first editions. Genre arrangement. Place, publisher, year, bibliographical notes by Kershaw. Includes translations and books edited or introduced by Aldington.

A convenient checklist which adds to Kershaw's bibliography.

SECONDARY

V. M. Parchevskaia. *Richard Aldington.* Moscow: Kniga Publishing House (Writers of Foreign Countries Series), 1965. Pp.[60] .

Pp. 21-29, primary bibliography. Pp. 30-47, secondary bibliography. Arranged: General Criticism; English and American Reviews, Russian Reviews (listed under titles by Aldington being reviewed). Books: place, publisher, date, pages. Periods: volume, pages, date. (In Russian)

GENERAL

Millett; Longaker & Bolles; Daiches; Temple & Tucker.

ALDISS, BRIAN WILSON   (1925-   )

PRIMARY

Margaret Manson. *Item Forty-three: Brian Wilson Aldiss, A Bibliography, 1954-1962.* Wisbech, 1963. Pp. 28.

Not seen.

GENERAL

W W 71.

ALDRIDGE, HAROLD EDWARD JAMES   (1918-   )

Hetherington; W W 71.

ALEXANDER, SAMUEL   (1859-1938)

Batho & Dobrée; CBEL, III, 861; V, 689.

ALLEN, WALTER ERNEST   (1911-   )

Temple & Tucker; WW 71.

ALVAREZ, ALFRED   (1929-   )

WW 71.

AMBLER, ERIC   (1909-   )

PRIMARY

[?Paxton Davis]. "Books by Eric Ambler." *Hollins Critic* 8 (February 1971): 6-7.

Primary books, all English-language editions. Chronological arrangement. Place, publisher, date, price, British and American titles. Filmscripts by Ambler listed on p. 5 with suggestion of other primary writings.

GENERAL

Bufkin; WW 71; Hagen.

AMIS, KINGSLEY WILLIAM   (1922-   )

SECONDARY

J. Don Vann and James T. F. Tanner. "Kingsley Amis. A Check-list of Recent Criticism." *Bulletin of Bibliography* 26 (1969): 115-117, 105, 111.

   Alphabetical by author arrangement. Books: place, publisher, date. Periods: volume, date, pages.

   A comprehensive list including reviews.

GENERAL

Temple & Tucker; Bufkin; WW 71.

ANGELL, SIR RALPH NORMAN   (1874-1967)

PRIMARY

Norman Angell. *After All. The Autobiography of Norman Angell.* London: Hamish Hamilton, 1951. Pp. 370.

   Pp. 357-358, primary books, 1903-1947. Dates. Other biblio-graphical information in text, *passim.*

GENERAL

Daiches; WW 68.

ANSON, SIR WILLIAM   (1843-1914)

Batho & Dobrée; CBEL, III, 920; V, 696.

ANSTEY, F. (1856-1934)

Pseudonym of Thomas Anstey Guthrie.

PRIMARY

Martin John Turner. *Bibliography of the Works of F. Anstey* [*Thomas Anstey Guthrie*]. London: Privately Published, 1931. Pp. 44. 150 copies.

Primary. Form arrangement. Transcribed TP, full collation, binding, date, variants, reprints, contents. Contributions to periodicals other than *Punch* listed. Index.

Lord Esher, *Book Collector's Quarterly*, No. 5 (January-March 1932), p. 36: "an almost perfect example of bibliographical work."

F. Anstey. *A Long Retrospect*. London and New York: Oxford University Press, 1936. Pp. 424.

Pp. 415-416, primary books, 1882-1936. Title, date. Occasional references to periodical contributions in text, *passim*.

GENERAL

Batho & Dobrée; Temple & Tucker; NCBEL, III, 1034.

ANTHONY, C. L. : see SMITH, DODIE

ARCHER, WILLIAM (1856-1924)

PRIMARY

Lt. Col. Charles Archer. *William Archer: Life, Work and Friendships*. London: George Allen and Unwin, 1931. Pp. 451.

Pp. 421-434, "Bibliographic Appendix." Primary. Chronological arrangement. Books: publisher, pages. Periods:

date. English works edited by Archer listed alphabetically by main author with publisher, date. Translations or books edited by Archer listed alphabetically by main author with publisher, date.

SECONDARY

Above, Archer, text and footnotes, *passim*.

GENERAL

Batho & Dobrée; Temple & Tucker; Salem; Palmer & Dyson; NCBEL, III, 1417-1418.

ARDEN, JOHN   (1930-   )

Coleman & Tyler; Adelman & Dworkin; WW 71.

ARLEN, MICHAEL   (1895-1956)

Pseudonym of Dikran Kuyumjian

PRIMARY

Hans Carl Guggenbühl. *Michael Arlen, Kritiker der Englischen Gesellschaft.* Zurich: Buchdruckerei Dr. J. Weiss, 1937. Pp. 139.

P. [vii], "Literaturverzeichnis." Selected primary and secondary bibliography. Books: publisher, date. Periods: date.

SECONDARY

Above, Guggenbühl, p. [vii].

GENERAL

Daiches; Temple & Tucker.

ARLOTT, LESLIE THOMAS JOHN   (1914-   )

WW 71.

ARMSTRONG, MARTIN DONISTHORPE   (1882-   )

PRIMARY

R. L. Mégroz. *Five Novelist Poets*. London: Joiner and Steele, 1933.

Pp. 245-246, primary books, first editions, 1912-1932. Chronological arrangement. Publisher, place, pages, date.

Martin Armstrong. Poet and Novelist: A Bibliography. Bristol: Public Libraries, 1937. Pp. [4].

Not seen.

GENERAL

Millett; Temple & Tucker; WW 71.

ARMSTRONG, TERENCE: see GAWSWORTH, JOHN

ASHTON, WINIFRED: see DANE, CLEMENCE

ASQUITH, LADY CYNTHIA   (-1960)

(Lady Cynthia, Mrs. Herbert Asquith).

WWW 51-60; Hagen.

ASQUITH, HON. HERBERT   (1881-1947)

WWW 41-50; Hagen.

AUDEN, WYSTAN HUGH   (1907-   )

PRIMARY

Edward Callan. "An Annotated Checklist of the Works of W. H.
Auden." *Twentieth Century Literature* 4 (1958): 30-50.
Separately published: Denver: Allan Swallow, 1958. Pp. 26.

P. 6, list of earlier bibliographies, not given in Bloomfield,
below.

B [arry] C [ambray] Bloomfield. *W. H. Auden. A Bibliography:
The Early Years through 1955.* Charlottesville: University of
Virginia Press, 1964. Pp. [xxii], [174].

Primary complete, secondary selected. Form arrangement.
Books: transcribed TP, part collation, pagination, binding,
date, price, contents, number of copies, textual and publish-
ing notes, reviews of primary books listed after each title.
Periods: volume, pages, date. Reviews by Auden include title
and author of book reviewed. Appendices list: Unpublished
Work; MSS; Anthologies; Musical Settings; Translations [of
Auden]. Pp. 136-142, secondary bibliography. Index.

R. J. Roberts, *Book Collector* 14 (1965): 389: "exemplary in
the accuracy of its descriptions, as it is in the completeness
of its contents."

Monroe K. Spears. *The Poetry of W. H. Auden. The Disen-
chanted Island.* London, New York: Oxford University Press,
1968. Pp. xx, 394.

Pp. 348-372, alphabetical list of first lines; title of poem,
places of publication and volumes in which collected. See
also the "Chronologies" (pp. x-xiii, 3-5, 75-79, 167-170,
251-261) for mention of other primary writings.

Edward Callan. "W. H. Auden. Annotated Checklist II. (1958-
1969)." *Twentieth Century Literature* 16 (1970): 27-56.

Primary complete for 1958-1969. Genre arrangement, subdivided by form. Books: place, publisher, date, contents,

limitations of issue. Periods: volume, pages, date. Reviews by Auden include title and author of book reviewed. Supplements earlier bibliographies by Callan and Bloomfield (above).

SECONDARY

Above, Bloomfield, pp. 1-64, reviews of books by Auden; also pp. 136-142; Spears, *passim*.

Joseph P. Clancy. "A. W. H. Auden Bibliography 1924-1955." *Thought* 30 (Summer 1955): 260-270.

Pp. 266-270, secondary bibliography arranged alphabetically by author.

George T. Wright. *W. H. Auden.* New York: Twayne Publishers, Inc. (TUSAS 144), 1969. Pp. 180.

Pp. 170-173, secondary bibliography. Form arrangement. Annotated.

John E. Stoll. *W. H. Auden: A Reading.* Muncie: Ball State University (Monograph No. 18; Publication in English No. 12), 1970. Pp. [iv], 40.

Pp. 38-40, secondary bibliography arranged alphabetically by author. "Especially relevant" items marked with an asterisk.

GENERAL

Longaker & Bolles; Daiches; Temple & Tucker; Coleman & Tyler; Adelman & Dworkin; Salem; Palmer & Dyson; WW 71.

AUSTIN, ALFRED (1835-1913)

PRIMARY

Norton B. Crowell. *Alfred Austin, Victorian.* Albuquerque: University of New Mexico Press; London: Weidenfeld and Nicolson, 1955. Pp. [x], 296.

Pp. 268-273, primary bibliography. Form arrangement. Books: place, publisher, date. Periods: volume, pages, date. Pp. 273-291, secondary bibliography.

SECONDARY

Above, Crowell, pp. 273-291.

GENERAL

NCBEL, III, 608-609.

AYER, SIR ALFRED JULES (1910-   )

Daiches; WW 71.

AYRTON, MICHAEL (1921-   )

WW 71.

BABINGTON-SMITH, CONSTANCE (1912-   )

PRIMARY

Rose Macaulay. *Last Letters to a Friend 1952-1958*, ed. Constance Babington-Smith. New York: Atheneum, 1963. Pp. [289].

P. [2] and p. 244, primary books with dates.

BAGNOLD, ENID (-   )

(Lady Jones)
Coleman & Tyler; Adelman & Dworkin; Salem; Palmer & Dyson; WW 71.

BAKER, JAMES FRANKLIN BETHUNE-　　　　　(1861-1951)

PRIMARY

Edward Ely. "James Franklin Bethune-Baker, 1861-1951." *Proceedings of the British Academy* 39 (1953): 355-362.

Pp. 361-362, primary books. Chronological arrangement. Place, year.

BALCHIN, NIGEL MARLIN　　　　　　　　　(1908-1970)

Pseudonym used: Mark Spade.

Bufkin; Temple & Tucker; WW 70.

BALFOUR, ARTHUR JAMES, LORD BALFOUR　　(1848-1930)

PRIMARY

Denis Judd. *Balfour and the British Empire. A Study in Imperial Evolution 1874-1932.* London: Macmillan; New York: St. Martin's Press, 1968. Pp. 392.

Pp. [361]-366, bibliography arranged: Manuscript sources; Parliamentary papers and documents; Periodical articles; Unpublished writings; Books (date and place). Primary and secondary writings together.

GENERAL

CBEL, III, 862; V, 689.

BARBELLION, W. N. P.　　　　　　　　　　(1889-1919)

Pseudonym of Bruce Frederick Cummings

Dictionary of National Biography, 1912-1921.

BARING, MAURICE   (1874-1945)

PRIMARY

"Bibliographies of Modern Authors. The Hon. Maurice Baring."
London Mercury 2 (1920): 346.

Primary books, 1899-1920. Genre arrangement. Publisher,
date.

Leslie Chaundy. *A Bibliography of the First Editions of the
Works of Maurice Baring.* Introduction by Desmond McCarthy.
London: Dulau, 1925. Pp. 48. 250 copies.

Primary books, first editions. Chronological arrangement.
Transcribed TP, part collation, binding, date, brief notes.

Louis Chaigne. *Maurice Baring. Biographie.* Paris: J. de
Gigord, 1935. Pp. 72.

Pp. 67-70, primary books. Chronological arrangement. Dates.
French translations listed separately: translator, publisher,
date. Pp. 71-72, secondary bibliography.

Paul Horgan, ed. *Maurice Baring Restored: Selections from his
Work.* New York: Farrar, Strauss, and Giroux, 1970. Pp.
[x], [444].

Pp. 439-440, primary books. Dates.

SECONDARY

Above, Chaigne, pp. 71-72.

GENERAL

Millett; Batho & Dobrée; Daiches; Temple & Tucker.

BARKER, SIR ERNEST   (1874-1960)

Daiches; WWW 51-60.

BARKER, GEORGE GRANVILLE   (1913-   )

PRIMARY

Martha Fodaski. *George Barker*. New York: Twayne Publishers, Inc. (TEAS 90), 1969. Pp. 190.

Pp. 182-184, primary bibliography. Genre arrangement. Books: place, publisher, date. Periods: volume, date, pages. Includes book reviews by Barker with author and title of book reviewed. Pp. 184-185, Secondary bibliography, annotated. Information as for primary; see notes, pp. 175-181, for additional secondary criticism.

Not a complete record of Barker's extensive writings, but at least a start toward it.

SECONDARY

Above, Fodaski, pp. 175-181, 184-185.

GENERAL

Longaker & Bolles; Daiches; Temple & Tucker; WW 71.

BARKER, H. GRANVILLE: see GRANVILLE-BARKER, H.

BARLOW, JAMES   (1921-   )

WW 71; Hagen.

BARLOW, JANE   (1857-1917)

NCBEL, III, 1908.

BARNSLEY, ALAN GABRIEL: see FIELDING, GABRIEL

BARRIE, SIR JAMES MATTHEW   (1860-1937)

PRIMARY

Herbert Garland. *A Bibliography of the Writings of Sir James M. Barrie.* London: Bookman's Journal, 1928. Pp. 146.

Primary complete, secondary selected, 1887-1924. Form arrangement. Books: transcribed TP, full collation, binding, date, contents, notes. Periods: dates; includes unsigned writings. Pp. 139-141, secondary books.

Bradley D. Cutler. *Sir James M. Barrie. A Bibliography, with Full Collations of the American Unauthorized Editions.* New York: Greenberg, 1931. Pp. 242. 1000 copies.

Primary books, secondary selected. Transcribed TP, part collation, pagination, binding, date, variants, notes. Pp. 223-233, prices and price trends of first editions. Pp. 215-220, secondary books.

Supplements Garland with the American edns. Additional prices are given in Andrew Block. *Sir James M. Barrie His First Editions: Points and Values.* London: W. and G. Foyle Ltd., 1933. Pp. 48. 500 copies. Alphabetical list of primary books: publisher, date, size, binding, value in sterling.

Roger Lancelyn Green. *James M. Barrie.* London: Bodley Head (Bodley Head Monograph), 1960. Pp. 64.

Pp. 59-64, "Book List." Genre, form arrangement. Publisher, date. Selected secondary bibliography.

Together these three works include most of the primary books; there is no complete list of Barrie's periodical contributions.

SECONDARY

Above, Garland, pp. 139-141; Cutler, pp. 215-220; Green, p. 64.

Katharine G. Shields. "Sir James M. Barrie, Bart., Being a Partial Bibliography." *Bulletin of Bibliography* 16 (1937): 44-46,

68-69, 97, 119, 140-141, 162.

Arranged under six topical divisions. Books: publisher, place, year, annotations. Periods: volume, pages, date, annotations.

Harry M. Geduld. Sir James Barrie. New York: Twayne Publishers, Inc. (TEAS 105), 1971. Pp. 187.

Pp. 180-184, bibliography. Books: place, publisher, date. Period: volume, pages, Date. Annotated. Additional items in notes, pp. 173-177.

GENERAL

Millett; Longaker & Bolles; Daiches; Temple & Tucker; Coleman & Tyler; Adelman & Dworkin; Salem; Palmer & Dyson; NCBEL, III, 1188-1192.

BARSTOW, STANLEY   (1928-   )

WW 71.

BATES, HERBERT ERNEST   (1905-   )

PRIMARY

John Gawsworth. *Ten Contemporaries. Notes Toward their Definitive Bibliography (Second Series).* London: Joiner & Steele Ltd., 1933. Pp. 240. 1000 copies.

Pp. 23-34, primary books, first editions, 1926-1932. Chronological arrangement. Transcribed TP, full collation, pagination, binding, date, bibliographical notes.

H. E. Bates. *The Vanished World. An Autobiography. Volume One.* London: Michael Joseph, 1969; Columbia: University of Missouri Press, 1971. Pp. [189].

Autobiography of childhood and adolescent years with little information concerning literary career; see p. [2] for list of primary books, arranged by genre.

GENERAL

Millett; Longaker & Bolles; Daiches; Temple & Tucker; WW 71.

BATES, RALPH   (1899-   )

Daiches; Bufkin; Temple & Tucker; WW 71.

BATESON, FREDERICK NOEL WILSE   (1901-   )

Temple & Tucker; WW 71.

BATHO, EDITH CLARA   (1895-   )

Daiches; WW 71.

BAX, SIR ARNOLD EDWARD TREVOR   (1883-1953)

PRIMARY

George Brandon Saul. "Of Tales Half-Forgotten." *Arizona Quarterly* 18 (1962): 151-154.

An essay with bibliographical information in text, *passim*.

BAX, CLIFFORD   (1886-1962)

Temple & Tucker.

BEACHCROFT, THOMAS OWEN   (1902-   )

Daiches; WW 71.

BEARDSLEY, AUBREY VINCENT   (1872-1898)

PRIMARY

A. E. Gallatin. *Aubrey Beardsley. Catalogue of Drawings and Bibliography.* New York: Grolier Club, 1945. Pp. 162. 300 copies.

Pp. 17-70, catalogue of drawings (1096 entries). Pp. 73-128, primary and secondary bibliography. Information arranged under these headings: Albums of Drawings, Monographs on Beardsley, Studies on Beardsley in Books and Periodicals, Beardsley's Literary Work, Collections of Beardsley's Letters, Catalogues of Beardsley Exhibitions. Appendices.

Additional information is provided by R. A. Walker. *Le Morte Darthur with Beardsley Illustrations. A Bibliographical Essay.* Bedford: Published by the Author, 1945. Pp. 24. 350 copies; and by A. E. Gallatin and Alexander D. Wainright, *The Gallatin Beardsley Collection in the Princeton University Library, A Catalogue.* Princeton University Press, 1952. Pp. 43. First published in the *Princeton University Library Chronicle* 10 (1949): 81-84; 12 (1951): 67-82; 126-147.

SECONDARY

Above, Gallatin (1945).

GENERAL

NCBEL, III, 610-611.

BEATON, CECIL WALTER HARDY   (1904-   )

WW 71.

BEAUMONT, CYRIL WILLIAM   (1891-   )

WW 71.

BECKETT, SAMUEL BARCLAY   (1906-   )

PRIMARY

Raymond Federman and John Fletcher. *Samuel Beckett. His
Works and His Critics. An Essay in Bibliography.* Berkeley:
University of California Press, 1970. Pp.[xiv], 383.

Pp. 1-109, primary complete. Pp. 113-319, secondary complete
(described below). Arranged by language in which written, or
by genre; chronological in each section. Books: transcribed
TP, part collation, pagination, binding, date, price, number of
copies, variants, reprints and subsequent editions, extensive bibliographical notes and annotations. Periods: volume, pages,
date, reprintings, notes. Extensive appendices and indices.
Pp. ix-xiii, explanation of arrangement.

SECONDARY

Federman and Fletcher, described above.

Pp. 113-319, secondary complete. Form arrangement. Books:
place, publisher, date, pages, contents, critical résumé, reviews. Periods: volume, date, pages, reprints, annotations.
Additional primary and secondary bibliographies listed on pp.
317-319.

The authoritative bibliography of primary writings and the
starting point for all study of Beckett.

James T. F. Tanner and J. Don Vann. *Samuel Beckett. A Checklist of Criticism.* Kent: Kent State University Press (Serif
Series No. 8), 1969. Pp. [vi], 85.

Secondary selected. Form arrangement with reviews of books
about Becket listed under book title; pp. 73-85, reviews of
Beckett's books listed under title of book reviewed. Books:
place, publisher, date, pages. Periods: volume, date, pages.

A useful checklist, particularly in its isolation of the book
reviews of Beckett's writings.

GENERAL
Temple & Tucker; Coleman & Tyler; Adelman & Dworkin; Salem;
Palmer & Dyson; WW 71.

BEDFORD, SYBILLE   (1911-   )

Temple & Tucker; Bufkin.

BEECHING, HENRY CHARLES   (1859-1919)

PRIMARY

George Arthur Stephen. "An Annotated Bibliography of the Writings of Dean Beeching and the Works Edited by Him." *Norwich
Public Library Reader's Guide* 7 (April 1919): 82-90.

Not seen.

GENERAL

NCBEL, III, 611.

BEEDING, FRANCIS: see PALMER, JOHN LESLIE.

BEERBOHM, SIR HENRY MAXIMILIAN   (1872-1956)

PRIMARY

A. E. Gallatin. *Sir Max Beerbohm: Bibliographical Notes.* Cambridge, Mass.: Harvard University Press, 1944. Pp. 121. 400
copies.

Primary complete, secondary selected. Form arrangement.
Transcribed TP, part collation, binding, date, contents.

-- and L. M. Oliver. *A Bibliography of the Works of Max Beerbohm.*
London: Rupert Hart-Davis (Soho Bibliography No. 3), 1952.
Pp. 60.

Primary books. Chronological arrangement. Transcribed TP, full collation, pagination, binding, date. Full account of subsequent editions; limits of publication. Full bibliographical notes. Pp. 57-60, description of MSS in the Gallatin and Harvard collections.

J. G. Riewald. *Sir Max Beerbohm, Man and Writer. A Critical Analysis with a Brief Life and a Bibliography.* Hague: Martinus Nijhoff, 1953. Pp. 369.

Pp. 213-333, bibliography. Primary complete, secondary complete. Form arrangement. Transcribed TP, full collation, pagination, binding, date, price, number of copies. Subsequent editions and reprints described briefly; extensive notes; for each title a list of early reviews. Pp. 306- 333, secondary bibliography. Pp. 333-343, subject index to Beerbohm's dramatic criticism.

P. 213: Riewald describes his work as a "reasonably complete list of the published works, both collected and uncollected... and of the secondary studies and notes." An overwhelmingly inclusive list--yet the differences between Riewald, Gallatin (1944), and Gallatin and Oliver are so great that the three books must be used together, no one being complete in itself.

Roy Huss. "Max Beerbohm's Drawings of Theatrical Figures." *Theatre Notebook* 21 (1966-1967): 75-86, 102-119, 169-180.

Described by Huss as a "*catalogue raisonné* of Max's drawings of theatrical figures...designed as the pictorial counterpart of J. G. Riewald's index..." (p. 75). A comprehensive catalogue giving all required information.

SECONDARY

Above, Gallatin (1944), pp. 93-100; Riewald, pp. 306-333.

GENERAL

Millett; Longaker & Bolles; Batho & Dobrée; Temple & Tucker.

21

BEHAN, BRENDAN (1922-1964)

PRIMARY

[?Benedict Kiely]. "Books by Brendan Behan." *Hollins Critic* 2 (February 1965): 7.

Primary books, all English-language editions. Chronological arrangement. Place, publisher, date, price.

SECONDARY

Sean McCann, ed. *The World of Brendan Behan.* London: New English Library Ltd. (Four Square Book), 1965.

Collection of 21 critical and biographical essays. Bibliographical information in the text, *passim.*

GENERAL

Temple & Tucker; Coleman & Tyler; Adelman & Dworkin; Palmer & Dyson.

BEITH, MAJOR GENERAL JOHN HAY: see HAY, IAN.

BELL, ADRIAN HANBURY (1901-   )

WW 71.

BELL, ARTHUR CLIVE HEWARD (1881-1964)

PRIMARY

Solomon Fishman. *The Interpretation of Art.* Berkeley and Los Angeles: University of California Press, 1963. Pp. 196.

Pp. 73-75, life chronology of Bell. Gives titles and dates of principal works.

GENERAL

Millett; Daiches; Temple & Tucker.

BELL, GERTRUDE MARGARET LOWTHIAN   (1868-1926)

PRIMARY

Winifred Cotterill Donkin. *Catalogue of the Gertrude Bell Collection in the Library of King's College, Newcastle-upon-Tyne.* University Library, 1960. Pp. 64.

Catalogue of the collection formed by Bell. P. 12, list of 15 items by and about Bell.

GENERAL

Daiches.

BELL, HENRY THOMAS MACKENZIE   (1856-1930)

NCBEL, III, 612; WWW 29-40.

BELL, QUENTIN CLAUDIAN STEPHEN   (1910-   )

WW 71.

BELLOC, JOSEPH HILAIRE PIERRE   (1870-1953)

PRIMARY

Norah Nicholls. "The First Editions of Hilaire Belloc." *Bookman* (London) 81 (1931): 62, 126-127.

Primary books. Chronological arrangement. Publisher, year, format, binding, illustrator. Bibliographical notes.

Patrick Cahill. *The English First Editions of Hilaire Belloc.*

London: [published by the author], 1953. Pp. 52.

Primary books. Chronological arrangement. Transcribed TP, part collation, binding, date, price, variants, extensive bibliographical notes.

N&Q 198 (1953): 365: "one or two small omissions [these are included in the review]...in this otherwise admirable bibliography." P. 452, reply by Cahill.

A list of books and pamphlets (with date and publisher) taken from Cahill is given in Robert Speaight. *The Life of Hilaire Belloc*. London: Hollis and Carter, 1957. Pp. 539-544; and is repeated in Herbert Van Thal, ed. *Belloc*. *A Biographical Anthology*. London: George Allen and Unwin, Ltd., 1970. Pp. 391-396.

Renée Haynes. *Hilaire Belloc*. London: Longmans, Green, and Co., Ltd. (WTW 35), 1958. Pp. 35.

Pp. 31-35, primary books. Chronological arrangement. Date, genre. P. 35, selected secondary books.

SECONDARY

Above, Haynes, p. 35.

GENERAL

Millett; Longaker & Bolles; Batho & Dobrée; Temple & Tucker.

BENNETT, ENOCH ARNOLD   (1867-1931)

PRIMARY

Georges Lafourcade. *Arnold Bennett*. *A Study*. London: Frederick Muller Ltd., 1939. Pp. 300.

Pp. 281-291, bibliography of primary books, first editions. Genre arrangement. Publisher, date, contents. Pp. 291-293, secondary bibliography.

James G. Hepburn. *The Art of Arnold Bennett*. Bloomington: Indiana University Press, 1963. Pp. 247.

Pp. 222-233, bibliography of primary books, first editions, and of selected periodical contributions. Genre arrangement. Place, publisher, date, important bibliographical notes. Pp. 233-238, secondary bibliography. Form arrangement: alphabetical by author lists. Material with bibliographies marked with asterisk.

Lafourcade and Hepburn jointly provide much information, but not a complete bibliography.

Norman Emery. *Arnold Bennett 1867-1931. A Bibliography*. Stoke-on-Trent Central Library, 1967.

Not seen.

John D. Gordan. "Arnold Bennett. The Centenary of his Birth. An Exhibition in the Berg Collection." *Bulletin of the New York Public Library* 72 (1968): 72-122.

Chronological arrangement of primary, secondary, and association material, both published and unpublished. Little specifically bibliographical information; extensive historical and biographical annotations. The catalogue is designed to show that the Berg holds "one of the most extensive accumulations of Arnold Bennett materials in the world."

SECONDARY

Above, Lafourcade, pp. 291-293; Hepburn, pp. 233-238.

James G. Hepburn. "Arnold Bennett Bibliography." *English Fiction in Transition* 1 (1957): 7-12.

Annotated secondary bibliography. Books: publisher, place, year. Periods: volume, date, pages. Subsequent issues of this periodical (later *English Literature in Transition*) add to this list, particularly 6 (1963): i, 19-25; 10 (1967): 204-208; 14 (1971): 55-59.

GENERAL

Millett; Longaker & Bolles; Batho & Dobrée; Temple & Tucker;
Adelman & Dworkin; Palmer & Dyson.

BENNETT, HENRY STANLEY   (1889-   )

WW 71.

BENSON, ARTHUR CHRISTOPHER   (1862-1925)

Longaker & Bolles; NCBEL, III, 1420; WWW 16-28.

BENSON, EDWARD FREDERICK   (1867-1940)

Batho & Dobrée; Temple & Tucker; WWW 29-40; Hagen.

BENSON, STELLA   (1892-1933)

PRIMARY

John Gawsworth. *Ten Contemporaries. Notes Toward their Definitive Bibliography (Second Series).* London: Joiner & Steele
Ltd., 1933. Pp. 240. 1000 copies.

Pp. 43-51, primary books, first editions, 1915-1932. Chronological arrangement. Transcribed TP, full collation, pagination,
binding, date, bibliographical notes.

Siegfried Steinbeck. *Der Ausgesetzte Mensch. Zum Leben und
Werk von Stella Benson.* Bern: Francke Verlag (Schweizer Anglistische Arbeiten 48), 1959. Pp. 117.

P. 115. Primary books. Dates.

GENERAL

Millett; Daiches, Temple & Tucker.

BENTLEY, EDWARD CLERIHEW   (1875-1956)

Batho & Dobrée; WWW 51-60; Hagen.

BENTLEY, PHYLLIS   (1894-   )

PRIMARY

Phyllis Bentley. *'O Dreams, O Destinations' An Autobiography.*
London: Victor Gollancz Ltd., 1962. Pp. 272.

P. [2], list of 25 primary books. Other bibliographical information in text, *passim*.

GENERAL

Millett; Temple & Tucker; WW 71.

BERESFORD, JOHN DAVYS   (1873-1947)

PRIMARY

Helmut Gerber. "John Davys Beresford: A Bibliography." *Bulletin of Bibliography* 21 (1956): 201-204.

Primary British and American first editions. Genre arrangement.
Books: publisher, place, year. Periods: volume, pages, date.
Contents of collections listed with information about previous
publication.

-- "John Davys Beresford." *English Fiction in Transition* 1
(1957): 12-13.

Locates Beresford's MSS; refers to Gerber's bibliography
(above) as "most complete and most accurate"; adds three
items to it.

GENERAL

Millett; Batho & Dobrée; Temple & Tucker; Hagen.

BERKELEY, REGINALD CHEYNE   (1890-1935)

WWW 29-40.

BESANT, ANNIE   (1847-1933)

PRIMARY

Theodore Besterman. *A Bibliography of Annie Besant*. London: Theosophical Society in England, 1924. Pp. 114.

Not seen.

Besterman later published *The Mind of Annie Besant*. London: Theosophical Publishing House, Ltd., 1927. Pp. [xii], 122, providing in the bibliography, pp. 115-117, a selected list of primary books, arranged under four topic headings, with place and date for each book; the footnotes, *passim*, provide additional primary titles.

BESIER, RUDOLPH   (1878-1942)

WWW 41-50; Adelman & Dworkin; Salem; Palmer & Dyson.

BETJEMAN, SIR JOHN   (1906-   )

PRIMARY

Jocelyn Brooke. *John Betjeman and Ronald Firbank*. London: Longmans, Green and Co. (WTW 153), 1962. Pp. 46.

Pp. 45-46, selected primary books. Year, genre.

GENERAL

Daiches; Temple & Tucker; WW 71.

BEVERIDGE, WILLIAM HENRY, LORD BEVERIDGE   (1879-1963)

PRIMARY

Lord Beveridge. *Power and Influence.* London: Hodder and
Stoughton, 1953. Pp. [xii], [448].

Pp. 415-419, primary bibliography. Form arrangement. Books:
publisher, date, pages; all editions. Periods: date. Complete
list of books; selected periodical contributions. Sources of
other primary writings described on p. 415.

GENERAL

WW 63.

BINYON, ROBERT LAURENCE   (1869-1943)

PRIMARY

"Bibliographies of Modern Authors. Robert Laurence Binyon."
London Mercury 2 (1920): 114-115.

Primary books, 1890-1919. Genre arrangement. Publisher,
year, brief notes.

GENERAL

Millett; Longaker & Bolles; Batho & Dobrée; Temple & Tucker;
NCBEL, III, 612-613.

BIRMINGHAM, G. A.   (1865-1950)

Pseudonym of James Owen Hannay

PRIMARY

W. E. Mackey. "The Novels of George A. Birmingham. A List
of First Editions." *Trinity College Dublin Annual Bulletin,*
Number 14-16 (1955).

Not seen.

GENERAL

WWW 41-50; Hagen.

BIRRELL, AUGUSTINE   (1850-1933)

PRIMARY

"Bibliographies of Modern Authors. The Rt. Hon. Augustine
Birrell, K. C. " *London Mercury* 4 (1921): 435-436.

Primary books. Chronological arrangement. Publisher, year,
bibliographical notes.

GENERAL

Batho & Dobrée; NCBEL, III, 1421-1422.

BLACKWOOD, ALGERNON   (1869-1951)

Millett; WWW 51-60; Hagen.

BLAIR, ERIC HUGH: *see* ORWELL, GEORGE

BLAKE, GEORGE   (1893-1961)

Daiches; WW 61.

BLAKE, NICHOLAS: *see* LEWIS, CECIL DAY

BLAND, HUBERT   (1855-1914)

See NESBIT, EDITH.

BLATCHFORD, ROBERT   (1851-1943)

PRIMARY

Laurence Thompson. *Robert Blatchford: Portrait of an English-man.* London: Victor Gollancz Ltd., 1951. Pp. [viii], 242.

Primary books listed in Index under Blatchford; other references to primary writings in text, *passim*.

GENERAL

WWW 41-50.

BLOOM, URSULA   (-   )

(Mrs. Gower Robinson).

WW 71.

BLUNDEN, EDMUND CHARLES   (1896-   )

PRIMARY

A. J. Gasworth and Jacob Schwartz. *Bibliography of Edmund Blunden with Preface and Copious Notes by Edmund Blunden.* London: Ulysses Bookshop, 1931.

Not seen. Although cited by several authorities, this work is not listed in the British Museum Catalogue and may not actually exist.

Alec M. Hardie. *Edmund Blunden.* London: Longmans, Green and Co. (WTW 93), 1958. Pp. 43.

Pp. 39-42, selected primary books. Form and genre arrangement. Place, year. Pp. 42-43, selected secondary bibliography.

GENERAL

Millett; Longaker & Bolles; Daiches; Temple & Tucker; WW 71.

BLUNT, WILFRID SCAWEN   (1840-1922)

PRIMARY

Edith Finch (Countess Russell). *Wilfrid Scawen Blunt 1840-
1922*. London: Jonathan Cape, 1938. Pp. 415.

Pp. 397-399, primary books. Genre arrangement. Place,
publisher, year. Pp. 400-402, general secondary bibliography.
Additional criticism in text, *passim*.

Sister Mary Joan Reinehr. *The Writings of Wilfrid Scawen Blunt.
An Introduction and a Study*. Milwaukee: Marquette University,
1941. Pp. [x], 223 .

Pp. 199-217, primary and secondary bibliography. One alphabetical by author list (entries for Blunt on pp. 199-202). Books:
place, year. Periods: volume, date.

Earl of Lytton. *Wilfrid Scawen Blunt*. London: MacDonald, 1961.
Pp. 368.

No bibliography. Information in text, *passim*.

SECONDARY

Above, Finch; Reinehr.

GENERAL

Longaker & Bolles; Batho & Dobrée; Temple & Tucker; NCBEL,
III, 614-615.

BLYTON, ENID MARY   (-1968)

(Mrs. K. F. D. Waters).

WW 68.

BOAS, FREDERICK SAMUEL   (1862-1957)

Daiches; WWW 51-60.

BODKIN, THOMAS PATRICK   (1887-1961)

PRIMARY

Alan Denson. *Thomas Bodkin A Bio-Bibliographical Survey
with a Bibliographical Survey of his Family.* Dublin: Bodkin
Trustees, 1966. Pp. 236 [Reproduction of typescript].

Primary and secondary bibliography. Form arrangement.
Books: place, publisher, date, pages, binding, price, extensive notes, especially of its printing history; reviews of the
book. Periods: volume, pages, date, notes. Secondary bibliography, *passim*. Includes correspondence, iconography,
radio and television work, paintings and sketches. Pp. 204-
228, bibliographies of other members of the Bodkin family.

SECONDARY

Above, Denson, *passim*.

BOLITHO, HENRY HECTOR   (1898-   )

WW 71.

BOLITHO, WILLIAM   (1890-1930)

Salem.

BOLT, ROBERT OXTON   (1924-   )

Coleman & Tyler; Adelman & Dworkin; Salem; Palmer &
Dyson; WW 71.

BOLTON, GUY   (1884-   )

Salem; WW 71.

BONE, SIR DAVID WILLIAM   (1874-1959)

PRIMARY

Harry R. Skallerup. "Sir David Bone 1874-1959: A Selected
Bibliography." *Bulletin of Bibliography* 23 (1963): 234-236.

Primary and secondary bibliography. Form arrangement.
Books: place, publisher, year, reprints, subsequent editions.
Periods: volume, pages, date. Secondary bibliography, pp.
235-236. Reviews of books listed under title of book.
Includes obituary notices.

BOOTH, CONSTANCE GORE-: *see* MARKIEVICZ, COUNTESS DE

BOSANQUET, BERNARD   (1848-1923)

Batho & Dobrée; NCBEL, III, 1519-1522.

BOTTOME, PHYLLIS   (1884-1963)

PRIMARY

Phyllis Bottome. *The Goal*. London: Faber and Faber, 1962.
Pp. 306.

Limited bibliographical information in this autobiography,
passim.

GENERAL

Temple & Tucker.

BOTTOMLEY, GORDON   (1874-1948)

PRIMARY

Claude Colleer Abbott, "Introduction" in Gordon Bottomley,

Poems and Plays. London: Bodley Head, 1953. Pp. 464.

Pp. 9-19, "Introduction." Bibliographical information in text, *passim.*

-- and Anthony Bertram, eds. *Poet and Painter, Being the Correspondence between Gordon Bottomley and Paul Nash, 1910-1946.* London: Oxford University Press, 1955. Pp. 272.

Bibliographical information in "Introduction," pp. xi-xix, and text, *passim.*

GENERAL

Millett; Longaker & Bolles; Batho & Dobrée; Temple & Tucker.

BOTTRALL, FRANCIS JAMES RONALD   (1906-   )

Daiches; Temple & Tucker; WW 71.

BOURDILLON, FRANCIS WILLIAM   (1852-1921)

NCBEL, III, 615.

BOURN, GEORGE: see STURT, GEORGE.

BOURNE, PETER: see GRAEME, BRUCE.

BOWEN, ELIZABETH DOROTHEA COLE   (1899-   )

PRIMARY

J'nan Sellery. "Elizabeth Bowen: A Check List." *Bulletin of the New York Public Library* 74 (1970): 219-274.

Primary, secondary. Form arrangement, chronological within each section. Books: place, publisher, date, all editions, contents; reviews of books listed under title of book. Periods:date, volume, pages. Reviews by Bowen include title and author of book reviewed. Some cross-referencing to indicate reprinting of separate pieces. Includes translations of primary writings (pp. 263-264) and list of MSS with lengthy descriptions and location (pp. 265-271).

But for the lack of physical descriptions a full-fledged bibliography.

SECONDARY

Above, Sellery, especially pp. 271-274.

GENERAL

Millett; Longaker & Bolles; Daiches; Temple & Tucker; WW 71.

BOWEN, JOHN GRIFFITH   (1924-   )

Bufkin; WW 71.

BOWEN, MARJORIE: see LONG, G. M. V. C.

BOWES-LYON, LILIAN HELEN: see LYON, LILIAN HELEN BOWES.

BOWRA, SIR CECIL MAURICE   (1898-   )

Daiches; Temple & Tucker; WW 71.

BOYLE, WILLIAM   (1853-1922)

NCBEL, III, 1939.

BRADBROOK, MURIEL CLARA   (1909-   )

WW 71.

BRADBURY, MALCOLM   (1932-   )

Temple & Tucker.

BRADLEY, ANDREW CECIL   (1851-1935)

PRIMARY

Mary Blish, R. S. C. J. "Andrew Cecil Bradley. A Summary Account." *Papers of the Bibliographical Society of America* 62 (1968): 607-612.

Primary bibliography. Form and genre arrangement. Books: place, publisher, date; also dates of subsequent editions. Periods: volume, date, pages. Includes works edited by Bradley and his letters to editors.

GENERAL

Batho & Dobrée.

BRADLEY,FRANCIS HERBERT   (1846-1924)

PRIMARY

A. E. Taylor. "Francis Herbert Bradley 1846-1924." *Proceedings of the British Academy* 11 (1924-1925): 458-468.

Pp. 466-468, primary bibliography. Form arrangement. Books: place, publisher, year. Periods: volume, pages, date.

GENERAL

Batho & Dobrée; NCBEL, III, 1522-1525.

BRADLEY, HENRY   (1845-1923)

PRIMARY

[A. S. Ferguson]. "Bibliography" in *The Collected Papers of Henry Bradley*. Oxford: Clarendon Press, 1928. Pp. x, 296.

Pp. 262-279, primary bibliography. Chronological arrangement. Books: date, pages, subsequent editions. Periods: date, pages. Reviews by Bradley include title and author of book reviewed.

GENERAL

NCBEL, III, 1639.

BRADLEY, KATHARINE: see FIELD, MICHAEL.

BRAGG, SIR WILLIAM HENRY   (1862-1942)

Daiches; WWW 41-50.

BRAILSFORD, HENRY NOEL   (1873-1958)

WWW 51-60.

BRAINE, JOHN GERARD   (1922-   )

PRIMARY

James W. Lee. *John Braine*. New York: Twayne Publishers, Inc. (TEAS 62), 1968. Pp. 127.

Pp. 123-124, bibliography. Primary, secondary selected. Form arrangement. Books, British and American editions: place, publisher, year. Periods: volume, pages, date, genre. Six critical studies, annotated. Notes, pp. 118-122, provide additional secondary criticism.

SECONDARY

Above, Lee.

GENERAL

Temple & Tucker; WW 71.

BRAMAH, ERNEST   (1869?-1942)

PRIMARY

William White. "Ernest Bramah. A First Checklist." *Bulletin of Bibliography* 22 (1958): 127-131.

Primary and secondary. Form arrangement. Books: place, publisher, date, pages, price, reprints, subsequent editions, contents. Periods: volume, pages, date. Pp. 130-131, secondary bibliography. Reviews listed under title of book reviewed. Annotations for secondary criticism.

-- "Some Uncollected Authors, XXXVII: Ernest Bramah 1869?-1942." *Book Collector* 13 (1964): 54-63.

Primary books. Chronological arrangement. Transcribed TP, part collation, binding, date, variants, notes. The authoritative bibliography.

-- "Two Bramah Variants." *Papers of the Bibliographical Society of America* 62 (1968): 254-256.

Two additions to *Book Collector* bibliography (above).

SECONDARY

Above, White (1958).

BRICKHILL, PAUL CHESTER JEROME   (1916-   )

Hetherington; WW 71.

BRIDGES, ROBERT SEYMOUR (1844-1930)

PRIMARY

George L. McKay. *A Bibliography of Robert Bridges*. London:
Oxford University Press; New York: Columbia University
Press, 1933. Pp. xii, 215. 550 copies.

Primary first edns. Form arrangement. Books: transcribed
TP, part collation, pagination, illustrations, binding, date,
number of copies, notes, contents, subsequent editions with important textual changes. Periods: volume, pages, date. Index
of first lines; general index. Pp. 12-13, previous bibliographies
of Bridges' work.

The standard bibliography. (See below, Kable).

Simon Nowell-Smith. "A Checklist of the Works of Robert Bridges."
Book Collector's Quarterly 16 (1934): 30-40.

Not seen.

William S. Kable. *The Ewelme Collection of Robert Bridges: A
Catalogue*. Columbia: University of South Carolina (Department
of English, Bibliographical Series No. 2), 1967. Pp. 35. 350
copies.

Catalogue of the collection formed by Simon Nowell-Smith.
Pp. 5-32, primary bibliography. Additions to McKay; notes
on variants from McKay's descriptions; annotations, quotations.
Pp. 32-35, secondary criticism. Books: place, publisher, date.
Periods: volume, pages, date. Annotations.

L. S. Thompson, *Papers of the Bibliographical Society of America* 62 (1968): 288: "a useful supplement to...McKay."

SECONDARY

Above, Kable, pp. 32-35.

GENERAL

Millett; Longaker & Bolles; Batho & Dobrée; Temple & Tucker;
NCBEL, III, 593-597.

BRIDIE, JAMES OSBORNE HENRY MAVOR   (1888-1951)

PRIMARY

Winifred Bannister. *James Bridie and his Theatre.* London:
Rockliffe Publishing Co., 1955. Pp. xii, 262.

P. ix, list of Bridie's plays, published and unpublished.
Other bibliographical information in text, *passim.*

Helen L. Luyben. *James Bridie Clown and Philosopher.* Philadelphia: University of Pennsylvania Press, 1965. Pp. 180.

Pp. 177-178, primary books, secondary selected. Publisher,
place, date, contents. Other secondary references in text,
passim.

SECONDARY

Above, Bannister; Luyben.

GENERAL

Daiches; Temple & Tucker; Coleman & Tyler; Adelman & Dworkin;
Salem.

BRIGGS, ASA   (1921-   )

WW 71.

BRIGHOUSE, HAROLD   (1882-1958)

PRIMARY

Harold Brighouse. *What I Have Had. Chapters in Autobiography.*
London: Harrap & Co., 1953. Pp. 192.

Bibliographical information in text, *passim.*

GENERAL

Millett; Longaker & Bolles.

BRITTAIN, VERA MARY   (1897-1970)

(Mrs. George E. G. Catlin).

PRIMARY

Vera Brittain. *Testament of Youth. An Autobiographical Study of the Years 1900-1925.* New York: Macmillan Co., 1933. Pp. [663].

-- *Testament of Experience. An Autobiographical Story of the Years 1925-1950.* New York: Macmillan Co., 1957. Pp. 480.

Bibliographical information in text, *passim.*

-- *On Becoming an Author* [English title: *On Becoming a Writer*]. New York: Macmillan Co., 1948. Pp. [xviii], 218.

Pp. 144-170 give Brittain's account of her writing career.

GENERAL

WW 70; *also, see below,* HOLTBY, WINIFRED.

BROCK, ARTHUR CLUTTON-   (1868-1924)

PRIMARY

"Bibliographies of Modern Authors: Arthur Clutton-Brock." *London Mercury* 1 (1920): 366.

Primary books. Chronological arrangement. Publisher, year, brief notes.

There appears to be no list of Clutton-Brock's contributions to periodicals and books.

BROCKWAY, ARCHIBALD FENNER, LORD BROCKWAY

(1888-   )

WW 71.

BROGAN, SIR DENIS WILLIAM   (1900-   )

WW 71.

BROME, VINCENT   (-   )

WW 71.

BRONOWSKI, JACOB   (1908-   )

Daiches; WW 71.

BROOKE, JOCELYN   (1908-   )

PRIMARY

Anthony Rota. *Jocelyn Brooke. A Checklist of his Writings, together with some appreciations.* London: Bertram Rota Ltd., 1963. Pp. 4.

Not seen.

GENERAL

Temple & Tucker.

BROOKE, RUPERT   (1887-1915)

PRIMARY

Richard M. G. Potter. *Rupert Brooke. A Bibliographical Note on his Works published in Book Form 1911-1919.* Hartford, Connecticut: Privately Published, 1923. Pp. 28. 52 copies.

Primary books. Chronological arrangement. Transcribed TP, part collation, pagination, binding, subsequent editions, variants, notes.

Keynes (below), p. 19: "a description of the more obvious books."

Geoffrey Keynes. *A Bibliography of Rupert Brooke*. London: Rupert Hart-Davis (Soho Bibliography No. 4, Third Edition Revised), 1964. Pp. 158.

Primary, secondary selected books. Genre and form arrangement. Transcribed TP, part collation, pagination, binding, date, price. number of copies, variants, reprints, contents, extensive notes. MSS described and located. Indices of poem titles, first lines, general.

The authoritative bibliography.

John Schroder. *A Catalogue of Books and Manuscripts by Rupert Brooke, Edward Marsh and Christopher Hassall.* [Collected, compiled and annotated by John Schroder.] Cambridge: Rampant Lions Press, 1970.

Not seen. Described as "the catalogue of an extensive collection, comprising some 481 items."

SECONDARY

Above, Keynes, pp. 137-141.

GENERAL

Millett; Longaker & Bolles; Batho &Dobrée; Temple & Tucker.

BROOKE, STOPFORD AUGUSTUS   (1832-1916)

PRIMARY

Fred L. Standley. "Stopford Augustus Brooke (1832-1916): A Primary Bibliography." *Bulletin of Bibliography* 24 (1964): 79-82.

Pp. 79-81, primary bibliography. Form arrangement. Books: place, date. Periods: volume, pages, date. Pp. 81-82, secondary bibliography. One alphabetical by author or title list.

SECONDARY

Above, Standley, pp. 81-82.

GENERAL

NCBEL, III, 1422-1423.

BROOKE-ROSE, CHRISTINE: see ROSE, CHRISTINE BROOKE.

BROPHY, BRIGID ANTONIA   (1929-   )

(Mrs. Michael Levey).

Temple & Tucker; Bufkin; WW 71.

BROPHY, JOHN   (1899-1965)

WW 65; Hagen.

BROWN, GEORGE DOUGLAS   (1869-1902)

PRIMARY

James Veitch. *George Douglas Brown*. London: Herbert Jenkins, 1952. Pp. 197.

P. 189, selected primary and secondary bibliography. Chronological arrangement. Dates. Other bibliographical information in text, *passim*; also in Cuthbert Lennox and Andrew Melrose, *George Douglas Brown*, introduced Andrew Lang. London: Hodder and Stoughton, 1903. Pp. xiv, 248.

SECONDARY

Above, Veitch.

GENERAL

Batho & Dobrée; NCBEL, III, 1046.

BROWN, IVOR JOHN CARNEGIE   (1891-   )

Temple & Tucker; WW 71.

BROWNE, MAURICE   (1881-1955)

PRIMARY

Montrose J. Moses and Oscar J. Campbell, eds. *Dramas of Modernism and Their Forerunners*. Boston: Little, Brown and Co., 1941. Pp. xvi, 946.

Pp. 925, 941, bibliography. Primary selected, secondary selected. One alphabetical list. Books: place, publisher, date. Periods: volume, pages, date. Studies or reviews of *Wings over Europe* listed thereunder.

Maurice Browne. *Too Late to Lament. An Autobiography*. London: Victor Gollancz, 1955; Bloomington: Indiana University Press, 1956. Pp. 403.

No bibliography, but references to primary and secondary writings in text, *passim*; also in Index.

GENERAL

WWW 51-60.

BRYANT, SIR ARTHUR WYNNE MORGAN   (1899-   )

Daiches; WW 71.

BRYHER (ANNIE WINIFRED ELLERMAN)   (1894-   )

PRIMARY

Bryher. *The Heart to Artemis. A Writer's Memoirs.* London:
Collins, 1963. Pp. 320.

Bibliographical information in text, *passim.* Index.

GENERAL

Temple & Tucker; WW 71.

BUCHAN, JOHN, LORD TWEEDSMUIR   (1875-1940)

PRIMARY

Archibald Hanna, Jr. *John Buchan 1875-1940. A Bibliography.*
Hamden, Connecticut: Shoe String Press, 1953. Pp. 135.

Primary complete, secondary selected. Form arrangement.
Books: publisher, place, date, pages, contents, notes.
Periods: volume, pages, date. Pp. 115-119, secondary
bibliography.

B. C. Wilmot. *A Checklist of Works by and about John Buchan
in the John Buchan Collection, Douglas Library, Queen's University, Kingston, Ontario.* Boston: G. K. Hall, 1961. Pp. 38,
24.

Primary complete, secondary selected. Form and genre arrangement. Publisher, place, date, pages, height, notes on
special bindings and MSS notations.

Janet Adam Smith. *John Buchan.* London: Rupert Hart-Davis,
1965. Pp. 524.

Pp. 476-479, bibliography of primary books. Date, contents.
Pp. 480-507, "Sources and References": bibliographical information, *passim.*

47

Hanna, Wilmot, and Smith together give an almost complete list of primary writings, although the bibliographical descriptions are incomplete.

SECONDARY

Above, Hanna, pp. 115-119; Wilmot, pp. 31-36.

J. Randolph Cox. "John Buchan, Lord Tweedsmuir. An Annotated Bibliography of Writings about Him." *English Literature in Transition* 9 (1966): 241-291, 292-325; 10 (1967): 209-211; *et seq.*

Books: place, publisher, year. Periods: volume, pages, date.

GENERAL

Longaker & Bolles; Daiches; Temple & Tucker; Hagen.

BULLEN, ARTHUR HENRY   (1857-1920)

NCBEL, III, 1640.

BULLETT, GERALD WILLIAM   (1893-1958)

Millett; WW 51-60.

BULLOUGH, GEOFFREY   (1901-   )

Daiches; WW 71.

BURDETT, OSBERT HENRY   (1885-1936)

Millett; WWW 29-40.

BURFORD, ELEANOR: see HIBBERT, ELEANOR.

BURGESS, ANTHONY   (1917-   )

Pseudonym of John Burgess Wilson.

PRIMARY

C[ornelia] D[ozier] E[merson]. "Books by Anthony Burgess."
Hollins Critic 6 (April 1969): 6-7.

Primary books, all English-language editions. Chronological
arrangement. Place, publisher, date, price.

GENERAL

Bufkin; Temple & Tucker; WW 71.

BURKE, THOMAS   (1886-1945)

PRIMARY

John Gawsworth. *Ten Contemporaries. Notes Toward their
Definitive Bibliography. (Second Series).* London: Joiner &
Steele Ltd., 1933. Pp. 240. 1000 copies.

Pp. 61-82, primary books, first editions, 1910-1932. Chronological arrangement. Transcribed TP, full collation, pagination,
binding, date, bibliographical notes.

GENERAL

Millett; Hagen.

BURNETT, FRANCES ELIZA HODGSON   (1849-1924)

PRIMARY

Marghanita Laski. *Mrs. Ewing, Mrs. Molesworth, and Mrs. Hodgson Burnett.* London: Arthur Barker Ltd., 1950. Pp. 121.

Pp. 113-117, bibliography. Primary books, unpublished plays.

Publisher, date. P. 113: "almost certainly incomplete as far as Burnett's magazine work is concerned."

BURNETT, IVY COMPTON- : see COMPTON-BURNETT, IVY.

BURY, JOHN B.   (1861-1927)

Batho & Dobrée.

BUSHNELL, GEORGE HERBERT   (1896-   )

WW 71.

BUTLER, SAMUEL   (1835-1902)

PRIMARY

A. J. Hoppé. *A Bibliography of the Writings of Samuel Butler and of Writings about Him*. London: Bookman's Journal, 1925. Pp. [xvi], 184. 500 copies.

Primary complete, secondary complete. Form arrangement. Books: transcribed TP, complete collation, pagination, binding, date, price, variants, contents, complete notes. Periods: page, date, reprintings, quotations. Pp. 129-160, secondary bibliography. Form arrangement. Annotations. Harkness (below), p. 11: "a solid and comprehensive record of Butler's achievement up to the year 1925...especially notable for the fullness and precision of its information under 'Editiones Principes'..."

Stanley B. Harkness. *The Career of Samuel Butler (1835-1902): A Bibliography*. London: Bodley Head, 1955. Pp. 154.

Primary complete, secondary complete. Pp. 29-67, primary bibliography. Chronological arrangement. Books: place, publisher, date, variants, reprints, location of MSS, notes. Periods: volume, pages, date, reprintings. Pp. 71-150, secondary bibliography. Form arrangement. Pp. 153-154, translations of primary writings listed under name of language.

Gerber (below), p. 13: Hoppé and Harkness together give an almost complete record of Butler's writings and of the secondary bibliography.

SECONDARY

Above, Hoppé, pp. 129-160; Harkness, pp. 71-150.

Helmut Gerber. "Samuel Butler." *English Fiction* (later *English Literature*) *in Transition* 1 (1957): 13-18; 6 (1963): i, 23-31; continued in subsequent issues.

Annotated additions to Harkness.

Lee E. Holt. *Samuel Butler.* New York: Twayne Publishers, Inc. (TEAS 2), 1964. Pp. 183.

Pp. 171-176, selected secondary bibliography. Alphabetical by author arrangement. Annotated.

A useful selected bibliography.

GENERAL

Batho & Dobrée; Temple & Tucker; NCBEL, III, 1406-1411.

BUTTERFIELD, SIR HERBERT   (1900-   )

Daiches; WW 71.

BUTTS, MARY FRANCIS   (1893-1937)

PRIMARY

Douglas Goldring. *South Lodge. Reminiscences of Violet Hunt, Ford Madox Ford, and the English Review Circle.* London: Constable and Co., Ltd., 1943. Pp. [xx], [240].

P. [240], bibliography of primary books. Genre arrangement.
Publisher, date.

BYRNE, BRIAN OSWALD DONN   (1889-1928)

PRIMARY

Winthrop Wetherbee, Jr. *Donn Byrne: A Bibliography*. New York:
New York Public Library, 1949. Pp. [xii], 89.

Primary and secondary. Form and genre arrangement. Books:
transcribed TP, part collation, binding, subsequent editions,
contents, bibliographical notes, reviews. Periods: volume, pages
date. Includes translations, dramatizations, cinematizations,
anthologies, MSS. Pp. 68-84, secondary bibliography.

The original typescript of this bibliography (available in the
New York Public Library) lists even more titles.

SECONDARY

Above, Wetherbee, pp. 1-47 (reviews of the primary books); pp.
68-84, general secondary bibliography.

BYRNE, MURIEL ST. CLARE   (1895-   )

WW 71.

BYRON, ROBERT   (1905-1941)

WWW 41-50.

CAINE, SIR THOMAS HENRY HALL   (1853-1931)

Batho & Dobrée; Temple and Tucker; NCBEL, III, 1042.

CALDER-MARSHALL, ARTHUR   (1908-   )

Daiches; WW 71.

CAMPBELL, IGNATIUS ROY DUNNACHIE   (1902-1957)

PRIMARY

David Wright. *Roy Campbell*. London: Longmans, Green and Co.
(WTW 137), 1961. Pp. 44.

P. 44, selected primary books. Genre arrangement. Place,
date.

GENERAL

Millett; Longaker & Bolles; Daiches; Temple & Tucker.

CAMPBELL, JOSEPH   (1879-1944)

PRIMARY

Patrick Sarsfield O'Hegarty. "Bibliography of Joseph Campbell."
Dublin Magazine 15 (October-December 1940): 58-61. [Also
published as a separate pamphlet.

Primary books. Chronological arrangement. Transcribed TP,
part collation, pagination, binding, variants, brief notes.]

CANNAN, DENNIS   (1919-   )

WW 71.

CANNAN, GILBERT   (1884-1955)

Millett; Batho & Dobrée; Bufkin; Temple & Tucker.

CANNING, VICTOR   (1911-   )

WW 71; Hagen.

CANTON, WILLIAM   (1845-1926)

NCBEL, III, 617.

CARDUS, SIR NEVILLE   (1889-   )

WW 71.

CARPENTER, EDWARD   (1844-1929)

PRIMARY

[?Edward Carpenter]. *A Bibliography of the Writings of Edward Carpenter*. London: George Allen and Unwin, 1916. Pp. 14. 150 copies.

Primary, secondary selected. Form arrangement. Books: publisher, place, date, reprints. Periods: dates. Excludes periodical contributions reprinted in book form. Includes translations and musical settings of primary writings. P. 14, secondary bibliography.

Reprinted from pp. 323-332 of Edward Carpenter. *My Days and Dreams*. London: George Allen and Unwin; New York: Charles Scribner's Sons, 1916. Pp. 340.

A Bibliography of Edward Carpenter. A Catalogue of the...Collection. Sheffield: Free Public Libraries and Museums, 1949.

Not seen.

GENERAL

Millett; Batho & Dobrée; Temple & Tucker; NCBEL, III, 1423.

CARR, EDWARD HALLETT   (1892-   )

WW 71.

CARROLL, PAUL VINCENT   (1900-1968)

PRIMARY

Montrose J. Moses and Oscar J. Campbell, eds. *Dramas of Modernism and Their Forerunners*. Boston: Little, Brown and Co., 1941. Pp. xvi, 946.

Pp. 933-934, 945, bibliography. Primary selected, secondary selected. Alphabetical by author arrangement. Books: place, publisher, date. Periods: volume, pages, date. Reviews of the two primary books listed under titles. Useful secondary checklist.

P. V. Carroll. *Irish Stories and Plays*. New York: Devin-Adair Co., 1950. Pp. 278.

No bibliography. "Contents," p. vii, gives titles of selected primary stories and plays; "Acknowledgements," p. vi, provides printing history.

These two entries, with the WW list, give a starting point for compiling the Carroll bibliography.

GENERAL

Temple & Tucker; WW 69; Adelman & Dworkin; Palmer & Dyson; Salem.

CARSWELL, CATHARINE ROXBURGH   (1879-1946)

WWW 41-50.

CARTER, FREDERICK   (-1967)

PRIMARY

John Gawsworth. *Ten Contemporaries. Notes Toward their Definitive Bibliography. (Second Series).* London: Joiner & Steele, Ltd., 1933. Pp. 240. 1000 copies.

Pp. 93-103, primary books, first editions, 1914-1932. Chronological arrangement. Transcribed TP, full coll ation, pagination, binding, date, bibliographical notes.

GENERAL

WW 67.

CARTER, JOHN WAYNFLETE (1905-   )

WW 71.

CARTLAND, BARBARA HAMILTON (?1905-   )

(Mrs. Barbara McCorquodale).

WW 71.

CARY, ARTHUR JOYCE LUNEL (1888-1957)

PRIMARY

Andrew Wright. *Joyce Cary: A Preface to his Novels.* London: Chatto and Windus; New York: Harper, 1958. Pp. 186.

Pp. 174-181, bibliography. Primary, secondary selected. Genre arrangement. Books: place, publisher, date. Periods: volume, pages, date. Pp. 180-181, secondary bibliography.

James B. Meriwether. "The Books of Joyce Cary: A Preliminary Bibliography of English and American Editions." *Texas Studies in Literature and Language* 1 (1959): 399-310.

Primary books. Chronological arrangement. Transcribed TP, part collation, binding, date, reprints, notes.

Together Wright and Meriwether give a fairly complete list.

SECONDARY

Above, Wright, pp. 180-181.

Robert Bloom. *The Indeterminate World: A Study of the Novels of Joyce Cary.* Philadelphia: University of Pennsylvania Press, 1962. Pp. 212.

Pp. 205-208, selected secondary. Books: place, publisher, date. Periods: volume, pages, date.

Maurice Beebe, James W. Lee, and Sam Henderson. "Criticism of Joyce Cary: A Selected Checklist." *Modern Fiction Studies* 9 (Autumn 1963): 284-288.

Alphabetical by author arrangement. Books: place, publisher, date. Periods: volume, pages, date.

M. M. Mahood. *Joyce Cary's Africa.* London: Methuen and Co., 1964. Pp. 206.

Pp. 197-201, "List of Sources." Important unpublished material in the Osborn collection, Bodleian Library; official government papers relating to Africa; other African studies.

Peter J. Reed. "Joyce Cary. A Selected Checklist of Criticism." *Bulletin of Bibliography* 25 (1968): 133-134, 151.

Alphabetical by author arrangement. Books: place, publisher, year. Periods: volume, pages, date.

GENERAL

Longaker & Bolles; Daiches; Temple & Tucker.

CASEMENT, ROGER DAVID   (1864-1916)

PRIMARY

Patrick Sarsfield O'Hegarty. "Bibliographies of 1916 and the Irish Revolution. No. XVII. Roger Casement." *Dublin Magazine* 24 (April-June 1949): 31-34. [Also published as a separate pamphlet.]

Primary books and pamphlets. Chronological arrangement. Transcribed TP, part collation, pagination, binding, bibliographical and textual notes.

Roger Casement. *The Crime against Europe. The Writings and Poetry of Roger Casement.* Collected and edited by Herbert O. Mackey. Dublin: C. J. Fallon Ltd., 1958. Pp. [xvi], 227.

Pp. 91-148, miscellaneous journalism; footnotes give periodical and date of original publication; pp. 159-214, poems (no bibliographical information).

CATLIN, SIR GEORGE EDWARD GORDON　　　　(1896-　　)

WW 71.

CATO, NANCY　　　　　　　　　　　(1917-　　)

(Mrs. Eldred Norman).

Hetherington.

CAUDWELL, CHRISTOPHER, pseudonym of Christopher Sr. John Sprigg: see SPRIGG, CHRISTOPHER St. JOHN.

CECIL, LORD EDWARD CHRISTIAN DAVID GASCOYNE (1902-)

Millett; Longaker & Bolles; Daiches; Temple & Tucker; WW 71.

CHAMBERS, CHARLES HADDON　　　　　(1860-1921)

Salem; WWW 16-28.

CHAMBERS, SIR EDMUND KERCHEVER   (1866-1954)

Batho & Dobrée; Daiches; Temple & Tucker.

CHAMBERS, RAYMOND WILSON   (1874-1942)

PRIMARY

H. Winifred Husbands. "A Bibliography of the Works of Raymond Wilson Chambers." *Proceedings of the British Academy* 30 (1944): 440-445.

Primary. Chronological arrangement. Books: place, publisher, date, pages. Periods: volume, pages, date. Reviews by Chambers include title and author of book reviewed.

GENERAL

Daiches.

CHAPMAN, ROBERT WILLIAM   (1881-1960)

WWW 51-60.

CHARLTON; HENRY BUCKLEY   (1890-1961)

Daiches; WW 61.

CHARTERIS, HUGO FRANCIS GUY   (1922-   )

WW 71.

CHARTERIS, LESLIE   (1907-   )

WW 71; Hagen.

CHESTERTON, GILBERT KEITH   (1874-1936)

PRIMARY

John Sullivan. *G. K. Chesterton. A Bibliography*. London: University of London Press; New York: Barnes and Noble, 1958. Pp. 208.

Primary first editions, secondary selected. Form arrangement. Books: transcribed TP, full collation, binding, date, price, variants, notes, number of copies. Selected contributions to periodicals, mainly of writings subsequently collected in book form: alphabetical list of periods: dates. Chronological list of books and periodicals illustrated by Chesterton. Chronological list of collections and selections from Chesterton. Chronological list of translations of primary writings. Pp. 161-171, secondary bibliography. Chronological arrangement. Index, pp. 197-208.

TLS, No. 2945 (8 August 1958): 452: "admirably thorough, informative, lucid record."

John Sullivan. *Chesterton Continued. A Bibliographical Supplement*. London: University of London Press, 1968. Pp. [xvi], 120.

Pp. 9-84, additions and corrections to Sullivan's *G. K. Chesterton* (above) in its style and order.

Joseph W. Sprug. *An Index to G. K. Chesterton*. Washington: Catholic University Press, 1965. Pp. xx, 427.

Pp. xiii-xvii, alphabetical list of titles by Chesterton herein indexed. Place, publisher, date, pages.

SECONDARY

Above, Sullivan (1958), pp. 161-171.

GENERAL

Millett; Longaker & Bolles; Batho & Dobrée; Temple & Tucker; Adelman & Dworkin.

CHILDE, WILFRED ROWLAND MARY   (1890-1952)

WWW 51-60.

CHILDERS, ROBERT ERSKINE   (1870-1922)

PRIMARY

Patrick Sarsfield O'Hegarty. "Bibliographies of 1916 and the Irish Revolution. No. XVI. Erskine Childers." *Dublin Magazine* 23 (April-June 1948): 40-43.

Primary books. Chronological arrangement. Transcribed TP, part collation, pagination, binding.

CHITTY, SIR THOMAS WILLES: see HINDE, THOMAS.

CHRISTIE, DAME AGATHA MARY CLARISSA   (1891-   )

(Lady Max E. L. Mallowan).

PRIMARY

G. C. Ramsey. *Agatha Christie. Mistress of Mystery.* New York: Dodd and Co., 1967. Pp. [xiv], 124.

Pp. 77-124, bibliographical appendices. Arranged: alphabetical list of all titles with genre; alphabetical list of novels including plot summary, publisher, and date; alphabetical list of short story collections with contents; alphabetical list of books and stories made into plays, including author of the dramatization; list of books and stories made into films; list of titles published only in America or in Britain; selected writings about Christie excluding reviews.

SECONDARY

Above, Ramsey, pp. 123-124.

GENERAL

Salem; Palmer & Dyson; WW 71; Hagen.

CHUBB, RALPH NICHOLAS   (1892-1960)

PRIMARY

Anthony Reid. "Ralph Chubb, the Unknown. Part II. His Work."
Private Library (2nd Series) 3 (1970): 193-213.

Primary, secondary. Form arrangement. Transcribed TP
without lineation bars, description of illustrations, binding,
number of copies, price, extensive bibliographical notes
concerning reprints, variants, and unique copies. Periods:
volume, pages, date, annotations.

SECONDARY

Above, Reid.

CHURCH, RICHARD THOMAS   (1893-   )

Daiches; Temple & Tucker; Bufkin; WW 71.

CHURCHILL, SIR WINSTON LEONARD SPENCER   (1874-1965)

PRIMARY

Frederick Woods. *A Bibliography of the Works of Sir Winston
Churchill, KG, OM, CH.* Second, revised edition. London:
Kaye and Ward; Toronto: University of Toronto Press, 1969.
Pp. 396, interleaved with unnumbered blank pages.

Primary complete; secondary books. Form arrangement. Books:

transcribed TP, full collation, pagination, binding, descriptions of type-face, paper, and endpapers, date, price, variations, reprints, number of copies, extensive textual and bibliographical notes. Periods: volume, pages, date. Appendices include bibliographical history of *The Second World War* and *The British Gazette;* list of *The Political Warfare Leaflets* (translations of Churchill's writings). Index of titles.

The standard primary bibliography.

SECONDARY

Above, Woods, pp. 325-348. Chronological arrangement. Place, publisher, date.

There appears to be no complete secondary bibliography, but by examining all of the bibliographies in all of the books named by Woods one would begin to get an idea of the size of such a list.

GENERAL

Daiches.

CLAPHAM, SIR JOHN   (1873-1946)

WWW 41-50.

CLARK, SIR GEORGE NORMAN   (1890-   )

Daiches; WW 71.

CLARK, KENNETH MACKENZIE, LORD CLARK   (1903-   )

PRIMARY

Lynette Eleanor Stagg. *Sir Kenneth MacKenzie Clark 1903-: A Bibliography of His Published Works Including Letters to "The Times."* Johannesburg: University of the Witwatersrand,

Department of Bibliogr aphy, Librarianship and Typography, 1969. Pp. [xiv], 30. Reproduced from typescript.

Pp. 1-20, primary bibliography. Arranged alphabetically by title. Books: place, publisher, date, subsequent editions; for first editions, height in centimeters, pages, list of reviews. Periods: volume, pages, date. Pp. 21-25, index of subjects and authors; pp. 26-30, chronological list of primary writings, 1928-1967.

SECONDARY

Above, Stagg, pp. 1-20, *passim* (reviews only).

GENERAL

Daiches; WW 71.

CLARK, LEONARD   (1905-)

WW 71.

CLARKE, ARTHUR CHARLES   (1917-)

WW 71.

CLARKE, AUSTIN   (1896-)

PRIMARY

M. J. MacManus. "Bibliographies of Irish Writers. No. 8. Austin Clarke." *Dublin Magazine* 10 (April-June 1935): 41-43.

Primary books. Chronological arrangement. Transcribed TP, part collation, pagination, binding, bibliographical notes.

Liam Miller. "The Books of Austin Clarke. A Checklist" in *A Tribute to Austin Clarke on his Seventieth Birthday*, ed.

John Montague and Liam Miller. Dublin: Dolmen Edns, 1966. Pp. 28. 1000 copies.

Primary books. Chronological arrangement. Transcribed TP without lineation bars, genre, part collation, binding. Notice of later editions and reprints with varying information. Occasional textual or bibliographical notes. [Revised and extended version of list first appearing in *The Dubliner*, No. 6, 1963.]

GENERAL

Temple & Tucker; Coleman & Tyler; WW 71.

CLARKE, THOMAS JAMES (- 1916)

PRIMARY

Patrick Sarsfield O'Hegarty. "Bibliographies of 1916 and the Irish Revolution. VII. Thomas James Clarke." *Dublin Magazine* 11 (July-September 1936): 57.

Primary books. Chronological arrangement. Transcribed TP, part collation, pagination, binding, bibliographical notes.

CLEARY, JON (1917-)

Hetherington.

COGHILL, NEVILL HENRY KENDAL AYLMER (1899-)

WW 71.

COHEN, JOHN MICHAEL (1903-)

WW 71.

COIT, STANTON (1857-1944)

NCBEL, III, 1528.

COLE, GEORGE DOUGLAS HOWARD   (1889-1959)

Millett; Daiches; WWW 51-60; Hagen.

COLE, DAME MARGARET ISABEL   (1893-   )

(Mrs. G. D. H. Cole).

WW 71; Hagen.

COLERIDGE, MARY ELIZABETH   (1861-1907)

PRIMARY

Mary E. Coleridge. *Poems* [ed. Henry Newbolt]. London: Elkin
Matthews, 1907. Pp. [xxii], 214.

Pp. v-xii, Preface by Newbolt: bibliographical details about
previous book publication of the poems, *passim*.

Mary Coleridge. *The Collected Poems*, ed. Theresa Whistler.
London: Rupert Hart-Davis, 1954. Pp. 266.

Pp. 21-81, Introduction by Whistler: bibliographical information, *passim*.

GENERAL

NCBEL, III, 618-619.

COLLIER, JOHN   (1901-   )

PRIMARY

John Gawsworth. *Ten Contemporaries. Notes Toward their
Definitive Bibliography (Second Series)*. London: Joiner and

Steele, Ltd., 1933. Pp. 240. 1000 copies.

Pp. 112-117, primary first editions, 1930-1932. Chronological arrangement. Transcribed TP, full collation, pagination, binding, date, bibliographical notes.

GENERAL

Temple & Tucker.

COLLINGWOOD, ROBIN GEORGE   (1889-1943)

PRIMARY

T. M. Knox. "Bibliography: exclusive of book reviews and of historical works and articles." *Proceedings of the British Academy* 29 (1943): 474-475.

Genre arrangement. Books: place, publisher, date, pages. Periods: volume, pages, date.

[I. M. Richmond]. "Bibliography of Writings on Ancient History and Archaeology." *Proceedings of the British Academy* 29 (1943): 481-485.

Chronological arrangement. Information as in Knox, above.

E. W. F. Tomlin. *R. G. Collingwood.* London: Longmans, Green and Co. (WTW 42), 1961. Pp. 40.

Pp. 39-40, selected primary books. Chronological arrangement. Place, year, genre.

Alan Donagan. *The Later Philosophy of R. G. Collingwood.* Oxford: Clarendon Press, 1962. Pp. 332.

Pp. 311-313, Appendix II: information about primary writings additional to Knox.

W. M. Johnston. *The Formative Years of R. G. Collingwood.* The Hague: M. Nijhoff, 1969. Pp. [xiv], 167.

Pp. 156-163, primary, secondary selected bibliography. List of writings on philosophy said to be "as complete as possible." Arranged by form and topic. Books: place, date. Periods: volume, date, pages, details of reprinting. Secondary bibliography arranged alphabetically by author, includes other bibliographies of Collingwood. Described as "although not exhaustive...the most thorough yet published."

SECONDARY

Above, Johnston, pp. 160-163.

William Debbins, ed. *Essays in the Philosophy of History by R. G. Collingwood.* Austin: University of Texas Press, 1965. Pp. xxxiv, 160.

Pp. 143-148, secondary bibliography. Alphabetical by author. Books: place, publisher, date. Periods: volume, date, pages. Special section of reviews of Collingwood's books, arranged under title of book reviewed (pp. 146-148).

Lionel Rubinoff. *Collingwood and the Reform of Metaphysics.* Toronto: University of Toronto Press, 1970. Pp. xiv, 413.

Pp. 398-405. Secondary bibliography. Alphabetical by author. Information as in Debbins, above. P. 406, list of doctoral dissertations on Collingwood. P. 394: The "Debbins and Johnston [bibliographies] have been the most complete. The Debbins volume contains an invaluable list of most of the reviews of Collingwood's philosophical books. A further comprehensive bibliography will be included in a [Collingwood anthology] edited by Michael Krausz, to be published by the Clarendon Press, Oxford."

GENERAL

Daiches.

COLLINS, MICHAEL   (1890-1922)

PRIMARY

Patrick Sarsfield O'Hegarty. "Bibliographies of 1916 and the Irish Revolution. XIII. Michael Collins." *Dublin Magazine* 12 (January-March 1937): 66-67.

Primary books. Chronological arrangement. Transcribed TP, part collation, pagination, binding, bibliographical and biographical notes.

SECONDARY

Rex Taylor. *Michael Collins*. London: Hutchinson, 1958. Pp. 352.

Pp. 335-337, secondary bibliography. Form arrangement. Also notes, pp. 324-333.

Margery Forester. *Michael Collins--The Lost Leader*. London: Sidgwick and Jackson, 1971. Pp. 371.

Not seen.

COLLIS, JOHN STEWART   (1900-   )

WW 71.

COLLIS, MAURICE   (1889-   )

WW 71.

COLTON, JOHN   (1886-1946)

Salem.

COLUM, PADRAIC   (1881-   )

PRIMARY

Alan Denson. "Padraic Colum: An Appreciation with a Checklist of His Publications." *Dublin Magazine* 6 (1967): i, 50-67, ii, 83-85.

Not seen.

A list of primary books with place and date of all edns, drawn from Denson, is given in Zack Bowen. *Padraic Colum A Biographical-Critical Introduction.* Carbondale: Southern Illinois University Press, 1970. Pp. [xiv], 162. Pp. 155-157.

GENERAL

Millett; Longaker & Bolles; Temple & Tucker; NCBEL, III, 1942-1943; WW 71.

COLVIN, SIR SIDNEY   (1845-1927)

Batho & Dobrée; NCBEL, III, 1425-1426.

COMFORT, ALEXANDER   (1920-   )

PRIMARY

Robert D. Callahan. "Alexander Comfort: A Bibliography in Progress." *West Coast Review* 3 (Winter, 1969): 48-67.

Primary, secondary. Form and genre arrangement. Books: place, publisher, date; includes British and American editions. Periods: volume, pages, date. Includes translations by Comfort; editing by Comfort; letters to editors by Comfort; and reviews by Comfort with title and author of book reviewed; also anthologies including his work. Pp. 64-67, secondary bibliography includes reviews of primary writings. Complete to 31 December 1967.

SECONDARY

Above, Callahan, pp. 64-67.

GENERAL

Daiches; Longaker & Bolles; Bufkin; Temple & Tucker; WW 71.

COMPTON-BURNETT, IVY   (1892-1969)

PRIMARY

Frank Baldanza. *Ivy Compton-Burnett*. New York: Twayne Publishers, Inc. (TEAS 11), 1964. Pp. 142.

Pp. 135-138, primary books, secondary selected. Chronological arrangement. Books: place, publisher, date. Periods: volume, pages, date. Annotations for secondary entries.

R. Glynn Grylls. *I. Compton-Burnett*. London: Longman Group Ltd. (WTW 220), 1971. Pp. 30.

P. 29, primary books. Chronological arrangement. Place, date. Pp. 29-30, secondary selected. Periods: volume, date, pages.

SECONDARY

Above, Baldanza and Grylls.

Charles Burkhart. *Ivy Compton-Burnett*. London: Victor Gollancz, 1965. Pp. 142.

Pp. 135-137, secondary selected, including reviews. Periods: volume, page, date.

GENERAL

Daiches; Temple & Tucker.

CONNOLLY, CYRIL VERNON   (1903-   )

Daiches; Temple & Tucker; WW 71.

CONNOLLY, JAMES   (-1916)

PRIMARY

Patrick Sarsfield O'Hegarty. "Bibliographies of 1916 and the Irish Revolution. No. V. James Connolly. Hand List, Notes and Queries." *Dublin Magazine* 11 (April-June 1936): 62-64.

Primary books. Chronological arrangement. All titles listed, but described only if O'Hegarty had seen a copy. Place, publisher, year, part collation, binding, extensive notes and queries.

CONRAD, JOSEPH   (1857-1924)

BIBLIOGRAPHIES OF BIBLIOGRAPHIES

Theodore George Ehrsam. *A Bibliography of Joseph Conrad.* Metuchen, New Jersey: Scarecrow Press, Inc., 1969. Pp. 448.

Pp. 373-386, bibliographical materials. Arranged alphabetically by author or title. Pp. 9-258, biographical and critical material. Pp. 259-330, primary bibliography. Arranged alphabetically by title. Books: place, publisher, year, pages. Periods: volume, pages, date. Occasional bibliographical notes and reviews under each primary book title. Other divisions: pp. 331-334, primary prefatory material; pp. 335-372, translations of Conrad (alphabetically arranged by English title of work, including translator's name and occasionally reviews); pp. 387-393, iconography; pp. 394-395, motion picture films; pp. 397-448, index.

The most important of all the Conrad bibliographical aids. Thomas M. Whitehead, *Papers of the Bibliographical Society of America* 63 (1969): 350: "perhaps its greatest achievement [is] a full treatment of books and articles about Conrad and [of] reviews of his works...a very useful guide to Conrad and 'Conradiana'."

PRIMARY

Thomas J. Wise. *A Bibliography of the Writings of Joseph Conrad (1895-1920)*. London: Privately Printed, 1920. Pp. 128. 150 copies. Second edn, revised and enlarged. 1921. 170 copies. Reprinted, London: Dawsons, 1964. *A Conrad Library. A Catalogue of Printed Books, Manuscripts and Autograph Letters by Joseph Conrad*. London: Privately Printed, 1928. Pp. [xx], [68]. 205 (?) copies.

Primary books, miscellaneous letters and MSS; secondary books. Transcribed TP, part collation, pagination, occasionally binding; bibliographical notes mainly concerning unique copies in Wise's library; occasionally subsequent editions.

Wise provides the standard bibliography of Editiones Principes in these two volumes (the 1921 and 1928 edns), each one of which "gives material not contained in the other" (W. Partington, *T. J. Wise in the Original Cloth*. London, 1946. p. 325).

Oliver Warner. Joseph Conrad. London: Longmans, Green and Co. (WTW 2), 1964. Pp. 40.

Pp. 34-40, bibliography. Primary books. Chronological arrangement. Date, genre. Also includes French and Polish translations with translator, place; a list of secondary books, chronologically arranged; and an alphabetical list of stories with title of volume in which collected.

A convenient checklist of titles.

Above, Ehrsam, pp. 259-334.

The most inclusive listing.

SECONDARY

Kenneth A. Lohf and Eugene P. Sheehy. *Joseph Conrad at Mid-Century: Editions and Studies, 1895-1955*. Minneapolis: University of Minneapolis Press, 1957. Pp. 114. Reprinted 1968.

Pp. 3-42, primary bibliography. Pp. 43-102, secondary bibliography. Arrangement: Memorial Issues of Periodicals; General; Individual Works (including reviews); Letters; Prefaces ; Drama; Parody and Miscellaneous. Index.

Ludwik Krzyzanowski, ed. *Joseph Conrad Centennial Essays.* New York: Polish Institute of Arts and Sciences in America, 1960. Pp. 174.

Pp. 166-174, secondary bibliography of items, mainly in Polish, not in Lohf and Sheehy.

Maurice Beebe. "Criticism of Joseph Conrad: A Selected Check-list." *Modern Fiction Studies* 1 (1955); 30-45; 10 (1964): 81-106.

Arranged: General; Studies of Separate Works, listed under title of work studied.

A selected list of studies conveniently arranged according to the primary work studied; particularly useful to the beginning student.

Above, Ehrsam, pp. 9-258; also pp. 259-330, pp. 335-372.

The most inclusive listing. Thorough study of the Conrad criticism begins with this volume, supplemented by the listings in *Conradiana* and in the Teets-Gerber *Annotated Bibliography.*

Conradiana 1 (1968): 87-88 (continuing).

This periodical, devoted to Conrad studies, includes in each issue a continuing bibliography which supplements Ehrsam.

Edmund A. and Henry T. Bojarski. "Three Hundred and Thirty Six Unpublished Papers on Joseph Conrad. A Bibliography of Masters Theses and Doctoral Dissertations, 1917-1963." *Bulletin of Bibliography* 26 (1969): 61-66, 79-83.

An incomplete list, the deficiencies being noted on p. 61.

Bruce E. Teets and Helmut E. Gerber. *Joseph Conrad An Annotated Bibliography of Writings about Him.* DeKalb: Northern Illinois University Press, 1971. Pp. [xii], 671.

Pp. 3-6, primary books. Genre arrangement. Place, date, contents of collections. Pp. 7-12, essay survey of secondary criticism. Pp. 13-614, secondary bibliography; 1977 entries, 1895 to 1967. Books: place, publisher, date. Period: volume, date, pages. Full annotations. Indices of authors, of titles of secondary works, of periodicals and newspapers, of foreign languages, and of primary titles.

GENERAL

Millett; Longaker & Bolles; Batho & Dobrée; Temple & Tucker.

CONWAY, OLIVE, pseudonym of Harold Brighouse and John Walton: see BRIGHOUSE, HAROLD.

COOPER, ALFRED DUFF, LORD NORWICH   (1890-1954)

WWW 51-60.

COOPER, EDITH: see FIELD, MICHAEL.

COOPER, WILLIAM   (1910-   )

Pseudonym of Harry Summerfield Hoff.

Temple & Tucker; Bufkin; WW 71.

COPPARD, ALFRED EDGAR   (1878-1957)

PRIMARY

Jacob Schwartz. *The Writings of A. E. Coppard. A Bibliography with Foreword and Notes by A. E. Coppard.* London: Ulysses Bookshop, 1931. Pp. [x], 73. 650 copies, signed by Coppard.

Primary complete. Form arrangement. Transcribed TP, full collation, binding, date, contents with details of previous publication, subsequent editions, extensive notes. Includes sections listing anthologies, translations, selected periodical contributions (including reviews by Coppard with title and author of book reviewed).

Gilbert H. Fabes. *The First Editions of A. E. Coppard, A. P. Herbert, and Charles Morgan, with Values and Bibliographical Points.* London: Myers and Co., 1933. Pp. 154.

Transcribed TP, binding, variants, value in sterling. A book for dealers or collectors.

Schwartz and Fabes together give a fairly complete list to 1933.

GENERAL

Millett; Longaker & Bolles; Daiches; Temple & Tucker.

CORELLI, MARIE   (1855-1924)

PRIMARY

William Stuart Scott. *Marie Corelli, the Story of a Friendship.* London: Hutchinson, 1955. Pp. 280.

Pp. 265-266, bibliography. Primary books, secondary selected. Publisher, date. Additional secondary criticism in text, *passim.*

GENERAL

Batho & Dobrée; Temple & Tucker; NCBEL, III, 1043-1044.

CORKERY, DANIEL   (1878-?1967)

Millett; WW 67.

CORNFORD, FRANCES CROFTS   (1886-1960)

Longaker & Bolles; Daiches; WWW 51-60.

CORVO, BARON: *see* ROLFE, FREDERICK WILLIAM.

COULTON, GEORGE GORDON (1858-1947)

WWW 41-50.

COURTHOPE, WILLIAM JOHN (1842-1917)

NCBEL, III, 1426.

COWARD, SIR NOEL PIERCE (1899-   )

PRIMARY

Raymond Mander and Joe Mitchenson. *Theatrical Companion to
Coward*. London: Rockliff, 1957. Pp. 407.

Pp. 391-396, bibliography of primary first publications. Form
arrangement. Publisher, date, of British and American editions.
Bibliographical information in text, *passim*.

Milton Levin. *Noel Coward*. New York: Twayne Publishers, Inc.
(TEAS 73), 1968. Pp. 158.

Pp. 149-151, primary selected. Genre arrangement. Books:
place, publisher, year, contents. Periods: volume, pages,
date. Pp. 151-153, secondary selected. Alphabetical-by-
author arrangement. Annotated.

SECONDARY

Above, Mander and Mitchenson, *passim;* Levin, pp. 151-153.

GENERAL

Millett; Longaker & Bolles; Daiches; Temple & Tucker; Coleman
& Tyler; Adelman & Dworkin; Salem; Palmer & Dyson; WW 71.

COX, WILLIAM TREVOR: see TREVOR, WILLIAM.

CRACKANTHORPE, HUBERT   (1870-1896)

PRIMARY

Henry Danielson. *Bibliographies of Modern Authors*. London:
Bookman's Journal, 1921. Pp. [xii], [212].

Pp. 21-23, primary books. Chronological arrangement. Transcribed TP, part collation, pagination, binding, variants, miscellaneous bibliographical notes.

SECONDARY

Wendell Harris. "A Bibliography of Writings about Hubert
Crackanthorpe." *English Literature in Transition* 6 (1963):
85-91.

Alphabetical by author. Books: place, publisher, year.
Periods: volume, pages, date. All entries annotated.

GENERAL

NCBEL, III, 1044.

CRAIG, EDWARD GORDON   (1872-1966)

PRIMARY

Ifan Kyrle Fletcher and Arnold Rood. *Edward Gordon Craig. A
Bibliography*. London: Society for Theatre Research, 1967.
Pp. 117.

Primary. Form arrangement, chronological within each section.
Books: part collation, binding, place, publisher or printer, date,
number of copies, subsequent editions, bibliographical notes.
Periods: volume, pages, date, annotations. Reviews by Craig
include title and author of book reviewed. Periodicals edited

by Craig treated like primary books. A complete and authoritative bibliography. For information about specific items and additional notes: Donald Oenslager and Arnold Rood. "Edward Gordon Craig. Artist of the Theatre, 1872-1966: Introduction and Catalogue." *Bulletin of the New York Public Library* 71 (1967): 431-467, 524-541.

SECONDARY

Enid Rose. *Gordon Craig and the Theatre.* New York: Frederick A. Stokes Co., n.d. Pp. [x], 250.

Pp. 225-228, catalogues of Craig's exhibitions: place, date. Pp. 229-239, selected secondary books. Chronological arrangement. Place, publisher, date.

CRAIGIE, PEARL MARY TERESA: see HOBBES, JOHN OLIVER.

CRAIGIE, SIR WILLIAM ALEXANDER   (1867-1957)

PRIMARY

A Memoir and a List of the Published Writings of Sir W. A. Craigie. Oxford: Clarendon Press, 1952. Pp. 38.

Not seen.

CRANE, WALTER   (1845-1915)

PRIMARY

Gertrude C. E. Massé. *A Bibliography of First Editions of Books Illustrated by Walter Crane.* London: Chelsea Publishing Co., 1923. Pp. 59.

Not seen.

CRANKSHAW, EDWARD   (1909-   )

WW 71.

CROCKETT, SAMUEL RUTHERFORD   (1860-1914)

NCBEL, III, 1044-1045.

CRONIN, ARCHIBALD JOSEPH   (1896-   )

Millett; Daiches; Temple & Tucker; Bufkin; WW 71.

CROSS, BEVERLEY   (1931-   )

WW 71.

CROSSMAN, RICHARD HOWARD STAFFORD   (1907-   )

Daiches; WW 71.

CROWLEY, ALEISTER   (1875-1947)

PRIMARY

Gerald Yorke. "Bibliography of Aleister Crowley" in John
Symonds. *The Great Beast. The Life of Aleister Crowley.*
London: Rider and Co., 1951. Pp. 316.

Pp. 301-310, bibliography. Primary complete. Genre arrangement. Books: publisher, place, date, pages, number of copies.
Periods: dates, pages. Secondary criticism in text, *passim.*

Edward Noel Fitzgerald. "The Works of Aleister Crowley, Pub-
lished or Privately Printed. A Bibliographical List" in Charles
Richard Cammell. *Aleister Crowley. The Man. The Mage.
The Poet.* London: Richards Press, 1951; New York: University
Books, 1962. Pp. 230.

Pp. 207-218, bibliography. Primary first editions. Chronological arrangement. Transcribed TP, binding, pages. Secondary
criticism in text, *passim*.

Fitzgerald is less comprehensive than Yorke, but adds bibliographical details.

SECONDARY

Above, Yorke; Fitzgerald.

CUMMINGS, BRUCE FREDERICK: see BARBELLION, W. N. P.

CURZON, GEORGE NATHANIEL, LORD CURZON   (1859-1925)

PRIMARY

Kenneth Rose. *Superior Person. A Portrait of Curzon and his
Circle in Late Victorian England.* London: Weidenfeld and
Nicolson, 1969. Pp. [xiv], 475.

P. 397, primary books: publisher, year. Pp. 397-404, alphabetical by author list of secondary books: publisher, year.
Pp. 405-406, information about unpublished writings.

GENERAL

Batho & Dobrée.

DAICHES, DAVID   (1912-   )

Daiches; Temple & Tucker; WW 71.

DANE, CLEMENCE   (188?-1965)

Pseudonym of Winifred Ashton.

DAN

Millett; Temple & Tucker; Adelman & Dworkin; Salem.

D'ARCY, THE VERY REV. MARTIN CYRIL, S. J.   (1888-   )

WW 71.

DARWIN, BERNARD   (1876-1961)

WW 61.

DASHWOOD, ELIZABETH M.: see DELAFIELD, ELIZABETH M.

DAVIDSON, JOHN   (1857-1909)

PRIMARY

C. A. and H. W. Stonehill. *Bibliographies of Modern Authors*
(Second Series). London: John Castle, 1925. Pp. [xiv], 162.
750 copies.

Pp. 3-38, primary bibliography. Form arrangement (mainly
books). Transcribed TP, full collation, pagination, binding,
price, number of copies, variants, bibliographical notes.

J. A. Lester, Jr. *John Davidson. A Grub Street Bibliography.*
Charlottesville, Virginia: University of Virginia Press (Bibli-
ographical Society of University of Virginia, Secretary's News
Sheet No. 40), 1958. Pp. 30.

Not seen.

J. B. Townsend (below), p. 522: "very useful bibliography of
Davidson's journalistic work...probably as complete as at
present can be compiled."

Maurice Lindsay, ed. *John Davidson. A Selection of His Poems.*
London: Hutchinson, 1961. Pp. 220.

Pp. 1-46, introduction: gives titles of primary writings and of secondary criticism. Pp. 215-216, primary books. Genre arrangement. Dates, occasionally place.

SECONDARY

Above, Lindsay.

J. B. Townsend. *John Davidson. Poet of Armageddon.* New Haven: Yale University Press, 1961. Pp. 555.

No bibliography; notes include secondary criticism, quotations from MSS, location of Davidson collections.

GENERAL

Batho & Dobrée; Longaker & Bolles; Temple & Tucker; NCBEL, III, 619-621.

DAVIE, DONALD ALFRED   (1922-   )

Temple & Tucker; WW 71.

DAVIES, RHYS   (1903-   )

PRIMARY

John Gawsworth. *Ten Contemporaries. Notes Toward their Defin-itive Bibliography.* [First Series]. London: Ernest Benn Ltd., 1932. Pp. 224.

Pp. 44-52, primary books, first editions, 1927-1932. Chrono-logical arrangement. Transcribed TP, full collation, pagination, binding, date, bibliographical notes.

G. F. Adam. *Three Contemporary Anglo-Welsh Novelists: Jack Jones, Rhys Davies, and Hilda Vaughan.* Bern: A. Francke A. G. (University of Bern Monograph), [1950]. Pp. 109.

P. 197, bibliography. Selected primary. Genre arrangement.
Publisher, date.

GENERAL

Millett; Temple & Tucker; WW 71.

DAVIES, WILLIAM HENRY   (1870-1940)

PRIMARY

George F. Wilson. "A Bibliography of W. H. Davies." *Book-man's Journal* 5 (1922): 202; 6 (1922): 29-59.

Not seen.

Gwendolen Murphy. "Bibliographies of Modern Authors. No. III. W. H. Davies." *London Mercury* 17 (1927-1928): 76-80, 301-304, 684-688.

Primary books. Chronological arrangement. Transcribed TP, full collation, pagination, binding, price, contents, variants, reprints, subsequent editions, bibliographical notes.Pp. 687-688, chronological list of contributions to the *Nation*, 1907-1923: pages, date. Ends "To be continued," but no other entries appeared in the *London Mercury*.

Samuel J. Looker. "W. H. Davies. His Later Bibliography, 1922-1928." *Bookman's Journal* 17 (1929): 10, 122-127.

Not seen.

Richard J. Stonesifer. *W. H. Davies. A Critical Biography.* London: Jonathan Cape, 1963; Middletown, Connecticut: Wesleyan University Press, 1965. Pp. 256.

Pp. 233-234, "A Chronology of Davies' Works." Primary books. Place, publisher, year. Pp. 235-250, notes include references to secondary criticism, *passim*.

SECONDARY

Above, Stonesifer, pp. 235-250.

GENERAL

Millett; Longaker & Bolles; Batho & Dobrée; Temple & Tucker.

DAVIS, HENRY WILLIAM CARLESS   (1874-1928)

Batho & Dobrée.

DAWSON, CHRISTOPHER   (1889-1970)

WW 70.

DAY, JAMES WENTWORTH   (1899-   )

WW 71.

DAY LEWIS, CECIL: see LEWIS, CECIL DAY.

DEEPING, GEORGE WARWICK   (1877-1950)

Daiches; WWW 41-50.

DELAFIELD, ELIZABETH MONICA   (1890-1943)

PRIMARY

John Gawsworth. *Ten Contemporaries. Notes Toward their Definitive Bibliography (Second Series).* London: Joiner & Steele Ltd., 1933. Pp. 240. 1000 copies.

Pp. 123-135, primary books, first editions, 1917-1932. Chronological arrangement. Transcribed TP, full collation, pagination, binding, date.

GENERAL

Millett; Daiches; Temple & Tucker.

DE LA MARE, WALTER JOHN   (1873-1956)

PRIMARY

Gwendolyn Murphy. "Bibliographies of Modern Authors. I. Walter de la Mare." *London Mercury* 15 (1927): 526-531, 635-639; 16 (1927): 70-71.

Primary books. Genre arrangement. Transcribed TP, full collation, pagination, binding, price, variants, reprints, subsequent editions. Pp. 70-71, musical settings with name of composer.

Leonard Clark. "A Handlist of the Writings in Book Form (1902-1953) of Walter de la Mare." *Studies in Bibliography* 6 (1954): 197-217; "Addendum: A Check List of the Writings of Walter de la Mare." *Studies in Bibliography* 8 (1956): 269-270.

Primary books. Chronological arrangement. Place, publisher, date, price, illustrator, reprints, subsequent editions. Index of titles.

-- *Walter de la Mare. A Checklist prepared on the Occasion of an Exhibition of his Books and MSS at the National Book League April 20 to May 19, 1956.* Cambridge: University Press, 1956. Pp. 56.

Primary, secondary selected. Form arrangement. Books: place, publisher, date, size in inches, price, occasional notes. Periods: volume, date. Pp. 54-56, secondary bibliography.

Edward Wagenknecht. "A List of Walter de la Mare's Contributions to the London *Times Literary Supplement*." Boston

University *Studies in English* 1 (Winter 1955-1956): 243-255.

Chronological arrangement. Title of review, number of issue, pages, date; author and title of book reviewed. Pp. 211-212, other periodical contributions by de la Mare.

Of the above items, Clark (1956) provides the most complete single list; one must refer to all four items for a complete listing and descriptions.

SECONDARY

Above, Clark (1956), pp. 54-56.

Doris R. McCrosson. *Walter de la Mare*. New York: Twayne Publishers, Inc. (TEAS 33), 1966. Pp. 167.

Pp. 164-167, secondary bibliography. Alphabetical by author arrangement. Books: place, publisher, year. Periods: date, pages. Annotated.

GENERAL

Millett; Longaker & Bolles; Batho & Dobrée; Daiches; Temple & Tucker.

DELANEY, SHELAGH   (1929-   )

Coleman & Tyler; Adelman & Dworkin; Salem; Palmer & Dyson; WW 71.

DE LA PASTURE, EDMEÉ ELIZABETH MONICA: see DELAFIELD, ELIZABETH M.

DE LA ROCHE, MAZO   (-1961)

Millett; WW 61.

DEL

DELDERFIELD, RONALD FREDERICK   (1912-   )

WW 71.

DE MORGAN, WILLIAM FREND   (1839-1917)

Batho & Dobrée; Temple & Tucker.

DENNIS, GEOFFREY POMEROY   (1892-1963)

WW 63.

DENNIS, NIGEL FORBES   (1912-   )

Temple & Tucker; Coleman & Tyler; Bufkin; WW 71.

DENT, EDWARD J.   (1876-1957)

PRIMARY

Lawrence Haward. *Edward J. Dent. A Bibliography*. Cambridge: Privately Printed at the University Press for King's College, 1956.

Not seen.

DE POLNAY, PETER   (1906-   )

WW 71.

DE SELINCOURT, ERNEST   (1870-1943)

Millett; Temple & Tucker.

DICKENS, MONICA ENID   (1915-   )

(Mrs. R. O. Stratton).

WW 71; Hagen.

DICKINSON, GOLDSWORTHY LOWES   (1862-1932)

PRIMARY

R. E. Balfour. "Bibliography" in E. M. Forster. *Goldsworthy Lowes Dickinson*. London: Edwin Arnold and Co., 1934, 1938. Pp. 277.

Pp. 244-268, primary bibliography. Chronological arrangement. Books: place, publisher, date, format, pages, publisher of American edition. Periods: date, occasionally pages. Includes t ranslations of Dickinson and obituary notices.

GENERAL

Millett; Batho & Dobrée.

DICKINSON, PATRIC THOMAS   (1914-   )

Daiches; WW 71.

DILLON, HAROLD ARTHUR, LORD DILLON   (1844-1932)

PRIMARY

J. G. Mann. "Bibliography of Works by the Late Viscount Dillon." *Proceedings of the British Academy* 18 (1932): 341-344.

Primary writings. Chronological arrangement. Books: place, publisher, date. Periods: volume, date, pages.

DIVER, KATHERINE HELEN MAUD (-1945)

WWW 41-50.

DOBRÉE, BONAMY (1891-)

PRIMARY

Margaret Britton. "A Selected List of the Published Writings of Bonamy Dobrée" in John Butt, ed., *Of Books and Human-kind. Essays and Poems Presented to Bonamy Dobrée.* London: Routledge and Kegan Paul, 1964. Pp. 232.

Pp. 217-226, primary bibliography, 1919-1962. Chronological arrangement. Books: place, publisher, date, reprints, contents. Periods: volume, pages, date. Includes unsigned writings.

GENERAL

Millett; Daiches; Temple & Tucker; WW 71.

DOBRÉE, VALENTINE (1894-)

Daiches.

DOBSON, HENRY AUSTIN (1840-1921)

PRIMARY

Francis Edwin Murray. *A Bibliography of Austin Dobson.* Derby: Frank Murray, 1900. Pp. 347. 635 copies.

Primary, Form arrangement, genre subdivisions. Information varies for each entry. Extensive indices.

Alban Dobson. *A Bibliography of the First Editions of Published and Privately Printed Books and Pamphlets by Austin Dobson.*

London: First Edition Club, 1925. Pp. 88.

Primary books. Chronological arrangement. Transcribed TP, full collation, binding, date, reprints, notes.

-- *Austin Dobson. Some Notes...with Chapters by Sir Edmund Gosse and George Saintsbury.* London: Oxford University Press, 1928.

Adds a few items not in Dobson (1925).

Alban T. A. Dobson. *University of London Library, Catalogue of the Collection of the Works of Austin Dobson (1840-1921).* London: Chiswick Press, 1960. Pp. 62.

Primary, secondary. Form arrangement. Minimum of bibliographical details, but a list of the titles by and about Dobson in this virtually complete collection.

Together these four books provide a complete account of Dobson's writings.

SECONDARY

Above, Dobson (1960).

GENERAL

Longaker & Bolles; Batho & Dobrée; NCBEL, III, 1427-1428.

DOUGHTY, CHARLES MONTAGU   (1843-1926)

PRIMARY

"Bibliographies of Modern Authors. Charles Montagu Doughty." *London Mercury* 4 (1921): 87.

Primary books, 1866-1921. Genre arrangement. Publisher, year.

Anne Treneer. *Charles Montagu Doughty. A Study of his Prose and Verse.* London: Jonathan Cape, 1935. Pp. 350.

Pp. 333-339, bibliography. Primary books, secondary selected. Genre arrangement. Publisher, place, date. Reviews of Doughty listed under title of book reviewed.

SECONDARY

Above, Treneer.

GENERAL

Millett; Longaker & Bolles; Temple & Tucker; NCBEL, III, 622-623.

DOUGLAS, LORD ALFRED   (1870-1945)

PRIMARY

Rupert Croft-Cooke. *Bosie. Lord Alfred Douglas, His Friends and Enemies.* London: W. H. Allen; New York: Bobbs-Merrill Co., 1963. Pp. 414.

No bibliography, but bibliographical references in text, *passim;* also see pp. 385-386 for list of primary and secondary books used by Croft-Cooke.

SECONDARY

Above, Croft-Cooke, *passim.*

GENERAL

NCBEL, III, 623-624.

DOUGLAS, GEORGE NORMAN   (1868-1952)

PRIMARY

Edward D. McDonald. *A Bibliography of the Writings of Norman Douglas with Notes by Norman Douglas*. Philadelphia: Centaur Book Shop, 1927. Pp. 165. 400 copies.

Primary, secondary selected. Form arrangement. Books: transcribed TP, full collation, pagination, binding, date, variants, reprints, notes. Periods: volume, date, titles of books in which later collected. Includes unsigned writings. Reviews by Douglas include title of book reviewed. Pp. 149-165, secondary bibliography.

Cecil Woolf. *A Bibliography of Norman Douglas*. London: Rupert Hart-Davis (Soho Bibliography No. 6), 1954; Fair Lawn, New Jersey: Essential Books, 1957. Pp. 201.

Primary. Form arrangement. Books: transcribed TP, full collation, pagination, binding, date, contents, price, variants, reprints, full notes. Periods: volume, pages, dates. Indices.

Continues, supplements, but does not supplant, McDonald.

Ian Greenlees. *Norman Douglas*. London: Longmans, Green and Co. (WTW 82), 1957. Pp. 38.

Pp. 35-37, bibliography. Primary books. Chronological arrangement. Date, genre, textual notes. P. 38, secondary bibliography.

One of the most complete bibliographies in the WTW series.

SECONDARY

Above, McDonald, pp. 149-165; Greenlees, p. 38.

Ralph D. Lindeman. *Norman Douglas*. New York: Twayne Publishers, Inc. (TEAS 19), 1965. Pp. 208.

Pp. 199-200, bibliography. Annotated.

GENERAL

Millett; Longaker & Bolles; Daiches; Temple & Tucker.

DOUGLAS, KEITH CASTELLAIN (1920-1944)

PRIMARY

John Waller and G. S. Fraser, eds. *The Collected Poems of Keith Douglas*. London: Editions Poetry London, 1951. Pp. [xxii], 151.

Bibliographical information, *passim*, in "Preface," p. v; "Acknowledgements," p. xii; "Biographical Note," pp. xv-xxi; "Notes," pp. 137-151.

SECONDARY

G. S. Fraser. "Keith Douglas: A Poet of the Second World War" [Chatterton Lecture on an English Poet]. *Proceedings of the British Academy* 42 (1956): 89-108.

No bibliography, but references to secondary criticism.

DOUGLAS HOME, WILLIAM: see HOME, WILLIAM DOUGLAS.

DOWSON, ERNEST CHRISTOPHER (1867-1900)

PRIMARY

Guy Harrison. "Bibliography" in Victor Plarr. *Ernest Dowson 1888-1897. Reminiscences, Unpublished Letters, and Marginalia*. London: Elkin Matthews, 1914. Pp. 147.

Pp. 131-142, primary first editions, secondary selected bibliography. Genre arrangement. Books: publisher, place, date, part collation, notes. Periods: volume, date, pages.

C. A. and H. W. Stonehill. *Bibliographies of Modern Authors* (Second Series). London: John Castle, 1925. Pp. [xiv], 162.

750 copies.

Pp. 41-63, primary bibliography. Form arrangement. Transcribed TP, full collation, pagination, binding, price, number of copies, variants, bibliographical notes.

SECONDARY

Above, Harrison.

Thomas Burnett Swann. *Ernest Dowson.* New York: Twayne Publishers, Inc. (TEAS 15), 1964. Pp. 122.

Pp. 113-114, primary books, including translations by Dowson. Pp. 114-117, secondary books. Alphabetical by author arrangement. Place, publisher, year, annotations.

Jonathan Ramsey. "Ernest Dowson: An Annotated Bibliography of Writings about Him." *English Literature in Transition* 14 (1971): 17-42.

Alphabetical by author arrangement. Books: place, publisher, date. Periods: volume, pages, date. Full annotations. The best source of information about Dowson.

GENERAL

Longaker & Bolles; Batho & Dobrée; NCBEL, III, 624-625.

DOYLE, SIR ARTHUR CONAN   (1859-1930)

PRIMARY

Harold Locke. *A Bibliographical Catalogue of the Writings of Sir Arthur Conan Doyle, M. D., Ll. D., 1879-1928.* Tunbridge Wells: D. Webster, 1928. Pp. 84.

Primary. Form and genre arrangement. Transcribed TP, part collation, binding, date, notes on some reprints, other notes. Contributions to periodicals listed under title of the periodical: dates. Index.

A fairly complete bibliography, although difficult to use.

Pierre Nordon. *Conan Doyle. A Biography,* translated Frances
Partridge. New York: Rinehart and Winston, 1967. Pp. 370.

Pp. 347-350, bibliography. Nordon refers one to Locke (above)
for the primary bibliography, providing additions and corrections to it. Pp. 351-360, selected secondary bibliography.
Topic arrangement. Place, publisher, date, pages.

SECONDARY

Above, Nordon, pp. 351-360.

Ronal Burt de Waal. "A Bibliography of Sherlockian Bibliographies and Periodicals." *Papers of the Bibliographical Society of America* 64 (1970): 339-354.

A bibliography of bibliographies, checklists, and catalogues.
Form arrangement. Books: place, publisher, date, pages.
Periods: volume, date, pages. P. 340: "The present list was
prepared as an aid to the compiler in his forth-coming *World
Bibliography on Sherlock Holmes and Dr. Watson.*"

The beginning point for study of the sacred writings.

GENERAL

Longaker & Bolles; Batho & Dobrée; Temple & Tucker; NCBEL,
III, 1046-1049.

DRABBLE, MARGARET   (1939-   )

(Mrs. C. W. Swift).

Bufkin; WW 71.

DRINKWATER, JOHN   (1882-1937)

PRIMARY

Henry Danielson. *Bibliographies of Modern Authors*. London:
Bookman's Journal, 1921. Pp. [xii], [212].

Pp. 41-60, books and pamphlets. Chronological arrangement.
Transcribed TP, part collation, pagination, binding, variants,
miscellaneous bibliographical notes.

Alois Wilhelm Roeder. *John Drinkwater als Dramatiker*. Giessen:
Verlag des Englischen Seminars der Universität Giessen, 1927.
Pp. 58.

Pp. 40-44, primary, secondary selected. Genre arrangement.
Books: date, publisher, place. Periods: date, pages. Pp. 45-
57, footnotes including secondary criticism.

[Timothy d'Arch Smith]. *John Drinkwater, 1882-1937. Catalogue
of an Exhibition*. London: Times Bookshop, 1962. Pp. 51.
100 copies.

Primary books, also MSS, association items and iconography.
Transcribed TP without lineation bars, full collation, binding,
date, variants, reprints, notes.

This catalogue provides the most complete list of primary
books; there appears to be no list of Drinkwater's periodical
contributions.

SECONDARY

Above, Roeder, pp. 45-57.

GENERAL

Millett; Longaker & Bolles; Daiches; Temple & Tucker; Salem.

DUCLAUX, MARY   (1856-1944)

Née Agnes Mary Frances Robinson; (1) Mrs. James Dar-
mesteter; (2) Mrs. Émile Duclaux.

PRIMARY

Ruth Van Zuyle Holmes. "Mary Duclaux. 1856-1944." *English
Literature in Transition* 10 (1967): i, 27-46.

Pp. 32-39, primary bibliography. Form arrangement. Books:
place, publisher, year. Periods: volume, pages, date, genre.
Pp. 39-46, secondary bibliography. Chronological arrangement.
Fully annotated. Lists anthologies including Duclaux, also
translations by Duclaux; excludes her reviews for the *TLS*.

SECONDARY

Above, Holmes, pp. 39-46.

GENERAL

NCBEL, III, 646-647.

DUGGAN, ALFRED LEO   (1903-1964)

Bufkin; Temple & Tucker.

DUKES, ASHLEY   (1885-1959)

PRIMARY

Ashley Dukes. *The Scene is Changed*. London: Macmillan and
Co., 1942. Pp. 252.

Bibliographical information in the text, *passim*, of this autobiography.

GENERAL

Millett.

DU MAURIER, DAME DAPHNE   (1907-   )

(Lady Browning).

Bufkin; Temple & Tucker; WW 71; Hagen.

DU MAURIER, GEORGE LOUIS PALMELLA BUSSON (1834-1896)

PRIMARY

Trilbyana. The Rise and Progress of a Popular Novel. New
   York: Critic Company, 1895. Pp. 41.

   Material drawn largely from the *Critic* puffing *Trilby;* important
   information concerning American reception of the novel.

John T. Winterich, "George du Maurier and *Trilby*" in *Books and
   the Man.* New York: Greenberg, 1929. Pp. [xvi], 374.

   Pp. 102-122, discursive essay with bibliographical information,
   passim.

L. N. Feipel. "The American Issues of *Trilby.*" *Colophon* 2,
   iv (1937): 537-549.

   An essay on the variants in the American issues; detailed
   bibliographical information.

Derek Pepys Whiteley. *George du Maurier.* London: Art and
   Technics, 1948. Pp. 112.

   Pp. 6-7, list of books illustrated by du Maurier.

GENERAL

Batho & Dobrée; NCBEL, III,.1049.

DUNCAN, RONALD   (1914-   )

Temple & Tucker; WW 71.

DUNSANY, EDWARD JOHN MORETON DRAX PLUNKETT,
    LORD DUNSANY   (1878-1957)

PRIMARY

Henry Danielson. *Bibliographies of Modern Authors*. London:
Bookman's Journal, 1921. Pp. [xii], [212].

Pp. 67-75, primary books, 1905-1920. Chronological arrangement. Transcribed TP, part collation, pagination, binding,
variants, miscellaneous bibliographical notes.

F. G. Stoddard. "The Lord Dunsany Collection." *Library
Chronicle of the University of Texas* 9, iii (1967): 27-32.

A discursive essay with particular attention given to the MSS
at Texas.

[Zack Bowen. *Lord Edward Dunsany*. Publication announced by
Bucknell University Press in 1971 for its Irish Writers Series.]

GENERAL

Millett; Temple & Tucker; Adelman & Dworkin; Salem; NCBEL,
III, 1945-1948.

DURRELL, GERALD MALCOLM   (1925-   )

WW 71.

DURRELL, LAWRENCE GEORGE   (1912-   )

PRIMARY

Robert A. Potter and Brooke Whiting. *Lawrence Durrell: A*

Checklist. Los Angeles: UCLA Library, 1961. Pp. 50.

Primary. Chronological arrangement. Books (both British and American editions): place, publisher, date, brief notes. Periods: volume, pages, date. Pp. 47-50, title index.

An extremely full list, issued on the occasion of the presentation of the Powell collection to UCLA, and incorporating two earlier bibliographies: A. G. Thomas and L. C. Powell, "Some Uncollected Authors. XXIII. Lawrence Durrell." *Book Collector* 9 (1960): 56-63; and A. Knerr. "Regarding a Checklist of Lawrence Durrell." *Papers of the Bibliographical Society of America* 55 (1961): 142-152.

Alan Thomas. "Bibliography" in G. S. Fraser. *Lawrence Durrell: A Study.* London: Faber and Faber, 1968. Pp. 256.

Pp. 200-250, bibliography. Primary, secondary. Form and genre arrangement. Books: publisher, place, date, format, brief bibliographical notes, remarks by Durrell. Periods: place, volume, date, notes. Includes gramophone records, musical settings, unpublished radio and television appearances by Durrell. Pp. 216-225, secondary bibliography. Chronological arrangement.

Potter-Whiting and Thomas together provide an almost complete primary list.

G. S. Fraser. *Lawrence Durrell.* London: Longman Group Ltd. (WTW 216), 1970. Pp. 47.

Pp. 45-47, primary and secondary books. Chronological arrangement. Date, genre, place.

A convenient checklist of the primary books.

SECONDARY

Above, Thomas, pp. 216-225.

Bernard Stone. "Bibliography" in Alfred Perlès. *My Friend Lawrence Durrell*. London: Scorpion Press, 1961. Pp. 62.

Pp. 47-60, primary bibliography. Pp. 61-62, secondary bibliography, including reviews. Volume, pages.

John A. Weigel. *Lawrence Durrell*. New York: Twayne Publishers, Inc. (TEAS 29), 1965. Pp. 174.

Pp. 165-170, bibliography. Books: place, publisher, date. Period: volume, pages, date. Annotated.

Maurice Beebe. "Criticism of Lawrence Durrell. A Selected Checklist." *Modern Fiction Studies* 13 (1967): 417-421.

Alphabetical by author arrangement. Books: place, publisher, year. Periods: volume, pages, date.

GENERAL

Daiches; Temple & Tucker; WW 71.

DUTTON, GEOFFREY   (1922-   )

Hetherington.

DYER, CHARLES   (1928-   )

Salem; WW 71.

DYMENT, CLIFFORD HENRY   (1914-   )

Daiches; WW 71.

EARP, THOMAS WADE   (1892-1958)

WWW 51-60.

EAST, MICHAEL, pseudonym of Morris West: *see* WEST, MORRIS.

EDDINGTON, SIR ARTHUR STANLEY   (1882-1944)

PRIMARY

A. Vibert Douglas. *The Life of Arthur Stanley Eddington.*
London: Thomas Nelson & Sons, Ltd., 1956. Pp. 207.

Pp. 193-198, "Published Works." Form arrangement. Books:
place, date, foreign editions. Periods: volume, pages, date.

GENERAL

Daiches.

EDDISON, ERIC RUCKER   (1882-1945)

PRIMARY

George Rostrevor Hamilton. "Eric Rucker Eddison." *Book
Handbook: An Illustrated Quarterly* [Bracknell] 1, i (1947):
53-57.

Not seen.

GENERAL

WWW 41-50.

EGERTON, GEORGE   (1859-1945)

Pseudonym of Mary Chavelita Clairmonte, afterwards Mrs.
Bright.

PRIMARY

John Gawsworth. *Ten Contemporaries. Notes Toward their
Definitive Bibliography* [First Series]. London: Ernest Benn

Ltd., 1932. Pp. 224.

Pp. 61-65, primary books, first editions, 1893-1905. Chronological arrangement. Transcribed TP, full collation, pagination, binding date, bibliographical notes. Includes translations by Egerton.

Terence deVere White, ed. *A Leaf from the Yellow Book.*
The Correspondence of George Egerton. London: Richards
Press, 1958. Pp. 184.

No bibliography: the text gives information about published
and unpublished writings, including periodical contributions
and secondary criticism. Index, pp. 181-184.

EGLINTON, JOHN   (1868-1961)

Pseudonym of William Kirkpatrick Magee.

Temple & Tucker.

ELIOT, THOMAS STEARNS   (1888-1965)

PRIMARY

Hans Willi Bentz. *T. S. Eliot in Übersetzungen.* Frankfurt
am Main: Hans W. Bentz Verlag, 1963. Pp. 58. 500 copies.

List of 222 translations of Eliot after 1945. Titles, names
of translators, publishers, places, dates, prices. Various
indices.

Donald [Clifford] Gallup. "The 'Lost' Manuscripts of T. S.
Eliot." *TLS,* No. 3480 (7 November 1968), pp. 1237-1240
(including three photographs of mss); in *Bulletin of the
New York Public Library* 72 (1968): 641-652 (including two
leaves of photographs).

Essay concerning primary MSS, some of which are reproduced in T. S. Eliot. *The Waste Land A Facsimile and
Transcript of the Original Drafts including the Annotations
of Ezra Pound,* ed. Valerie Eliot. New York: Harcourt
Brace Jovanovich, Inc., 1971. Pp. [xxxii], 149. See the

"Introduction," pp. ix-xxx, for details concerning original publication of The Waste Land.

-- T. S. Eliot A Bibliography. London: Faber and Faber, Ltd., 1969. [Second, revised edition of the London, Faber and Faber, Ltd., 1952 and the New York, Harcourt, Brace, and Co., 1953, edition]. Pp. 414.

Primary. Form arrangement. Books: transcribed TP, part collation, binding, date, price, number of copies, variants, subsequent editions, extensive notes. Periods: volume, pages, date. Reviews by Eliot include title and author of book reviewed. Translations of Eliot listed separately under name of language into which translated. Index. "Introductory Note," pp. 11-14, provides concise statement of Gallup's bibliographical principles.

The authoritative bibliography.

SECONDARY

Richard M. Ludwig. "T. S. Eliot" in Fifteen Modern American Authors. A Survey of Research and Criticism, ed. Jackson R. Bryer. Durham, North Carolina: Duke University Press, 1969. Pp. [xviii], 493.

Pp. 139-174. Survey and evaluation in essay form of the Eliot bibliographies, editions, MSS and letters, biographies, and criticism, the latter section subdivided into five chronological areas.

The beginning point for study of the criticism of Eliot; particularly helpful listing of all primary and secondary bibliographies. Among the recommended secondary bibliog - raphies are the following three:

Leonard Unger, ed. T. S. Eliot. A Selected Critique. New York: Rinehart and Co., 1948. Pp. [xx], 478. Reprinted 1966.

Pp. 463-478, secondary bibliography. Alphabetical by author arrangement. Books: place, publisher, year. Periods: volume, pages, date.

David E. Jones. The Plays of T. S. Eliot. London, 1960; Toronto: University of Toronto Press, 1965. Pp. xiv, 242.

Pp. 223-238, secondary bibliography, selected. Restricted to criticism of Eliot's plays. Arranged under title of play studied. Books: publisher, place, date, relevant pages. Periods: volume, pages, date. Occasional annotations.

Fei-Pai Lu. *T. S. Eliot. The Dialectical Structure of his Theory of Poetry*. Chicago and London: University of Chicago Press, 1966. Pp.[xii], 170.

Pp. 139-147, primary bibliography, selected. Pp. 147-164, secondary bibliography, selected. Mainly concerned with Eliot the critic. Form arrangement. Books: place, publisher, date, pages. Periods: volume, pages, date.

GENERAL

Millett; Longaker & Bolles; Temple & Tucker; Coleman & Tyler; Adelman & Dworkin; Salem; Palmer & Dyson.

ELLERMAN, ANNIE WINIFRED: *see* BRYHER.

ELLIS, HENRY HAVELOCK   (1859-1939)

PRIMARY

Houston Peterson. *Havelock Ellis. Philosopher of Love*. Boston and New York: Houghton Mifflin Co.; London: Allen and Unwin Ltd., 1928. Pp. 432.

Pp. 394-417, bibliography of primary writings, August 1880 to January 1928. Chronological arrangement. Books: place, publisher, date, reprints. Periods: volume, pages, date. Translations listed under name of language. P. 394: "Although [Ellis] has himself gone over the list three times, it cannot be considered absolutely complete."

Burne (below), p. 100: "excellent bibliography up to 1928."

A. Calder Marshall. *Havelock Ellis. A Biography*. London: Rupert Hart-Davis, 1959. Pp. 292.

Pp. 283-286, bibliography of post-1928 titles; selected secondary bibliography.

Glenn S. Burne. "Havelock Ellis: An Annotated Selected Bibliography of Primary and Secondary Works." *English Literature in Transition* 9 (1966): 55-107.

Pp. 55-74, primary bibliography, excluding "work of a strictly and clearly medical nature." Form arrangement. Books: date, place, publisher, pages, reprints. Periods: volume, pages, date. Pp. 74-107, secondary bibliography. Alphabetical by author arrangement. Annotated.

SECONDARY

Above, Marshall, pp. 285-286, 11-16; Burne, pp. 74-107 (subsequent issues of *English Literature in Transition* continue this bibliography).

GENERAL

Millett; Batho & Dobrée; Temple & Tucker; NCBEL, III, 1429-1431.

ELLIS-FERMOR, UNA MARY   (1894-1958)

Daiches; WWW 51-60.

ELTON, GODFREY, LORD ELTON   (1892-   )

WW 71.

ELTON, OLIVER   (1861-1945)

Batho & Dobrée; WWW 41-50.

EMPSON, WILLIAM   (1906-   )

Millett; Longaker & Bolles; Daiches; Temple & Tucker; WW 71.

ENRIGHT, DENNIS JOSEPH   (1920-   )

Temple & Tucker; WW 71.

ESMOND, HENRY VERNON   (1869-1922)

Pseudonym of Henry Vernon Jack.

NCBEL, III, 1192.

ERVINE, ST. JOHN GREER   (1883-1971)

Millett; Longaker & Bolles; Batho & Dobrée; Temple & Tucker;
Adelman & Dworkin; Salem; NCBEL, III, 1945; WW 71.

ESSLIN, MARTIN J.   (1918-   )

WW 71.

EVANS, CARADOC   (1879-1945)

PRIMARY

Oliver Sandys. *Caradoc Evans*. London: Hurst and Blackett,
Ltd., 1946. Pp. 167.

Bibliographical information in text, *passim*, of this biography
by Mrs. Evans.

Brynmor Jones. *Caradoc Evans 1879-1945*. Welsh Arts Council
(Bibliographies of Anglo-Welsh Literature, 2), 1968.

Not seen.

GENERAL

Millett; Daiches; Temple & Tucker.

EVANS, JOAN   (-   )

WW 71.

EWING, ALFRED CYRIL   (1899-   )

WW 71.

FABER, SIR GEOFFREY CUST   (1889-1961)

WW 61.

FABIAN SOCIETY   (1884-   )

PRIMARY

Anne Fremantle. *This Little Band of Prophets. The British
Fabians.* London: George Allen and Unwin; New York: New
American Library (Mentor Book MT266), 1960. Pp. 320.

Pp. 268-285, "Fabian Publications 1884-1958." Chronological arrangement under three divisions: Tracts, Research
Pamphlets, Books and Other Publications. Date, number in
series, title and author. General secondary bibliography, pp.
308-314.

SECONDARY

Above, Fremantle, pp. 308-314.

FAGAN, JAMES BERNARD   (1873-1933)

WWW 29-40.

FAIRFIELD, CICILY ISABEL: see WEST, REBECCA.

FALKNER, JOHN MEADE   (1858-1932)

PRIMARY

Graham Pollard. "Some Uncollected Authors. XXV. John Meade
Falkner. 1858-1932." *Book Collector* 9 (1960): 318-325.

Primary books. Chronological arrangement. Transcribed
TP, part collation, binding, date, variants, reprints, notes.

GENERAL

NCBEL, III, 1051; Hagen.

FARJEON, ELEANOR   (1881-1965)

PRIMARY

Eileen H. Colwell. *Eleanor Farjeon*. London: Bodley Head
(Bodley Head Monograph), 1961. Pp. 94.

Pp. 89-94, bibliography. Primary books. Chronological under
these headings: Books by Eleanor Farjeon; Books by Eleanor
Farjeon and Harry Farjeon; Books by Eleanor Farjeon and
Herbert Farjeon; American Editions. Publisher, date, illustrator.

FARJEON, HERBERT   (1887-1945)

WWW 41-50; also above, FARJEON, ELEANOR.

FAUSSET, HUGH I'ANSON   (1895-1965)

Millett; Temple & Tucker; WW 65.

FERMOR, PATRICK MICHAEL LEIGH   (1915-   )

WW 71.

FERMOR, UNA MARY ELLIS-: see ELLIS-FERMOR, UNA MARY.

FFOULKES, MAUDE MARY   (1871-1949)

(Mrs. Chester Craven).

PRIMARY

Violet Powell. *A Substantial Ghost: The Literary Adventures
of Maude ffoulkes.* London: Heinemann, 1967. Pp. xii, [210].

No bibliography, but references in passing to Mrs. ffoulkes'
books. Additional information in Marguerite Steen, *Looking
Glass. An Autobiography.* London: Longmans, 1966, pp.
81-84.

FIELD, GUY CROMWELL   (1887-1955)

PRIMARY

D. J. Allan. "Guy Cromwell Field. 1887-1955." *Proceedings
of the British Academy* 42 (1956): 311-318.

Pp. 317-318, bibliography. Primary books. Chronological
arrangement. Year.

FIELD, MICHAEL

Pseudonym of:

BRADLEY, KATHERINE HARRIS (1846-1914)
                and

COOPER, EDITH EMMA (1862-1913).

PRIMARY

Mary Sturgeon. *Michael Field*. London: George Harrap and Co., 1922. Pp. 246.

Pp. 245-246, bibliography. Primary books. Chronological arrangement. Publisher, date, reprints. Information about periodical contributions and secondary criticism in text, *passim*.

T. and D. C. Sturge Moore, eds. *Works and Days. From the Journal of Michael Field*. London: John Murray, 1933. Pp. 338.

No bibliography. Information in text, *passim*, and in "Editors' Preface," pp. xv-xxii.

GENERAL

Temple & Tucker; NCBEL, III, 626-627.

FIELDING, GABRIEL   (1916-   )

Pseudonym of Alan Gabriel Barnsley.

Temple & Tucker; Bufkin; WW 71.

FIGGIS, DARRELL   (1882-1925)

PRIMARY

Patrick Sarsfield O'Hegarty. "Bibliographies of 1916 and the Irish Revolution. No. XV. Darrell Figgis." *Dublin Magazine* 12 (July-September 1937): 47-54.

Primary books. Chronological arrangement. Transcribed TP, part collation, pagination, binding, extensive biographical and and bibliographical notes.

FIRBANK, ARTHUR ANNESLEY RONALD   (1886-1926)

PRIMARY

Miriam J. Benkovitz. *A Bibliography of Ronald Firbank*. London: Rupert Hart-Davis (Soho Bibliography No. 16), 1963. Pp. 103.

Primary. Form arrangement. Transcribed TP, full collation, pagination, binding, date, price, variants, reprints, extensive notes, contents. Index.

The authoritative bibliography. Praised by Lord Horder, *Book Collector* 12 (1963): 380: "a work which takes Firbank studies in general so much further forward" (also additions and corrections).

SECONDARY

Robert Murray Davis. "Ronald Firbank. A Selected Bibliography of Criticism." *Bulletin of Bibliography* 26 (1969): 108-111.

Alphabetical by author arrangement. Books: place, publisher, date. Periods: volume, date, pages. Reviews are identified, and cross-references are given for related entries.

GENERAL

Temple & Tucker.

FIRTH, SIR CHARLES HARDING   (1857-1936)

PRIMARY

[Sir C. H. Firth]. *A Bibliography of the Writings of Sir Charles Firth*. London: Oxford University Press, 1928. Pp. 45.

Primary. Genre arrangement. Books: place, date, publisher, pages, reprints. Periods: volume, pages, date. Index.

GENERAL

Batho & Dobrée.

FISHER, HERBERT ALBERT LAURENS   (1865-1940)

PRIMARY

David Ogg. *Herbert Fisher 1865-1940. A Short Biography.*
London: Edward Arnold and Co., 1947. Pp. 205.

Bibliographical information in text, *passim.* Index.

GENERAL

Batho & Dobrée; Daiches.

FITZGIBBON, ROBERT LOUIS CONSTANTINE LEE-DILLON
                (1919-   )

WW 71.

FITZMAURICE, GEORGE   (1877-1963)

PRIMARY

The Plays of George Fitzmaurice. Dublin: Dolmen Press Ltd. I.
Dramatic Fantasies, ed. Austin Clarke. 1967. Pp. [xvi],
159; II. *Folk Plays,* ed. Howard K. Slaughter. 1969. Pp. xx,
153; III. *Realistic Plays,* ed. Howard K. Slaughter. 1970.
Pp. xviii, 166.

The title page for each play gives the title of the volume
or periodical, place, and date of first publication, while the
last pages of each volume provide details of the first production of each play: place, theatre, date, cast of characters,
producer. The three Introductions provide references to the
secondary bibliography.

GENERAL

NCBEL, III, 1941-1942.

FLECKER, JAMES ELROY   (1884-1915)

PRIMARY

Henry Danielson. *Bibliographies of Modern Authors.*   London:
Bookman's Journal, 1921. Pp. [xii], [212].

Pp. 81-89, primary books, 1906-1921. Chronological arrangement. Transcribed TP, part collation, pagination, binding,
variants, miscellaneous bibliographical notes.

Most of this information is reprinted in Douglas Goldring.
*James Elroy Flecker. An Appreciation with some Biographical
Notes.* London: Chapman and Hall, 1922. Pp. 200. Pp. 191-
195, bibliography. Adds the number of copies in each edition.

Thomas Stanley Mercer. *James Elroy Flecker. From School to
Samarkand.* Thames Ditton, Surrey, Merle Press, 1952. Pp. 56.
160 copies.

Pp. 47-56, primary bibliography. Genre and form arrangement.
Books: transcribed TP, part collation, binding, notes. Periods:
volume, pages, dates.

Mercer provides the most complete list of primary writings.

GENERAL

Millett; Longaker & Bolles; Batho & Dobrée; Temple & Tucker.

FLEMING, IAN LANCASTER   (1908-1964)

PRIMARY

Kingsley Amis. *The James Bond Dossier.* London: Jonathan
Cape, 1965. Pp. 159.

Pp. 156-159, chronological list of novels by Fleming with

details of plot.

John Pearson. *The Life of Ian Fleming*. New York: McGraw-Hill, 1966. Pp. [xii], 338.

Bibliographical information in text, *passim*.

David Randall. *The Ian Fleming Collection of 19th-20th Century Source Material concerning Western Civilization together with the Originals of the James Bond-007 Tales*. Bloomington, Indiana: Lilly Library, 1971. Pp. 53.

Not seen. *TLS*, 23 July 1971, p. 868: part III of this catalogue of an exhibition at the Lilly Library gives bibliographical details of primary manuscripts.

SECONDARY

Oreste de Buono and Umberto Edo. *The Bond Affair*, translated R. A. Downie. London: MacDonald, 1966. Pp. 173.

Pp. 171-173, secondary bibliography (mainly Continental in origin). Other information in text, *passim*.

GENERAL

Hagen.

FLETCHER, GEOFFREY SCOWCROFT   (1923-   )

WW 71.

FLETCHER, JOSEPH SMITH   (1863-1935)

PRIMARY

"A Bibliography of the Works of J. S. Fletcher." *The Borzoi 1925*. New York: Alfred A. Knopf, 1925. Pp. [xiv], 351.

Pp. 73-75, primary books. Genre arrangement. Titles only.

GENERAL

WWW 29-40; Hagen.

FLINT, FRANK STEWART   (1885-   )

Millett; Longaker & Bolles; Temple & Tucker.

FORD, ELBUR: see HIBBERT, ELEANOR.

FORD, FORD MADOX [HUEFFER]   (1873-1939)

PRIMARY

David Dow Harvey. *Ford Madox Ford, 1873-1939. A Bibliography
of Works and Criticism.* Princeton: Princeton University Press,
1962. Pp. xxiv, 633.

Primary, secondary. Form arrangement. Books: transcribed
TP, part collation, binding, date, price, variants, reprints, full
notes, MSS, previous publication of contents, contents. Periods: volume, pages, date. Sections on Manuscripts; Letters;
Miscellanea; Contributions to Periodicals: précis, annotations,
quotations. Complete, extensive annotations and quotations
for all secondary criticism and many of the primary writings.

H. E. Gerber, *English Literature in Transition* 6 (1963): 57:
"the basic bibliographical record...accurate, thorough, and as
nearly complete as any volume of this kind is ever likely to
be or need be even for the most discriminating scholar."

SECONDARY

Above, Harvey, pp. 275-610, for criticism before 1962. After
1962, consult issues of *English Literature in Transition* for
annotated lists of secondary bibliography.

Charles G. Hoffmann. *Ford Madox Ford.* New York: Twayne
Publishers, Inc. (TEAS 55), 1967. Pp. 156.

Pp. 145-147, primary books. Pp. 147-150, secondary bibliography. Alphabetical by author arrangement. Books: place, publisher, year. Periods: volume, pages, date. Annotated.

GENERAL

Millett; Longaker & Bolles; Temple & Tucker.

FORESTER, CECIL SCOTT   (1899-1966)

Temple & Tucker; Bufkin; WW 66; Hagen.

FORMAN, BUXTON   (1842-1917)

NCBEL, III, 1646.

FORSTER, EDWARD MORGAN   (1879-1970)

PRIMARY

Louis K. Greiff. "Edward Morgan Forster. A Bibliography." *Bulletin of Bibliography* 24 (1964): 108-112.

Primary books. Genre arrangement. Place, publisher, date, pages, reprints, subsequent editions, translations. Includes stage adaptations of Forster's writings.

B[rownlee] J[ean] Kirkpatrick. *A Bibliography of E. M. Forster.* London: Rupert Hart-Davis (Soho Bibliography No. 19, Revised Edition), 1968. Pp. 205.

Primary. Form arrangement. Books: transcribed TP, part collation, pagination, binding, date, price, number of copies, variants, reprints, subsequent editions, contents, extensive notes. Periods: volume, pages, date. Includes unsigned primary writings; reviews by Forster include title and author of book reviewed. Separate list of translations of Forster. Index.

R. J. Roberts, *Book Collector* 15 (1966): 75-79: "one of the most careful and useful of recent additions to the study of contemporary English literature" (review of the first edition).

John B. Shipley. "Additions to the E. M. Forster Bibliography." *Papers of the Bibliographical Society of America* 60 (1966): 224-225.

Adds six items to Kirkpatrick (first edition); other information.

SECONDARY

Helmut Gerber. "E. M. Forster: An Annotated Checklist of Writings about Him." *English Fiction in Transition* 2 (1959): 4-27.

Alphabetical by author arrangement. Books: place, publisher, date. Periods: volume, pages, date. Précis of each entry. Continued in subsequent issues of *English Fiction* (later *English Literature) in Transition* by various compilers, especially Frederick P. W. McDowell, to form the most comprehensive list of secondary criticism available..

For particularly lengthy checklists, see: 3, i (1960): 24-27; 3, ii (1960): 48-50; 4, ii (1961): 45-53; 4, iii (1961): 41-47; 5, i (1962): 38-43; 5, iv (1962): 25-32; 6, ii (1963): 97-105; 8, v (1965): 278-283; 10 (1967): 219-238; 11 (1968): 206-216; 14 (1970): 93-173.

Maurice Beebe and Joseph Brogunier. "Criticism of E. M. Forster: A Selected Checklist." *Modern Fiction Studies* 7 (1961): 284-292.

Arranged: General; Studies of Individual Works of Fiction (alphabetical list of primary titles). Books: place, publisher, date. Periods: volume, pages, date.

Although less comprehensive than the *English Fiction in Transition* checklist, the emphasis on quality and the arrangement make this checklist particularly helpful to the beginning student.

One should also note the announcement in 1971 by the Annotated Secondary Bibliography Series on English Literature in Transition, Helmut E. Gerber, general editor, Northern Illinois University Press, that Frederick P. W. McDowell is preparing the volume on Forster for publication in spring, 1973.

GENERAL

Millett; Longaker & Bolles; Batho & Dobrée; Daiches; Temple & Tucker.

FOWLER, HON. ELLEN THORNEYCROFT   (-1929)

(Mrs. A. L. Felkin).

WWW 29-40.

FOWLER, HENRY WATSON   (1858-1933)

WWW 29-40.

FOWLES, JOHN   (1926-   )

PRIMARY

Anne Grauer. "Books by John Fowles." *Hollins Critic* 6 (December 1969): 7.

Primary books, all English-language editions. Chronological arrangement. Place, publisher, date.

FOXWELL, HERBERT SOMERTON   (1849-1936)

PRIMARY

John Maynard Keynes. "Herbert Somerton Foxwell." *Economic Journal* 46 (1936): 611-614.

Primary. Chronological arrangement. Books: date, pages.
Periods: date, pages. Brief annotations.

FRANKAU, GILBERT   (1884-1952)

WWW 51-60; Hagen.

FRASER, CLAUD LOVAT   (1890-1921)

PRIMARY

Christopher S. Millard. *The Printed Work of Claud Lovat Fraser.*
London: Henry Danielson, 1921. Pp. x, 106. 275 copies.

Primary. Genre arrangement. Detailed description of Fraser's
art work.

SECONDARY

Haldane Macfall. *The Book of Claud Lovat Fraser.* London: J.
M. Dent and Sons, 1923. Pp. 183.

No bibliography; information in text, *passim.*

FRASER, GEORGE SUTHERLAND   (1915-   )

Daiches; Temple & Tucker.

FRAYN, MICHAEL   (1933-   )

WW 71; Hagen.

FRAZER, SIR JAMES GEORGE   (1854-1941)

PRIMARY

Theodore Bestermann. *A Bibliography of Sir James George
Frazer, O.M.*

London: Macmillan, 1934. Pp. xxi, 100. Reprinted, London: Dawsons of Pall Mall, 1968.

Primary complete, 1884-1933. Chronological arrangement. Books: transcribed TP without lineation bars, size, pages, brief notes on later reprints. Periods: volume, pages, date; notes on volumes in which later collected; reviews by Frazer include title and author of book reviewed. Pp. [85]-93, primary titles listed by form and genre. Index.

The standard bibliography.

GENERAL

Batho & Dobrée; NCBEL, III, 1482-1484.

FREEMAN, JOHN   (1880-1929)

PRIMARY

"Bibliographies of Modern Authors: John Freeman." *London Mercury* 1 (1920): 497.

Primary books. Genre arrangement. Publisher, date.

Gertrude Freeman and Sir John Squire, eds. *John Freeman's Letters*. London: Macmillan and Co., 1936. Pp. 395.

No bibliography; information in text, *passim*.

GENERAL

Millett; Longaker & Bolles; Batho & Dobrée; Daiches; Temple & Tucker.

FREEMAN, RICHARD AUSTIN   (1862-1943)

PRIMARY

"Checklist Bibliographies of Modern Authors. Richard Austin Freeman." *Book Trade Journal* 64 (July 1936): 20-21.

Not seen.

GENERAL

WWW 41-50; Hagen.

FRIEL, BRIAN   (1929-   )

Salem; WW 71.

FRY, CHRISTOPHER   (1907-   )

PRIMARY

Bernice Larson Schear and Eugene C. Prater. "A Bibliography
on Christopher Fry." *Tulane Drama Review* 4 (March 1960):
88-98.

Primary and secondary. Arranged: pp. 88-89, primary writings
in one list, alphabetical by title of book or name of periodical;
translations by Fry listed under name of original author. Pp.
89-98, secondary bibliography: books alphabetical by author,
periods alphabetical by title, reviews of Fry listed under title
of work reviewed. Books: place, publisher, date, pages.
Periods: volume, pages, date.

Derek Stanford. *Christopher Fry*. London: Longmans, Green and
Co. (WTW 54, Revised), 1962. Pp. 44.

P. 44, primary books. Date, genre.

SECONDARY

Above, Schear-Prater, pp. 89-98.

GENERAL

Daiches; Temple & Tucker; Coleman & Tyler; Adelman & Dworkin; Salem; Palmer & Dyson; WW 71.

FRY, ROGER ELIOT   (1866-1934)

PRIMARY

Solomon Fishman. *The Interpretation of Art*. Berkeley and Los
Angeles: University of California Press, 1963. Pp. 196.

Pp. 101-105, chronology of Fry's life; includes primary books.

Quentin Bell. *Roger Fry. An Inaugural Lecture.* Leeds University Press, 1964. Pp. [22]; and Arts Council of Great Britain. *Vision and Design. The Life, Work and Influence of Roger Fry* [Catalogue of an exhibition]. London: Shenval Press, 1966. Pp. [48].

No bibliographies in these two pamphlets; information in text and notes, *passim.*

While the primary books are listed in these books, there is no list of all of Fry's writings.

GENERAL

Millett; Daiches; Temple & Tucker.

FRYE, NORTHROP (1912-   )

PRIMARY

John E. Grant. "Checklist of Writings by and about Northrop Frye" in Murray Krieger, ed., *Northrop Frye in Modern Criticism: Selected Papers from the English Institute.* New York. London: Columbia University Press, 1966. Pp. [xii], 203.

Pp. 147-171, primary bibliography. Form arrangement. Books: place, publisher, year, subsequent editions, reprints, translations. Periods: date, pages; reviews by Frye include author and title of book reviewed. Pp. 171-172, topical index of primary writings. Pp. 172-188, secondary bibliography. Topical arrangement.

SECONDARY

Above, Grant, pp. 172-188.

FULFORD, ROGER THOMAS BALDWIN   GAL
                                     (1902-   )

WW 71.

FULLER, ROY BROADBENT   (1912-   )

Longaker & Bolles; Daiches; Bufkin; Temple & Tucker; WW 71;
Hagen.

GALE, NORMAN ROWLAND   (1862-1942)

PRIMARY

Alfred Hayes, Richard LeGallienne, Norman Gale. Rugby:
Rugby Press, 189?. Pp. 11.

Pp. 6-11, primary books. Chronological arrangement. Date,
part collation, publisher, binding, number of copies.

GENERAL

Millett; NCBEL, III, 627.

GALSWORTHY, JOHN   (1867-1933)

PRIMARY

H. V. Marrot. *A Bibliography of the Works of John Galsworthy.*
London: Elkin Matthews and Marrot; New York: Charles
Scribner's Sons, 1928. Pp. xiv, 252. 210 copies.

Primary, secondary selected. Form arrangement. Books (subdivided by genre): transcribed TP, part collation, pagination,
binding, date, contents, number of copies, variants, reprints,
notes; includes both British and American editions, although
descriptions of the latter are less complete than of the former.
Periods: dates. Includes translations of Galsworthy, iconography, index. Pp. 195-208, secondary bibliography.

Ralph Mottram. *John Galsworthy.* London: Longmans, Green
and Co. (WTW 38), 1953. Pp. 40.

Pp. 37-40, primary books. Date, genre.

Genji Takahashi. *Studies in the Works of John Galsworthy.*
Tokyo: Shinozaki Shorin, 1954, 1956.

Not seen. *English Fiction in Transition* 1 (1958): 27:
"Valuable bibliography of translations into Japanese of Galsworthy."

SECONDARY

Above, Marrot, pp. 195-208.

Alice T. McGirr. "Reading List of John Galsworthy." *Bulletin of Bibliography* 7 (1913): 113.

Reviews listed under title of book reviewed. Periods:
volume, pages, date, quotations.

Helmut Gerber, *et al.* "John Galsworthy." *English Fiction*
(later *English Literature) in Transition* 1 (1957): 23-24; 2
(1958): 7-29; 7 (1964): 93-110. (Continued in subsequent
issues).

Annotated. Books: place, publisher, year. Periods: volume,
pages, date.

One should also note the announcement in 1971 by the Annotated Secondary Bibliography Series on English Literature
in Transition, Helmut E. Gerber, general editor, Northern
Illinois University Press, that Earl E. Stevens and H. Ray
Stevens are preparing the volume on Galsworthy for publication in the fall, 1973.

E. H. Mikhail. *John Galsworthy the Dramatist: A Bibliography.*
Troy, New York: Whitston Publishing Co., 1971. Pp. [vi],
90.

Not seen. Described as "near-complete bibliography of
biographical, critical, and scholarly material surrounding
Galsworthy-as-dramatist."

GENERAL

Millett; Longaker & Bolles; Batho & Dobrée; Daiches; Temple & Tucker; Coleman & Tyler; Adelman & Dworkin; Salem; Palmer & Dyson.

GARDINER, ALFRED G.   (1865-1946)

WWW 41-50.

GARDNER, EDMUND GARRATT   (1869-1935)

PRIMARY

C. J. Sisson and C. Foligno. *Edmund Garratt Gardner. A Bibliography of his Publications.* London: J. M. Dent and Sons, 1937. Pp. 27.

Primary. Chronological arrangement. Books: publisher, date, reprints, subsequent editions. Periods: date. Book reviews by Gardner include author and title of book reviewed.

GARDNER, DAME HELEN LOUISE   (1908-   )

WW 71.

GARIOCH, ROBERT   (1909-   )

Pseudonym of Robert Garioch Sutherland.

Daiches.

GARNETT FAMILY

    CONSTANCE   (1862-1946)

    DAVID   (1892-   )

EDWARD WILLIAM (1868-1937)

RICHARD (1835-1906)

PRIMARY

Carolyn G. Heilbrun. *The Garnett Family*. London: George Allen and Unwin, 1961. Pp. 214.

Pp. 202-210, separate bibliographies for each of the four Garnetts. Primary books. Form and genre arrangement. Place, publisher, year.

GENERAL

Millett (Edward, David); Batho & Dobrée; NCBEL, III, 1431 (Richard); Daiches; WW 71; Hagen (David).

GARROD, HEATHCOTE WILLIAM (1878-1960)

WW 61.

GASCOYNE, DAVID EMERY (1916-   )

PRIMARY

Ann Atkinson. "David Gascoyne: A Check-List." *Twentieth Century Literature* 6 (1961): 180-192.

Primary, secondary selected. Form arrangement. Books: place, publisher, date, pages. Periods: volume, pages, date. Occasional annotations. List of anthologies including Gascoyne.

GENERAL

Longaker & Bolles; Daiches; Temple & Tucker.

GATHORNE-HARDY, HON. ROBERT   (1902-   )

WW 71.

GAUNT, WILLIAM   (1900-   )

WW 71.

GAWSWORTH, JOHN   (1912-1970)

Pseudonym of Terence Ian Fytton Armstrong.

Longaker & Bolles; WW 70.

GEORGE, WALTER LIONEL   (1882-1926)

GENERAL

Stanley J. Kunitz and Howard Haycraft. *Twentieth Century Authors.* New York: H. W. Wilson Co., 1942. Pp. [viii], 1577.

Pp. 524-525, titles by and about George.

Longaker & Bolles; WWW 16-28.

GERAHTY, DIGBY GEORGE: see STANDISH, ROBERT.

GERHARDIE, WILLIAM ALEXANDER   (1895-   )

Millett; Daiches; Bufkin; Temple & Tucker; WW 71.

GÉRIN, WINIFRED   (-)

(Mrs. John Lock).

WW 71.

GIBBINGS, ROBERT JOHN   (1889-1958)

PRIMARY

A. Mary Kirkus. *Robert Gibbings: A Bibliography*, ed. Patience Empson and John Harris. London: J. M. Dent and Sons, 1962. Pp. 170. 975 copies.

Primary, secondary. Form and genre arrangement. Transcribed TP, part collation, pagination, binding, date, price, number of copies, variants, reprints, contents, notes. Pp. 125-144, secondary bibliography. Chronological arrangement. Index.

P. H. Muir, *Book Collector* 12 (1963): 109: "an impressive record...the bibliographical rigmarole indulged in here is quite unnecessary [and not always accurate] ...with the precautions detailed [in this review] it can be recommended."

SECONDARY

Above, Kirkus, pp. 125-144.

GIBBON, LEWIS GRASSIC: see MITCHELL, JAMES LESLIE.

GIBBON, WILLIAM MONK   (1896-   )

WW 71.

GIBBONS, STELLA DOROTHEA   (1902-   )

(Mrs. Allan Bourne Webb).

Daiches; Bufkin; Temple & Tucker; WW 71.

GIBBS, SIR PHILIP HAMILTON   (1877-1962)

PRIMARY

Philip Gibbs. *The Pageant of the Years. An Autobiography.* London: Heinemann, 1946. Pp. 530. *Crowded Company.* London and New York: Allan Wingate, 1949. Pp. 286.

Bibliographical information in texts, *passim*, of these two autobiographies.

GENERAL

Millett; Temple & Tucker.

GIBSON, WILFRID WILSON   (1878-1962)

PRIMARY

John Gawsworth. *Ten Contemporaries. Notes Toward their Definitive Bibliography.* [First Series]. London: Ernest Benn Ltd., 1932. Pp. 224.

Pp. 74-94, primary books, first editions, 1902-1932. Chronological arrangement. Transcribed TP, full collation, pagination, binding, date, bibliographical and textual notes.

GENERAL

Millett; Longaker & Bolles; Batho & Dobrée; Daiches; Temple & Tucker.

GILBERT, MARTIN JOHN   (1936-   )

WW 71.

GILL, ARTHUR ERIC ROWTON   (1882-1940)

PRIMARY

Evan R. Gill. *Bibliography of Eric Gill.* London: Cassell and Co., 1953. Pp. 224. 1000 copies.

Primary, secondary. Form arrangement. Books: transcribed TP, full collation, pagination, binding, date, price, variants, reprints, contents, reviews of the book. Periods: volume, pages, date. Pp. 153-193, secondary bibliography. Index.

J. G. Physick. *The Engraved Work of Eric Gill.* London: HMSO (Victoria and Albert Museum Publication), 1963. Pp. 266.

Chronological list of the engravings with full information.

Evan R. Gill. *The Inscriptional Work of Eric Gill. An Inventory.* London: Cassell and Co., 1964. Pp. 140 plus plates.

Complete description of 762 inscriptions; informative prefaces; various indices.

SECONDARY

Above, Gill (1953).

Wolfgang Kehr. "Eric Gill als Schriftkünstler." *Archiv für Geschichte des Buchwesens* 4 (1962): 454-621.

Pp. 614-621, secondary bibliography.

GINSBURY, NORMAN   (1902-   )

WW 71.

GISSING, GEORGE ROBERT   (1857-1903)

PRIMARY

Temple Scott. "Bibliography" in George Gissing. *Critical Studies of the Works of Dickens,* ed. Temple Scott. New York: Greenberg, 1924. Pp. 165.

Pp. 161-165, bibliography of primary books. Chronological arrangement. Transcribed TP, without lineation bars, part collation, binding.

John D. Gordan. *George Gissing 1857-1903: An Exhibition from the Berg Collection.* New York Public Library, 1954. Pp. 45. Reprinted from *Bulletin of the New York Public Library* 58 (1954): 489-496, 551-566, 611-618; 59 (1955): 35-46.

Information in notes for each entry. No index.

Jacob Korg. *George Gissing. A Critical Biography.* Seattle: University of Washington Press, 1963. Pp. 311.

Pp. 301-305, bibliography. Primary selected, secondary selected. Arranged: primary books (place, publisher, date); letters; chief MSS sources. Pp. 303-305, secondary bibliography.

Pierre Coustillas. "Gissing's Short Stories: A Bibliography." *English Literature in Transition* 7 (1964): 59-72.

Arranged: collections; translations into Japanese; individual stories. Books: place, publisher, date, pages. Periods: volume, pages, date. Extensive bibliographical and textual notes.

These four works list all of the primary books; but there is no single listing of all of Gissing's writings.

SECONDARY

Above, Korg, pp. 303-305.

Jacob Korg. "George Gissing." *English Fiction* (later *English Literature*) *in Transition* 1 (1957): 24-28; Helmut Gerber, 2, i (1959): 45-46; 3, i (1960): 27-30; Joseph J. Wolff, 3, ii (1960): 3-33; Pierre Coustillas and Paul Goetsch, 7 (1964): 14-26; Joseph J. Wolff, 7 (1964): 73-92; continued in subsequent issues, especially 14 (1971): 62-71.

Alphabetical by author arrangement. Annotated.

One should also note the announcement in 1971 by the Annotated Secondary Bibliography Series on English Literature in Transition, Helmut E. Gerber, general editor, Northern

Illinois University Press, that Joseph Wolff is preparing the volume on Gissing for publication in the spring, 1974.

John Spiers and Pierre Coustillas. *A Reader's Guide* [Catalogue of the Exhibition, *The Rediscovery of George Gissing*]. London: National Book League, 1971.

Not seen. *TLS*, 2 July, 1971, p. 762: "a rich source of accurate information about all aspects of the novelist's life and work...[an] important...landmark in our understanding of the materials on which a definitive life might be based."

GENERAL

Longaker & Bolles; Batho & Dobrée; Temple & Tucker; NCBEL, III, 1000-1004.

GITTINGS, ROBERT WILLIAM VICTOR   (1911-   )

WW 71.

GLASKIN, GERALD MARCUS   (1923-   )

Hetherington; Hagen.

GLOAG, JOHN EDWARDS   (1896-   )

WW 71.

GLYN, ELINOR SUTHERLAND   (1864-1943)

(Mrs. Clayton Glyn).

PRIMARY

Anthony Glyn [Sir Anthony Geoffrey Leo Simon, né Davson]. *Elinor Glyn. A Biography*. London: Hutchinson and Co., 1968 (Revised Edition). Pp. 356.

P. [345], bibliography of primary books. Chronological arrangement. Publisher, date. Other important bibliographical information in text, *passim*. Index.

There is no list of the extensive periodical contributions, nor a complete account of the very detailed history of the primary books.

GENERAL

WWW 41-50.

GODDEN, RUMER   (1907-   )

(Mrs. James Haynes Dixon).

Longaker & Bolles; Bufkin; Temple & Tucker; WW 71.

GOGARTY, OLIVER ST. JOHN   (1878-1957)

PRIMARY

Michael Hewson. "Gogarty's Authorship of *Blight*." *Irish Book* 1 (Spring 1959): 19-20.

Not seen.

Ulick O'Connor. *Oliver St. John Gogarty. A Poet and His Times* London: Jonathan Cape, 1964. Pp. 317.

Pp. 305-310, general bibliography. Author, title. Other bibliographical information in text, *passim*. Index.

GENERAL

Longaker & Bolles; Temple & Tucker.

GOLDING, LOUIS   (1895-1958)

PRIMARY

Louis Golding. *The World I Knew*. London: Hutchinson and Co.,
[1940]. Pp. 328.

   Bibliographical information in text, *passim*, of this autobiography.

J. B. Simons. *Louis Golding. A Memoir*. London: Mitre Press,
[1958]. Pp. 139.

   Bibliographical information in text, *passim*.

GENERAL

Millett; Daiches; Temple & Tucker; Hagen.

GOLDING, WILLIAM GERALD   (1911-   )

PRIMARY

James R. Baker. *William Golding. A Critical Study*. New York:
St. Martin's Press, 1965. Pp. 106.

   Pp. 97-102, bibliography. Primary, secondary selected. Chronological arrangement. Books: place, publisher, year (first
   British edition). Periods: volume, pages, date. Pp. 99-102,
   secondary bibliography. Alphabetical by author arrangement.
   Annotated.

Bernard S. Oldsey and Stanley Weintraub. *The Art of William
Golding*. New York: Harcourt, Brace and World, Inc., 1965.
Pp. 178.

   Pp. 175-178, primary bibliography. Less complete than Baker,
   but lists all editions: place, publisher, date.

Bernard G. Dick. *William Golding*. New York: Twayne Publishers, Inc. (TEAS 57), 1967. Pp. 119.

   Pp. 109-111, primary bibliography. Form arrangement. Books:

place, publisher, year (first editions; also "most accessible" paperback edition). Periods: volume, pages, date. Pp. 111-113, secondary bibliography. Annotated.

A useful continuation of Baker.

Jack I. Biles. "A William Golding Checklist." *Twentieth Century Literature* 17 (1971): 107-121.

Pp. 108-112, primary. Pp. 112-121, secondary selected. Form arrangement. Books: place, publisher, date of British and American first editions; reviews listed under primary title. Periods: date, pages.

SECONDARY

Above, Baker, pp. 99-102; Dick, pp. 11-13; Biles, pp. 112-121.

GENERAL

Temple & Tucker; WW 71.

GOLDRING, DOUGLAS   (1887-1960)

PRIMARY

Douglas Goldring. *Odd Man Out. The Autobiography of a "Propaganda Novelist."* London: Chapman and Hall, 1935.

Bibliographical information in text, *passim*.

GENERAL

Temple & Tucker.

GOLLANCZ, SIR ISRAEL   (1863-1930)

NCBEL, III, 1649.

GOOCH, GEORGE PEABODY   (1873-1968)

WW 69.

GOOLDEN, BARBARA   (1900-   )

WW 71.

GORDON, ALEXANDER   (1841-1931)

PRIMARY

H. McLachlan. *Alexander Gordon (9 June 1841-21 February 1931) A Biography with a Bibliography.* Manchester University Press (University Publication No. 218), 1932. Pp. 197.

Pp. 125-186, primary bibliography. Chronological arrangement. Books: date, place, pages, format. Periods: volume, pages, date.

A comprehensive checklist with the few omissions detailed on p. vii.

GORDON, RICHARD   (1921-   )

Pseudonym of Gordon Ostlere.

WW 71.

GORDON, SETON   (1886-   )

WW 71.

GORE, CHARLES   (1853-1932)

Batho & Dobrée.

GORE-BOOTH, CONSTANCE: see MARKIEVICZ, COUNTESS DE

GOSSE, SIR EDMUND WILLIAM   (1849-1928)

PRIMARY

Norman Gullick, "Bibliography" in Evan Charteris. *The Life and Letters of Sir Edmund Gosse.* London: Heinemann; New York: Harper, 1931. Pp. 525.

Pp. 511-518, bibliography of primary books, restricted to Gosse's "more important writings." Chronological arrangement. Place, publisher, date, bibliographical notes.

Elias Bredsdorff, ed. *Sir Edmund Gosse's Correspondence with Scandinavian Writers.* Copenhagen: Gyldendal (Scandinavian University Books), 1960. Pp. 354.

Pp. 316-342, primary bibliography. Arranged: Gosse's writings on Scandinavian subjects; contributions to the *Encyclopaedia Britannica* on Scandinavian subjects; contributions to Scandinavian periodicals and newspapers. Pp. 343-346, secondary bibliography. Chronological arrangement. Books: place, date. Periods: number, pages, date. Reviews by Gosse include author and title of book reviewed.

There is no complete primary bibliography.

SECONDARY

Above, Bredsdorff, pp. 343-346.

James D. Woolf. "Sir Edmund Gosse. An Annotated Bibliography of Writings about Him." *English Literature in Transition* 11 (1968): 126-172. Continued in later issues, especially 14 (1971): 71-73.

Alphabetical by author arrangement. Books: place, publisher, year. Periods: volume, pages, date. Annotations.

GENERAL

Millett; Longaker & Bolles; Batho & Dobrée; Temple & Tucker; NCBEL, III, 1432-1435.

GOUDGE, ELIZABETH DE BEAUCHAMP   (1900-   )

WW 71; Hagen.

GOULD, GERALD   (1885-1936)

Millett; Temple & Tucker.

GRAEME, BRUCE   (-   )

Pseudonym of Graham Montague Jeffries.

WW 71; Hagen.

GRAHAM, ROBERT BONTINE CUNNINGHAME   (1852-1936)

PRIMARY

Leslie Chaundy. *A Bibliography of the First Editions of Robert Bontine Cunninghame Graham.* London: Dulau and Co., 1924. Pp. 16. 500 copies.

Primary books. Chronological arrangement. Transcribed TP, part collation, binding, date, notes.

Herbert Faulkner West. *The Herbert Faulkner West Collection of Robert Bontine Cunninghame Graham* [in the Dartmouth College Library]. Dartmouth: Privately Published, 1938. Pp. 20. 85 copies.

Primary, secondary selected. Form arrangement. Books: place, publisher, date, reprints, variants. Periods: volume, pages, dates. Includes MSS, letters. Pp. 18-19, secondary bibliography.

The catalogue of a *"virtually* complete" (p. 5) collection.

C. T. Watts. "Robert Bontine Cunninghame Graham 1852-1936. A List of his Contributions to Periodicals." *Bibliotheck* 4 (1965): v, 186-199.

Not seen.

SECONDARY

Above, West, pp. 18-19.

Helmut Gerber. "Robert Bontine Cunninghame Graham." *English Fiction* (later *English Literature) in Transition* 1 (1957): 19. Continued in later issues.

Annotated.

GENERAL

Millett; Longaker & Bolles; Batho & Dobrée; Temple & Tucker.

GRAHAM, STEPHEN   (1884-   )

WW 71; Hagen.

GRAHAM, WILLIAM SYDNEY   (1917?-   )

Daiches; Temple & Tucker.

GRAHAME, KENNETH   (1859-1932)

PRIMARY

Roger Lancelyn Green. "Kenneth Grahame." *TLS*, 9 June 1945, p. 276.

Primary first editions. Chronological arrangement. Books: transcribed TP, pages, number of copies for the limited

141

editions. Periods: date.

Green states that of Grahame's periodical contributions it is "unlikely that much remains unrecorded."

Eleanor Graham. *Kenneth Grahame*. London: Bodley Head (Bodley Head Monograph), 1963. Pp. 72.

Pp. 70-71, bibliography of primary books. Publisher, date, illustrator. Additional information about reprints and subsequent editions of the primary titles listed by Green (above).

SECONDARY

Peter Morris Green. *Kenneth Grahame 1859-1932. A Study of his Life, Work and Times*. London: John Murray; New York: World, 1959. Pp. 400.

Pp. 377-385, primary bibliography derived from Green (above). Pp. 381-385, general secondary bibliography. Additional secondary criticism in text and notes, *passim*.

GENERAL

Batho & Dobrée; Temple & Tucker.

GRANVILLE-BARKER, HARLEY   (1877-1946)

PRIMARY

Frederick May and Margery M. Morgan. "A List of Writings" in Charles B. Purdom. *Harley Granville-Barker. Man of the Theatre, Dramatist and Scholar*. London: Rockliff, 1955. Pp. 322.

Pp. 293-309, bibliography. Primary. Form and genre arrangement. Books: part collation, binding, variants, reprints, notes. Periods: volume, pages, date. Includes MSS and an account of works written in collaboration.

SECONDARY

Mary Louise Davis. "Reading List on Harley Granville-Barker." *Bulletin of Bibliography* 7 (1913): 130-132.

Primary, secondary. Topical arrangement. Books: place, publisher, date, reprints, contents (British and American editions. Periods: volume, pages, date, quotations, annotations.

Margery M. Morgan. *A Drama of Political Man. A Study in the Plays of Harley Granville-Barker.* London: Sidgwick and Jackson, 1961. Pp. 337.

No bibliography. References to secondary criticism in text and in notes, *passim*.

GENERAL

Millett; Longaker & Bolles; Batho & Dobrée; Temple & Tucker; Coleman & Tyler; Adelman & Dworkin.

GRAVES, ALFRED PERCEVAL   (1846-1932)

PRIMARY

Alfred Perceval Graves. *To Return to All That. An Autobiography.* London: Jonathan Cape, 1930. Pp. 350.

Pp. 347-350, bibliography of primary books. Genre arrangement. Publisher, occasionally date.

GENERAL

NCBEL, III, 1907-1908.

GRAVES, CHARLES PATRICK RANKE   (1899-   )

PRIMARY

Jane Gordon. *Married to Charles.* London: Heinemann, 1950. Pp. 283.

Bibliographical information in text, *passim*, of this informal biography by Mrs. Graves.

GENERAL

WW 71.

GRAVES, ROBERT RANKE (1895-)

PRIMARY

Fred H. Higginson. *A Bibliography of the Works of Robert Graves*. London: Nicholas Vane Ltd., 1966. Pp. 328.

Primary, secondary selected. Form arrangement. Books: transcribed TP, part collation, pagination, binding, date, price, number of copies, variants, reprints, subsequent editions, contents, notes. Periods: volume, pages, date, genre; reviews by Graves include title and author of book reviewed. Pp. 283-297, secondary bibliography; selected reviews of primary books listed under book titles. Pp. 300-328, Index.

The authoritative primary bibliography.

SECONDARY

Above, Higginson, pp. 283-297.

Douglas Day. *Swifter than Reason*. Chapel Hill: University of North Carolina Press, 1963. Pp. 228.

Bibliography, pp. 220-223.

GENERAL

Millett; Daiches; Temple & Tucker; WW 71.

GRAY, JOHN HENRY (1866-1934)

PRIMARY

Alan Anderson, "Bibliography" in Father Brocard Sewell, ed.
Two Friends, John Gray and André Raffalovich. Essays Biographical and Critical. Aylesford: St. Albert's Press, 1963.
Pp. 193.

Pp. 178-187, primary bibliography. Form arrangement. Books:
transcribed TP, size in inches, binding, occasional notes.
Books with contributions: dates. List of periodicals to which
Gray contributed; no specific entries.

Timothy D'Arch Smith, *Book Collector* 12 (1963): 379: "Apart
from a regrettable failure to give any pagination...the work is
admirably done"; provides corrections and additions.

SECONDARY

Above, Sewell, *passim.*

GENERAL

NCBEL, III, 628.

GREEN, HENRY   (1905-   )

Pseudonym of Henry Vincent Yorke.

PRIMARY

John Russell. *Henry Green: Nine Novels and an Unpacked Bag.*
New Brunswick: Rutgers University Press, 1960. Pp. 251.

Pp. 245-246, "Books, Stories, and Articles by Henry Green."
Chronological arrangement. Books: place, publisher, date.
Periods: volume, pages, date. Includes reviews by Green.
No secondary bibliography, although there are references to
secondary criticism in notes, pp. 237-243.

SECONDARY

Above, Russell, pp. 237-243.

Edward Stokes. *The Novels of Henry Green.* London: Hogarth Press, 1959. Pp. 248.

Notes, pp. 237-243, provide references to secondary bibliography.

Robert S. Ryf. *Henry Green.* New York: Columbia University Press (Columbia Essays on Modern Writers 29), 1967. Pp. 48.

Pp. 47-48, secondary bibliography. Alphabetical by author arrangement. Books: place, publisher, date. Periods: date.

GENERAL

Longaker & Bolles; Daiches; Temple & Tucker; WW 71.

GREEN, PETER MORRIS   (1924-   )

WW 71.

GREENE, GRAHAM   (1904-   )

PRIMARY

Phyllis Hargreaves. "Graham Greene. A Selected Bibliography." *Modern Fiction Studies* 3 (1957): 269-280.

Primary. Genre arrangement, alphabetical by title thereunder. Books: place, publisher, date, reprints, subsequent editions, contents. Periods: volume, pages, date. P. 280, "Chronology and Classification of Major Works."

Neil Brennan. "Bibliography" in Robert O. Evans, ed. *Graham Greene. Some Critical Considerations.* Lexington: University of Kentucky Press, 1963. Pp. 286.

Pp. 245-276, bibliography. Primary books, secondary selected. Chronological arrangement. Books: place, publisher, date, reviews and relevant secondary criticism. No details of periodical contributions, but titles and dates of periodicals for which

Greene has written. Pp. 263-274, secondary bibliography. Genre arrangement.

DeVitis (below), p. 161: "A nearly complete bibliography."

SECONDARY

Above, Brennan, pp. 263-274.

William Birmingham. "Graham Greene Criticism, A Bibliographical Study." *Thought* 27 (Spring, 1952): 72-100.

Pp. 72-98, essay on studies of Greene. Pp. 98-100, alphabetical by author list of secondary criticism (mainly in periodicals), highly selective.

Maurice Beebe. "Criticism of Graham Greene. A Selected Checklist with an Index to Studies of Separate Works." *Modern Fiction Studies* 3 (1957): 281-288.

Alphabetical by author list of general criticism; specific studies listed under alphabetically arranged titles of the primary books.

Donald P. Costello. "Graham Greene and the Catholic Press." *Renascence* 12 (Autumn 1959): 3-28.

Pp. 3-26, essay; pp. 26-28, bibliography of "items...representative of the interest the Catholic Press...has shown in Greene..."

A. A. DeVitis. *Graham Greene.* New York: Twayne Publishers, Inc. (TEAS 3), 1964. Pp. 175.

Pp. 161-165, primary bibliography. Form and genre arrangement. Books: place, publisher, year. Periods: volume, pages, date. Pp. 165-171, secondary bibliography. Alphabetical by author arrangement. Annotated.

J. Don Vann. *Graham Greene. A Checklist of Criticism.* Kent, Ohio: Kent State University Press (Serif Series No. 14), 1970. Pp. [viii], 69.

Form and genre arrangement. Book reviews listed under title

of book reviewed, primary books being chronologically arranged. Pp. 2-3, list of primary and secondary bibliographies. Books: place, publisher, date (reviews of books about Greene listed under title of the book reviewed). Periods: volume, date, pages.

Vann attempts to list omissions from previous bibliographies and to bring "Greene scholarship from [Brennan, above] up to date" (p. v). Together these secondary bibliographies give a fairly complete listing of the available information.

GENERAL

Longaker & Bolles; Daiches; Temple & Tucker; Coleman & Tyler; Adelman & Dworkin; Salem; Palmer & Dyson; WW 71; Hagen.

GREENWOOD, WALTER   (1903-   )

Palmer & Dyson; WW 71.

GREG, SIR WALTER WILSON   (1875-1959)

PRIMARY

F. C. Francis. "A List of Dr. Greg's Writings." *Library*, 4th Series, 26 (June 1945): 72-97.

Primary. Chronological arrangement, each year subdivided by genre. Books: place, publisher, date, format, pages. Periods: volume, pages, date. Includes unsigned periodical contributions. Pp. 73-74, list of the Malone Society Reprints.

D. F. McKenzie. "Writings of Sir Walter Greg, 1945-1959." *Library*, 5th Series, 15 (March 1960): 42-46.

Continuation of the list above.

GREGORY, LADY ISABELLA AUGUSTA PERSSE   (1859-1932)

PRIMARY

Eileen E. Coxhead. *Lady Gregory. A Literary Portrait.* London: Macmillan and Co., 1961. Pp. 241. (Second edition, revised and enlarged, 1966. Not seen).

Pp. 231-232, "Lady Gregory's Principal Publications." Primary books. Chronological arrangement. Publisher, year.

-- *John Millington Synge and Lady Gregory.* London: Longmans, Green and Co. (WTW 149), 1962. Pp. 35.

Pp. 34-35, bibliography of primary books. Chronological arrangement. Place, year, contents of collections.

SECONDARY

Edward Halim Mikhail. "The Theatre of Lady Gregory." *Bulletin of Bibliography* 27 (1970): 10, 9.

Alphabetical by author arrangement. Books: place, publisher, date. Periods: volume, pages, date. More emphasis on the Irish theatre in general than on Lady Gregory's plays.

GENERAL

Millett; Batho & Dobrée; Longaker & Bolles; Temple & Tucker; Coleman & Tyler; Adelman & Dworkin; Salem; NCBEL, III, 1939-1941.

GRENFELL, JULIAN   (1892-1915)

Longaker & Bolles.

GRIBBLE, LEONARD REGINALD   (1908-   )

WW 71; Hagen.

GRIERSON, SIR HERBERT JOHN CLIFFORD   (1865-1960)

Batho & Dobrée; Daiches; Temple & Tucker

GRIEVE, CHRISTOPHER MURRAY   (1892-   )

PRIMARY

William R. Aitken. "A Check List of Books and Periodicals--
Written, Translated, Edited, Published, or Introduced by Chris-
topher Murray Grieve (Hugh MacDiarmid)" in K. D. Duval and
Sydney Goodsir Smith, eds. *Hugh MacDiarmid, A Festschrift.*
Edinburgh: K. D. Duval, 1962. Pp. 221.

Pp. 213-221, "Check List." Primary. Chronological arrangement, with "Books introduced by Grieve" and "Periodicals
edited by Grieve" in separate lists. Books: place, publisher,
date, binding, bibliographical notes, reprints, illustrator: information varies with each entry. Periods: volume, pages,
date.

Duncan Glenn. *Hugh MacDiarmid (Christopher Murray Grieve)
and the Scottish Renaissance.* Edinburgh and London: W.
and R. Chambers Ltd., 1964. Pp. x, 294.

Pp. 245-280, bibliography. Primary, secondary selected. Form
and genre arrangement. Books: place, publisher, date, reprints,
subsequent editions. Periods: volume, pages, date. Includes
list of anthologies with contributions by Grieve. Pp. 256-257,
also in text, *passim*, selected, uncollected prose contributions
to periodicals. Pp. 263-280, secondary bibliography, including
association material.

Glenn includes more titles than Aitken, while giving less
information about individual titles. Together they provide
fairly complete lists.

SECONDARY

Above, Glenn, pp. 263-280.

Kenneth Buthlay. *Hugh MacDiarmid (Christopher Murray Grieve).*
Edinburgh: Oliver and Boyd (Writers and Critics Series), 1964.
Pp. 125.

P. 125, secondary bibliography.

GENERAL

Longaker & Bolles; Daiches; Temple & Tucker; WW 71.

GRIFFIN, GWYN   (1922-   )

Bufkin.

GRIFFITH, ARTHUR   (1872-1922)

PRIMARY

Patrick Sarsfield O'Hegarty. "Bibliographies of 1916 and the Irish Revolution. XII. Arthur Griffith." *Dublin Magazine* 12 (January-March 1937): 61-66.

Primary books. Chronological arrangement. Transcribed TP, part collation, pagination, binding, bibliographical and bio-graphical notes.

GRIGSON, GEOFFREY EDWARD HARVEY   (1905-   )

Longaker & Bolles; Daiches; Temple & Tucker; WW 71.

GUEDALLA, PHILIP   (1889-1944)

Millett; Longaker & Bolles; Daiches; Temple & Tucker.

GUINNESS, BRYAN WALTER, LORD MOYNE   (1905-   )

WW 71.

GUNN, NEIL MILLER   (1891-   )

PRIMARY

W. R. Aitken. "Neil Miller Gunn. A First Checklist of his
Books." *Bibliotheck* 3 (1961): 89-95.

Not seen.

GENERAL

Daiches; WW 71.

GUNN, THOMSON (THOM) WILLIAM   (1929-   )

Temple & Tucker; WW 71.

GUTHRIE, THOMAS ANSTEY: see ANSTEY, F.

GWYNN, STEPHEN LUCIUS   (1864-1950)

Temple & Tucker.

HADDON, CHRISTOPHER: see PALMER, JOHN LESLIE.

HADOW, SIR WILLIAM HENRY   (1859-1937)

NCBEL, III, 1435-1436.

HAGGARD, SIR HENRY RIDER   (1856-1925)

PRIMARY

George L. McKay. *A Bibliography of the Writings of Sir Rider
Haggard*. London: Bookman's Journal, 1930. Pp. 110. 475
copies.

Primary. Form arrangement. Books: transcribed TP, part

collation, pagination, binding, date, contents, number of copies, full notes. Periods: volume, pages, date. Publications other than books listed together in one list.

-- and J. E. Scott. *Additions and Corrections to the Haggard Bibliography*. London: Mitre Press, 1939. Pp. 28. 100 copies.

Considerable expansion of McKay (1930); especially pp. 3-9, list of American editions, 1886-1891; pp. 10-24, corrections and additional information concerning first editions; pp. 25-28, additional writings other than books.

J. E. Scott. *A Bibliography of the Works of Sir Henry Rider Haggard 1856-1925*. Bishop's Stortford, Herts, Elkin Matthews Ltd. , 1947. Pp. 258. 500 copies.

Primary, secondary selected. Form and genre arrangement. Books: transcribed TP, part collation, pagination, binding, date, number of copies, contents, variants, MSS, reprints, full bibliographical notes. Periods: date. Divisions include letters to the *Times* and other newspapers; reports of speeches; reviews by Haggard (including title and author of book reviewed); dramatizations and film productions of Haggard's novels; parodies of Haggard. Pp. 236-246, secondary bibliography. Dates, annotations. Index.

The authoritative bibliography.

SECONDARY

Above, Scott, pp. 236-246.

Morton Cohen. "Henry Rider Haggard." *English Fiction* (later *English Literature*) *in Transition* 1, iii (1958): 36-38. Continued in later issues.

Annotated.

-- *Rider Haggard. His Life and Works*. London: Hutchinson and Co., 1960. Pp. 327.

Pp. 310-322, secondary bibliography. Arranged: reviews of primary books listed under title of book; other writings about Haggard; general literary and historical background.

GENERAL

Batho & Dobrée; Temple & Tucker; NCBEL, III, 1055-1056.

HALDANE, JOHN SCOTT   (1860-1936)

Batho & Dobrée; WWW 29-40.

HALDANE, RICHARD BURDON, LORD HALDANE   (1856-1928)

PRIMARY

Richard Burdon Haldane (Viscount Haldane). An Autobiography. New York: Doubleday, Doran and Co., Inc., 1929. Pp. [xii], 391.

Pp. 379-380, primary books, British and American editions. Chronological arrangement. Publisher, date.

SECONDARY

Stephen E. Koss. *Lord Haldane. Scapegoat for Liberalism.* New York and London: Columbia University Press, 1969. Pp. [xvi], 263.

Pp. 247-251, secondary bibliography; mainly books, but also including important collections of unpublished papers of eminent figures connected with Lord Haldane.

GENERAL

Batho & Dobrée; WWW 16-28.

HALE, KATHLEEN   (1898-   )

(Mrs. Douglas McClean).

WW 71.

HALL, MARGUERITE RADCLYFFE   (1886-1943)

PRIMARY

Sheila Bolton. "A Radclyffe Hall Collection." *Private Library* 2 (1958-1959): 50-52.

An essay in which the primary books in their various editions are mentioned along with date, publisher, place, and genre. Extensive bibliographical notes.

GENERAL

Bufkin; Temple & Tucker.

HALL, WILLIS   (1929-   )

WW 71.

HAMBURGER, MICHAEL PETER LEOPOLD   (1924-   )

WW 71.

HAMILTON, CICELY   (1872-1952)

WWW 51-60.

HAMILTON, SIR GEORGE ROSTREVOR   (1888-1967)

Temple & Tucker; WW 67.

HAM

HAMILTON, MARY AGNES   (1883-1966)
  WW 66; Hagen.

HAMILTON, PATRICK   (1904-1962)

  Salem; WW 62; Hagen.

HAMMOND, JOHN LAWRENCE LE BRETON   (1872-1949)

  Daiches.

HANKIN, ST. JOHN EMILE CLAVERING   (1869-1909)

PRIMARY

St. John Hankin. *The Dramatic Works*, ed. John Drinkwater.
New York: Mitchell Kennerley, 1912. 3 vols. 1000 copies.

Bibliographical information in "Introduction," I, 3-28, by
Drinkwater. Casts and dates of original performances, III,
225-231. Collection includes essays and reviews by Hankin
with place and date of original publication.

HANLEY, JAMES   (1901-   )

  Millett; Daiches; Bufkin; Temple & Tucker; WW 71.

HANNAY, JAMES OWEN: see BIRMINGHAM, G. A.

HARDY, THOMAS   (1840-1928)

PRIMARY

Henry Danielson. *The First Editions of the Writings of Thomas
  Hardy and their Values*. London: George Allen and Unwin,
  1916. Pp. 40. A. P. Webb. *A Bibliography of the Works of
  Thomas Hardy*. London: Frank Hollings, 1916. Pp.[xiv], [128].

156

Two typical bibliographies of the first-edition-craze period: still informative, but inferior to Purdy (below).

Richard Little Purdy. *Thomas Hardy, A Bibliographical Study.* London: Oxford University Press, 1954. Pp.[x], [388]. New Impression, 1968.

Primary. Form arrangement. Books (pp. 3-276): transcribed TP, part collation, pagination, binding, variants, reprints, later editions; extensive textual and bibliographical notes. Collected Editions (pp. 279-288): brief descriptions, including contents. Uncollected Contributions to Books, Periodicals, Newspapers (pp. 291-325): dates, pages. Six appendices on special Hardy topics. Index, pp. 355-388.

The authoritative bibliography. F. B. Adams, *Book Collector* 4 (1955): 82-84: "this virtually flawless book."

SECONDARY

Above, Webb, pp. 103-117.

Margaret Hutchins. "A Selected List of References on Thomas Hardy's Works." *Bulletin of Bibliography* 12 (1924): 51-55.

Arranged under the Hardy titles and under topics.

Carl J. Weber. *The First Hundred Years of Thomas Hardy 1840-1940. A Centenary Bibliography of Hardiana.* Waterville, Maine: Colby College Library, 1942. Pp. 276. Reprinted: New York: Russell and Russell, Inc., 1965.

One list including studies, reviews, translations, etc., arranged alphabetically by author or title of periodical. Books: place, publisher, date. Periods: volume, pages, date. Occasional brief annotations.

One of the most comprehensive secondary bibliographies ever compiled for a modern author.

Maurice Beebe, Bonnie Culotta, Erin Marcus. "Criticism of Thomas Hardy: A Selected Checklist." *Modern Fiction Studies*

6 (Autumn, 1960): 258-279.

Mainly post-1940 material to supplement Weber (above); limitations listed p. 258. Arranged: General Studies, Studies of Hardy's Poetry (alphabetical by author), Studies of Individual Works of Fiction (arranged under the Hardy titles).

Weber and Beebe are the starting points for any study of the criticism of Hardy.

James Osler Bailey. *The Poetry of Thomas Hardy. A Handbook and Commentary.* Chapel Hill: University of North Carolina Press, 1970. Pp. xxviii, 712.

Titles of the poems are listed in the order of the collected editions, with comments and, often, bibliographical notes for each poem. Alphabetical list of alternate titles, pp. 632-672. Index.

Although not a bibliography, Bailey is a most valuable supplement to Purdy.

One should also note the announcement in 1971 by the Annotated Secondary Bibliography Series on English Literature in Transition, Helmut E. Gerber, general editor, Northern Illinois University Press, that Gerber and W. Eugene Davis are preparing the volume on Hardy for publication in the fall, 1972.

GENERAL

Millett; Batho & Dobrée; Longaker & Bolles; Temple & Tucker; NCBEL, III, 980-992.

HARRIS, FRANK   (1856-1931)

PRIMARY

Vincent Brome. *Frank Harris.* London: Cassells and Co., 1959. Pp. 254. Reprinted: London: World Distributors, 1965.

Pp. 242-248, primary, secondary select bibliography. Books:

publisher, date. Periods: date. List of letters used by Brome with date and information as to whether published or not, but no location thereof. "Foreword," pp. 5-7, describes MSS sources and gives other bibliographical information.

Incomplete--yet a starting point toward a list which can probably never be complete.

SECONDARY

Above, Brome, pp. 243-246.

GENERAL

Temple & Tucker.

HARRIS, JAMES RENDEL   (1852-1941)

WWW 41-50.

HARRISON, JANE ELLEN   (1850-1928)

WWW 16-28.

HARROWER, ELIZABETH   (1928-   )

Hetherington.

HART, SIR BASIL HENRY LIDDELL: see LIDDELL-HART, SIR BASIL HENRY.

HARTLEY, LESLIE POLES   (1895-   )

PRIMARY

Peter Bien. "A L. P. Hartley Bibliography." *Adam International Review* 29, Numbers 294-296 (1961): 63-70.

Primary. Form arrangement. Books: date, publisher, place, reprints or subsequent editions, translations, contents with details of original publication. Periods: volume, date, pages; information concerning later publication in book form.

More informative and extensive than the bibliography in Bien's book (below).

-- *L. P. Hartley*. London: Chatto and Windus; University Park: Pennsylvania State University Press, 1963. Pp. 288.

Pp. 267-269, bibliography. Primary. Genre arrangement. Dates. P. 268, list of book reviews by Hartley (N. B.: "The reviews are too numerous to list in detail. A fuller listing is available from University Microfilms, Ann Arbor, Michigan, publication No. 62-1912.") Pp. 268-269, selected secondary bibliography.

Paul Bloomfield. *L. P. Hartley*. London: Longman Group Ltd. (WTW 217, Revised Edition), 1970. Pp. 36.

Pp. 35-36, primary books, selected secondary criticism. Chronological arrangement. Date, genre.

SECONDARY

Above, Bien (1963), pp. 268-269; Bloomfield, pp. 35-36.

GENERAL

Daiches; Temple & Tucker; WW 71; Hagen.

HARWOOD, HAROLD MARSH   (1874-1959)

Salem; WWW 51-60.

HASKELL, ARNOLD LIONEL   (1903-   )

WW 71.

HASSALL, CHRISTOPHER VERNON   (1912-1963)

PRIMARY

Christopher Hassall. *Ambrosia and Small Beer. The Record
of a Correspondence between Edward Marsh and Christopher
Hassall.* London: Longmans, 1964. Pp. 374.

Although there is no bibliography, these letters (mainly from
Marsh) throw light on the literary work of both men. Especially informative about Marsh's editorial work.

See above: BROOKE, RUPERT. John Schroder. *A Catalogue...*

GENERAL

Temple & Tucker.

HAWKES, JACQUETTA HOPKINS   (1910-   )

(Mrs. J. B. Priestley).

Palmer & Dyson; WW 71.

HAWKINS, SIR ANTHONY HOPE: see HOPE, ANTHONY.

HAY, IAN   (1876-1952)

Pseudonym of John Hay Beith.

WWW 51-60.

HAYES, ALFRED   (1857-1936)

PRIMARY

Alfred Hayes, Richard LeGallienne, Norman Gale. Rugby: Rugby

Press, 189?. Pp. 11.

P. 1, primary books. Chronological arrangement. Date, part collation, publisher, binding, number of copies.

GENERAL

NCBEL, III, 629.

HEANEY, SEAMUS   (1930-   )

PRIMARY

[?Benedict Kiely]. "Books by Seamus Heaney." *Hollins Critic* 7 (October, 1970): 9.

Primary books, all English-language editions. Chronological arrangement. Place, publisher, date, price.

HEATH-STUBBS, JOHN FRANCIS ALEXANDER   (1918-   )

Daiches; Temple & Tucker; WW 71.

HENDERSON, PHILIP PRICHARD   (1906-   )

WW 71.

HENDRY, JAMES FINDLAY   (1912-   )

Daiches.

HENLEY, WILLIAM ERNEST   (1849-1903)

PRIMARY

Kennedy Williamson. *William Ernest Henley. A Memoir.* Harold Shaylor, 1930. Pp. 296.

Pp. 287-290, bibliography. Primary, secondary selected. Arranged: Magazine and Newspaper Articles on Henley; Books containing material on Henley; Works edited by Henley; Writings by Henley not included in the *Collected Works* (1921). Dates. Additional primary writings mentioned in text, *passim*.

Michael Sadleir. "Some Uncollected Authors, X. William Ernest Henley." *Book Collector* 5 (1956): 162-168.

Primary books. Chronological arrangement. Publisher, date, format, pages, binding, subsequent editions.

SECONDARY

Above, Williamson.

Jerome Hamilton Buckley. *William Ernest Henley. A Study in the 'Counter-Decadence' of the 'Nineties.* Princeton: Princeton University Press, 1945. Pp. xii, 234.

Pp. 217-224, all inclusive secondary bibliography.

Joseph M. Flora. *William Ernest Henley.* New York: Twayne Publishers, Inc. (TEAS 107), 1970. Pp. 171.

Pp. 157-159, primary bibliography. Form and genre arrangement. Pp. 159-162, secondary bibliography. Alphabetical by author arrangement. Annotated. Additional information in notes, *passim*, pp. 149-156.

GENERAL

Longaker & Bolles; Batho & Dobrée; NCBEL, III, 629-631.

HEPPENSTALL, JOHN RAYNER   (1911-   )

Temple & Tucker; WW 71.

HERBERT, SIR ALAN PATRICK   (1890-   )

PRIMARY

Gilbert Fabes. *The First Editions of A. E. Coppard, A. P.
Herbert, and Charles Morgan, with Values and Bibliographical
Points.* London: Myers and Co., 1933. Pp. 154.

Pp. 55-125, bibliography of primary books. Chronological
arrangement. Transcribed TP, binding, variants, current
price.

GENERAL

Millett; Daiches; Temple & Tucker; WW 71.

HERFORD, CHARLES HAROLD   (1853-1931)

Batho & Dobrée; WWW 29-40; NCBEL, III, 1439.

HESELTINE, PHILIP   (1894-1930)

PRIMARY

Cecil Gray. *Peter Warlock: A Memoir of Philip Heseltine.* London: Jonathan Cape, 1934. Pp. 319.

Pp. 307-313, "Complete List of Published Works." Pp. 307-
313, original music. P. 313, literary works: publisher, date.

HEWITT, REGINALD MAINWARING   (1887-1948)

PRIMARY

Vivian de Sola Pinto, ed. *Reginald Mainwaring Hewitt (1887-
1948) A Selection from his literary remains...with a memoir.*
Oxford: Blackwell (for the subscribers), 1955. Pp. 149.

No bibliography, but many references in passing to Hewitt's
contributions to periodicals and to other writings.

HEWLETT, MAURICE HENRY   (1861-1923)

PRIMARY

Percy H. Muir. "A Bibliography of the First Editions of Books
by Maurice Henry Hewlett (1861-1923)" in *Bibliographies of
Modern Authors*, 3rd Series. London: Bookman's Journal, 1927.
Pp. 9-36, plus 4 pp. "Addenda and Corrigenda" (1931).

Primary books. Chronological arrangement. Transcribed TP,
full collation, pagination, binding, variants, notes. The "Addenda and Corrigenda" adds important information.

Very much a "collector's bibliography."

Bruce Sutherland. "A Bibliography of Maurice Henry Hewlett."
Bulletin of Bibliography 15 (1935): 126-129.

Primary. Arranged: Books and Pamphlets; Translations of
Hewlett's novels; Books reviews and prefaces by Hewlett.
Chronological in each section. Place, publisher, date, occasional notes. Author and title of books reviewed or introduced by Hewlett. Pp. 127-129, secondary select bibliography. Arranged alphabetically by author. Includes reviews.

SECONDARY

Above, Sutherland, pp. 127-129.

Marie T. Tate. "Maurice Hewlett." *English Literature in Transition* 6 (1963): 33-36.

Annotated. Continued in subsequent issues of *ELT*.

GENERAL

Millett; Longaker & Bolles; Batho & Dobrée; Temple & Tucker.

HIBBERT, ELEANOR   (1906-   )

Pseudonyms used: Jean Plaidy, Eleanor Burford, Ellalice

Tate, Elbur Ford, Kathleen Kellow, Victoria Holt.

WW 71; Hagen.

HICHENS, ROBERT SMYTHE   (1864-1950)

PRIMARY

Robert Hichens. *Yesterday. The Autobiography of Robert Hichens.* London: Cassell and Co., Ltd., 1947. Pp. 464.

No bibliography, but much information concerning Hichen's literary career. Index.

GENERAL

Temple & Tucker; Hagen.

HIGGINS, FREDERICK ROBERT   (1896-1941)

PRIMARY

M. J. MacManus. "Bibliography of F. R. Higgins." *Dublin Magazine* 21 (July-September 1946): 43-45.

Primary books. Chronological arrangement. Transcribed TP, part collation, pagination, binding, price, occasional notes.

HILTON, JAMES   (1900-1954)

PRIMARY

"Checklist Bibliographies of Modern Authors. James Hilton." *Book Trade Journal* 64 (July, 1936): 20.

Not seen.

GENERAL

Temple & Tucker; WWW 51-60.

HINDE, THOMAS   (1926-   )

Pseudonym of Sir Thomas Willes Chitty.

WW 71; Hagen.

HOBBES, JOHN OLIVER   (1867-1906)

Pseudonym of Pearl Mary Theresa Craigie.

Batho & Dobrée; NCBEL, III, 1058.

HOBHOUSE, LEONARD TRELAWNEY   (1864-1929)

Batho & Dobrée.

HOBSON, HAROLD   (1904-   )

WW 71.

HODGSON, RALPH   (1871-1962)

PRIMARY

Colin Fenton, ed. Ralph Hodgson, *Collected Poems*. London: Macmillan and Co., Ltd., 1961. Pp. 185.

Pp. 179-181, poems by Hodgson arranged alphabetically by title. For each, name of periodical in which first published and date.

Neda M. Westlake. "Ralph Hodgson Exhibition." *Library Chronicle* [of the University of Pennsylvania] 30 (1964): 85-87.

Bibliographical information for three poems.

GENERAL

Millett; Longaker & Bolles; Batho & Dobrée; Temple & Tucker.

HOFF, HARRY SUMMERFIELD: see COOPER, WILLIAM.

HOLLOWAY, JOHN   (1920-   )

Temple & Tucker; WW 71.

HOLME, CONSTANCE   (?1913-1955)

(Mrs. F. B. Punchard).

PRIMARY

E. A. Osborne. "Bibliography of Constance Holme." *Book Trade Journal* 63 (1936): 28.

Not seen.

Bertram Rota. "Some Uncollected Authors, XI: Constance Holme." *Book Collector* 5 (1956): 250-255.

Primary books. Chronological arrangement. Publisher, date, binding, bibliographical notes. Includes books with contributions by Holme.

GENERAL

Daiches.

HOLMES, THOMAS RICE EDWARD   (1855-1933)

PRIMARY

"Materials for a Bibliography of the Writings published by T. R. E. Holmes." *Proceedings of the British Academy*

22 (1936): 372-379.

Primary bibliography. Chronological arrangement. Books: place, publisher, date, pages. Periods: volume, date, pages.

HOLT, VICTORIA: see HIBBERT, ELEANOR.

HOLTBY, WINIFRED   (1898-1935)

PRIMARY

Geoffrey Handley-Taylor. *Winifred Holtby. A Concise and Selected Bibliography together with Some Letters.* London: A. Brown and Sons, Ltd., 1955. Pp. 76. 1000 copies.

Primary, secondary select. Form arrangement. Part collation, publisher, place, date, contents; notes on subsequent editions, reprints, and translations. Periodical contributions arranged alphabetically by subject matter: dates. Includes list of MSS with locations. Index.

References to primary writings not listed here are made in the following:

Vera Brittain. *Testament of Friendship. The Story of Winifred Holtby.* London: Macmillan and Co., Ltd., 1940. Pp. 442.

-- and Geoffrey Handley-Taylor, eds. *Selected Letters of Winifred Holtby and Vera Brittain (1920-1935).* London: A. Brown and Sons, Ltd., 1960. Pp. 384. 500 copies.

SECONDARY

Above, Handley-Taylor (1955), pp. 41-52.

GENERAL

Temple & Tucker.

HOME, HON. WILLIAM DOUGLAS - (1912-   )

PRIMARY

William Douglas Home. *Half-Term Report, An Autobiography.* London: Longmans, Green and Co., 1954. Pp. 209.

A certain amount of bibliographical assistance can be deduced from this volume.

-- *The Plays of William Douglas Home.* London: Heinemann, 1958. Pp. 434.

Bibliographical references in the introduction, pp. 7-11.

GENERAL

Palmer & Dyson; WW 71.

HOPE, ANTHONY (1863-1933)

Pseudonym of Sir Anthony Hope Hawkins.

PRIMARY

Sir Charles Mallet. *Anthony Hope and his books, Being the Authorised Life of Sir Anthony Hope Hawkins.* London: Hutchinson and Co., 1935. Pp. 290.

Bibliographical information in text, *passim*.

GENERAL

Batho & Dobrée; Temple & Tucker; NCBEL, III, 1058-1059.

HOPE, SIR WILLIAM HENRY ST. JOHN (1854-1919)

PRIMARY

Alexander Hamilton Thompson. *A Bibliography of the Published*

Writings of Sir William St. John Hope...With a brief introductory Memoir. Leeds: J. Whitehead and Son, 1929. Pp. 50.

Not seen.

GENERAL

WWW 16-28.

HOPKINS, GERARD MANLEY   (1844-1889)

PRIMARY

Edward H. Cohen. *Works and Criticism of Gerard Manley Hopkins : A Comprehensive Bibliography.* Washington, D. C.: Catholic University of America Press, 1969. Pp. [xvi], 217.

Pp. 1-5, primary; pp. 15-163, secondary. Chronological within each section; alphabetical by author within the year in the secondary bibliography. Books: place, publisher, date, pages; reviews within year of publication listed after book title, other- wise book title is repeated for following year(s) and reviews are listed there. Periods: volume, date, pages. Index of Critics.

A checklist of primary and secondary titles, one-fifth of the latter composed of unpublished theses and dissertations.

Ruth Seelhammer. *Hopkins Collected at Gonzaga.* Chicago: Loyola University Press, 1970. Pp. xiv, 272.

Catalogue of the collection in the Crosby Library, Gonzaga University, Spokane, Washington. Arranged: Primary writings; Association items; Secondary writings. Alphabetical by author within second and third section, by title within first. Books: place, publisher, date; brief description of any unique auto- graph inscriptions. Periods: volume, date, pages. The col- lection includes every edition and impression of the primary writings. Index of names and relevant topics.

Cohen and Seelhammer together provide an almost complete list of primary and secondary titles; but there is no complete, descriptive bibliography of Hopkins's writings.

SECONDARY

Above, Cohen, pp. 15-163; Seelhammer, pp. 63-226.

GENERAL

Longaker & Bolles; NCBEL, III, 581-593.

HOPKINSON, HENRY THOMAS   (1905-   )

Daiches; WW 71.

HOUGH, GRAHAM GOULDER   (1908-   )

WW 71.

HOUGHTON, CLAUDE   (1889-1961)

Pseudonym of Claude Houghton Oldfield.

PRIMARY

Sir Hugh S. Walpole and Clemence Dane. *Claude Houghton. Appreciations...with a bibliography.* London: William Heinemann, 1935. Pp. 15.

Not seen.

Ben Abramson. "Claude Houghton Bibliography." *Reading and Collecting* 2 (December, 1937): 6.

Primary books. Chronological arrangement. Place, date.

GENERAL

WW 61; Hagen.

HOUGHTON, STANLEY   (1881-1913)

Longaker & Bolles; Batho & Dobrée; Salem.

HOULT, NORAH   (1901-   )

Millett; WW 71; Hagen.

HOUSMAN, ALFRED EDWARD   (1859-1936)

PRIMARY

A. S. F. Gow. *A. E. Housman. A Sketch together with a List of his Writings and Indexes to his Classical Papers.* Cambridge: University Press; New York: Macmillan Company, 1936. Pp. [xiv], [137].

Pp. 65-78, Writings on Greek and Latin. Alphabetical list of subjects (reviews included). For books: place, publisher, date. For periodicals: volume and page numbers, date. Reviews by Housman include author and title of book reviewed. Indexes, pp. 83-[137], divided Passages in Greek and Latin Authors (alphabetical list of authors with references to specific pages in Housman's writings) and subjects. Pp. 79-80, English Writings (information as above). Pp. 58-59, icongraphy; pp. 60-61, lectures by Housman with dates.

The definitive list of Housman's classical work.

John Carter and John Sparrow. "A. E. Housman. An Annotated Checklist," *The Library*, N. S. 21 (September, 1940): 160-191.

Primary first editions, secondary selected. Chronological arrangement. Information varies, but generally for books: place, publisher, date, size, number of leaves, binding, number of copies, various annotations. For periodicals: date and page number. Includes brief account of The Poetical Manuscripts. This work is reproduced in *A. E. Housman An Annotated Hand-List.* London: Rupert Hart-Davis (Soho Bibliography Number 2), 1952. Pp. 54. Reviewed by W. White, *Library* 7 (December,

173

1952): 285: "It has been corrected and slightly revised, the appendix on the poetical manuscripts being considerably enlarged...only two new entries are listed...authoritatively written small gem of a bibliographical hand-list."

William White, *et al.* "A. E. Housman, An Annotated Check-List. Additions and Corrections," *The Library* 23 (June, 1942): 31-44; (September-December, 1942): 133.

Information as in Carter and Sparrow (1940), above.

William White, "A. E. Housman, An Annotated Check-List. Additions and Corrections: III, " *The Library* 7 (September, 1952): 201-210.

Information as in Carter and Sparrow (1940), above. Particularly informative concerning reprints and numbers of copies in editions. Note especially White's introduction, p. 201, for brief survey of Housman bibliography.

G. B. A. Fletcher. "A. E. Housman Bibliography," *The Library* 8 (March, 1953): 51.

Addition to White (1952), above.

William White. "A. E. Housman Anthologized," *Bulletin of Bibliography* 21 (1954): 43-48, 68-72.

Chronological list of anthologies containing Housman. For each title: publisher, place, date, title of Housman contribution.

William White. "An Unrecorded Housman MS Item," *Papers of the Bibliographical Society of America* 49 (1955): 78-79.

Letters and a poem in the Fitzwilliam Museum, Cambridge.

William White. "Published Letters of A. E. Housman," *Bulletin of Bibliography* 22 (1957): 80-82.

Alphabetical listing by authors of printed sources. For books: publisher, place, date. For periodicals: volume and page numbers, date. Extensive annotations and quotations.

William White. "A Checklist of A. E. Housman's Writings in Latin," *Papers of the Bibliographical Society of America* 54 (1960): 188-190.

A list of the twelve known items with finding information.

William White. "Housman in French and Music," *Papers of the Bibliographical Society of America* 56 (1962): 257-259.

A short study of translations of Housman.

Tom Burns Haber. "Three Unreported Letters of A. E. Housman." *Papers of the Bibliographical Society of America* 57 (1963): 230-233.

There are no short-cuts in finding Housman's writings: in order to locate all of the primary material one should consult all of the above entries, noting as well the references within these items to other bibliographies of Housman.

SECONDARY

Above, Carter and Sparrow (1940, 1952); White (1942, 1952); Fletcher (1953).

Theodore G. Ehrsam. *A Bibliography of Alfred Edward Housman.* Boston: F. W. Faxon Company (Useful Reference Series No. 66), 1941. Pp. 44.

Put forward as a primary bibliography, this work was described by White (1942) as "incomplete and inaccurate": its value lies in its listing of secondary material, although there are inaccuracies here. Pp. 11-21, titles by Housman, followed by listing of reviews: volume and page numbers, dates. Pp. 21-43, Material written about Housman: alphabetical by author. Pp. 43-44, Bibliographical Material about Housman.

Robert W. Stallman. "Annotated Bibliography of A. E. Housman: A Critical Study," *PMLA* 60 (1945): 463-502.

Essay with checklists; material arranged by topics, which are listed on p. 464, fn. 1. Books: publisher, place, date, pages.

Periods: volume, date, pages.

GENERAL

Millett; Batho & Dobrée; Longaker & Bolles; Temple & Tucker; NCBEL, III, 601-606.

HOUSMAN, LAURENCE   (1865-1959)

PRIMARY

Anna Rudolf. *Die Dichtung von Laurence Housman.* Breslau: Priebatschs Buchhandlung (English Series Volume II), 1930. Pp. 93.

Pp. 85-89, bibliography. Primary books, secondary selected. Chronological arrangement. Place, publisher, year (88 items to 1928). Includes reviews of Housman.

GENERAL

Millett; Longaker & Bolles; Batho & Dobrée; Temple & Tucker; Salem; NCBEL, III, 632.

HOWARD, ELIZABETH JANE   (1923-   )

(Mrs. Kingsley Amis).

Temple & Tucker; WW 71.

HOWARD, PETER DUNSMORE   (1908-1965)

PRIMARY

Anne Wolrige Gordon. *Peter Howard. Life and Letters.* London: Hodder and Stoughton, 1969. Pp. 318.

Pp. 313-314, "Books and Plays by Peter Howard." Primary books. Chronological arrangement. Publisher, date. Additional primary and secondary references in text, *passim*, including unpublished letters. Index.

HOYLE, FRED   (1915-   )

WW 71.

HUBBARD, WILFRANC   (1857-   )

Millett.

HUDDLESTON, SISLEY   (1883-1952)

WWW 51-60.

HUDSON, STEPHEN   (1868-1944)

Pseudonym of Sydney Alfred Schiff.

PRIMARY

John Gawsworth. *Ten Contemporaries. Notes Toward their Definitive Bibliography.* [First Series]. London: Ernest Benn Ltd., 1932. Pp. 224.

Pp. 102-109, primary first editions, 1913-1931. Chronological arrangement. Transcribed TP, full collation, pagination, binding, date, bibliographical notes.

Theophilus E. M. Boll. "Biographical Note" and "Critical Essay" in Stephen Hudson. *Richard, Myrtle and I.* Philadelphia: University of Pennsylvania Press, 1962. Pp. 140.

Pp. 15-89. No bibliography, but text and notes provide primary and secondary references. See also the review by Helmut Gerber of this volume: *English Fiction in Transition* 5, ii (1962): 35-36.

SECONDARY

Above, Boll, pp. 15-89.

GENERAL

Millett; Daiches; Temple & Tucker.

HUDSON, WILLIAM HENRY   (1841-1922)

PRIMARY

George F. Wilson. *A Bibliography of the Writings of W. H. Hudson.* London: Bookman's Journal, 1922. Pp. 80. Reprinted 1968.

Primary. Two sections: "First editions, pamphlets, leaflets, etc." and "Contributions to periodical literature, prefaces to books, etc., which--unless otherwise stated--have not been reprinted." Chronological arrangement. Books: transcribed TP, part collation, pagination, binding, date, variants, notes; subsequent editions included with full descriptions. Periods: genre, date, pages.

[*The Collected Works of W. H. Hudson, in Twenty-four Volumes.* London and Toronto: J. M. Dent and Sons Ltd.; New York: E. P. Dutton and Co., 1923. 885 copies.

Includes almost all of Hudson's writings.]

Sidonia C. Rosenbaum. "W. H. Hudson: Bibliografía." *Revista Hispánica Moderna* 10 (1944): 222-230.

Primary, secondary select. Form arrangement. Books: place, publisher, date, subsequent editions listed under first edition; translations in separate list. Periods: volume, date, pages. Secondary bibliography: arranged alphabetically by author. In Spanish.

SECONDARY

Above, Rosenbaum.

Helmut Gerber. "W. H. Hudson." *English Fiction in Transition*
1 (1957): 28-29; Marie T. Tate, *English Literature in Transition*
6 (1963): 36-48, 164-165; continued in subsequent issues.

Annotated.

GENERAL

Millett; Batho & Dobrée; Longaker & Bolles; Temple & Tucker;
NCBEL, III, 1059-1060.

HUGHES, RICHARD ARTHUR WARREN   (1900-   )

Millett; Daiches; Temple & Tucker; WW 71.

HUGHES, TED   (1930-   )

Temple & Tucker; WW 71.

HULME, THOMAS ERNEST   (1883-1917)

PRIMARY

Alun Richard Jones. *Life and Opinions of T. E. Hulme*. London: Victor Gollancz Ltd., 1960. Pp. 233.

Pp. 221-224, "Bibliography of T. E. Hulme's Published Writings." Primary. Chronological arrangement. Books: place,
publisher, date. Periods: volume, date, pages. Pp. 225-226,
secondary bibliography. Arranged alphabetically by author.
Additional secondary criticism in footnotes, *passim*.

T. E. Hulme. *Further Speculations*, ed. Sam Hynes. Minneapolis: University of Minnesota Press, 1955. Pp. 226.

Pp. 221-223, bibliography. Primary. Chronological arrangement. Books: place, publisher, date. Periods: date, volume,

pages. P. 224, secondary bibliography.

Wallace Martin. "T. E. Hulme: A Bibliographical Note." *Notes and Queries*, N. S., 9 (1962): 307.

Adds twelve items to Jones and Hynes.

SECONDARY

Above, Jones, pp. 225-226; Hynes, p. 224.

GENERAL

Longaker & Bolles; Temple & Tucker.

HUNT, VIOLET   (1862-1942)

PRIMARY

Douglas Goldring. *South Lodge. Reminiscences of Violet Hunt, Ford Madox Ford, and the English Review Circle.* London: Constable and Co., Ltd., 1943. Pp. [xx], [240].

Pp. 238-[240], bibliography of primary books. Chronological arrangement. Publisher, date. Suggestions of periodical contributions are found in the text, *passim*.

GENERAL

WWW 41-50.

HUTCHINSON, ARTHUR STUART MENTETH   (1879-   )

WW 71.

HUTCHINSON, RAY CORYTON   (1907-   )

Daiches; Temple & Tucker; WW 71.

HUTTON, EDWARD   (1875-1969)

PRIMARY

Dennis Everard Rhodes. *The Writings of Edward Hutton. A Bibliographical Tribute Compiled and Presented to Edward Hutton on his Eightieth Birthday.* London: Hollis and Carter, 1955. Pp. 64.

Not seen.

GENERAL

WW 69.

HUXLEY FAMILY

ALDOUS (Also below).   (1894-1963)

ANTHONY (WW 71)   (1920-   )

ELSPETH JOSCELINE (WW 71; Hagen)   (1907-   )
   (Mrs. Gervas Huxley).

FRANCIS

GERVAS (WW 71)   (1894-   )

HENRIETTA

JULIAN (Also below).   (1887-   )

JULIETTE

LAURA

LEONARD   (1860-1933)

PRIMARY

Ronald W. Clark. *The Huxleys.* London: Heinemann, 1968.

Pp. xvi, 398.

Pp. 367-373, selected primary books. Arranged by author (as above). Place, publisher, date.

HUXLEY, ALDOUS LEONARD   (1894-1963)

PRIMARY

Hanson R. Duval. *Aldous Huxley. A Bibliography.* New York: Arrow Editions, 1939. Pp. 205.

Primary. Form arrangement. Books: transcribed TP, full collation, pagination, binding, date, variants, contents, bibliographical notes; all English language editions described, foreign editions listed with publisher. Reprints of books listed separately. Books with contributions by Huxley listed alphabetically by main author. Periods: arranged alphabetically by title of periodical with Huxley's contributions listed chronologically thereunder: date, pages. Includes reviews by Huxley with title of book reviewed. Index.

Complete to September, 1939.

Claire John Eschelbach and Joyce Lee Shober. *Aldous Huxley. A Bibliography 1916-1959.* Berkeley and Los Angeles: University of California Press, 1961. Pp. x, 150.

Primary, secondary. Form and genre arrangement. Books: publisher, place, date, pages. Periods: volume, date, pages. Arrangement within each division is alphabetical by title. All editions and contents of books and pamphlets listed. For poems, essays and short pieces, all places of publication listed. Books reviewed by Huxley listed alphabetically by author, as are books with contributions by Huxley. Secondary bibliography (pp. 91-123) arranged by form. Includes list of earlier bibliographies (p. 91) and criticism of primary works under the title of the work.

Nicholas Barker, *Book Collector* 11 (1962): 109-110: "a checklist only in the literal sense of the word: it is a list you can check by; it contains no other information." The best available bibliography, but by no means authoritative.

Thomas D. Clareson and Carolyn S. Andrews. "Aldous Huxley: A Bibliography, 1960-1964." *Extrapolation* 6 (1964): 2-21.

Not seen.

H. H. Watts (below), p. 169: "a valuable supplement" to Eschelbach and Shober.

Harold H. Watts. *Aldous Huxley*. New York: Twayne Publishers, Inc. (TEAS 79), 1969. Pp. 182.

Pp. 169-171, primary books and pamphlets. Place, publisher, date of British and American first editions. Complete to 1963. Pp. 172-176, secondary bibliography, selected. Periods: volume, pages, date. Annotated.

SECONDARY

Above, Eschelbach and Shober, pp. 91-123; Clareson and Andrews, pp. 17-20; Watts, pp. 172-176.

GENERAL

Millett; Longaker & Bolles; Daiches; Temple & Tucker; Coleman & Tyler; Salem.

HUXLEY, SIR JULIAN SORELL   (1887-   )

PRIMARY

Ronald W. Clark. *Sir Julian Huxley, F. R. S.* London: Phoenix House Ltd.; New York: Roy Publishers (Living Biographies Series), 1960. Pp. 109.

P. 108, "Some of Sir Julian Huxley's Books": titles.

GENERAL

Millett; Daiches; WW 71.

HYDE, DOUGLAS (1860-1949)

PRIMARY

Patrick Sarsfield O'Hegarty. "A Bibliography of Dr. Douglas Hyde." *Dublin Magazine* 14 (January-March, 1939): 57-66; (April-June, 1939): 72-78. Reprinted as pamphlet, Dublin: Privately Published, 1939. Pp. 19. 40 copies.

Primary books, and books edited by Hyde. Chronological arrangement. Transcribed TP, part collation, pagination, binding, notes. Includes "the more important" of Hyde's contributions to books and a two-paragraph description of contributions to periodicals.

Tomas De Bhaldraithe. "Aguisin le clar saothair An Chraoibhin." *Galvia* 4 (1957): 18-24.

Not seen.

GENERAL

Millett; NCBEL, III, 1909-1910.

HYDE, HARFORD MONTGOMERY (1907-   )

WW 71.

INGE, WILLIAM RALPH (1860-1954)

Longaker & Bolles; Batho & Dobrée; NCBEL, III, 1613.

INNES, MICHAEL: see STEWART, JOHN.

IRWIN, MARGARET   (-1967)

WW 68.

ISHERWOOD, CHRISTOPHER WILLIAM BRADSHAW (1904-   )

PRIMARY

Selmer Westby and Clayton M. Brown. *Christopher Isherwood. A Bibliography 1923-1967.* Los Angeles: California State College, for the J. F. Kennedy Memorial Library, 1968. Pp. [xii], 51.

Pp. 3-29, primary bibliography. Form and genre arrangement. Books: first and subsequent editions: place, publisher, year, pages. Periods: volume, pages, date, reprintings; reviews by Isherwood include title and author of book reviewed. Pp. 33-51, secondary bibliography. Two sections: general criticism (alphabetical by author) and reviews of the primary books (listed under titles of books, alphabetically arranged).

SECONDARY

Above, Westby-Brown, pp. 33-51.

Alan Wilde. *Christopher Isherwood.* New York: Twayne Publishers, Inc. (TUSAS 173), 1971. Pp. 171.

Pp. 161-162, checklist of selected primary titles. Pp. 162-164, general secondary bibliography, annotated. P. 165, eighteen reviews of Isherwood's books.

GENERAL

Daiches; Temple & Tucker; Palmer & Dyson; WW 71.

JACK, HENRY VERNON: see ESMOND, HENRY VERNON.

JACKSON, HOLBROOK   (1874-1948)

Millett; WWW 41-50.

JACOBS, WILLIAM WYMARK   (1863-1943)

PRIMARY

E. A. Osborne. ''Epitome of a Bibliography of W. W. Jacobs.''
American Book Collector 5 (1934): 201-204, 268-272, 286-
288, 331-334, 358-362.

A bibliographically informative, chatty, informal essay. No
listings provided.

GENERAL

Millett; Longaker & Bolles; Batho & Dobrée; Temple & Tucker;
Hagen.

JAMES, DAVID GWILYM   (1905-1968)

Daiches; WW 68.

JAMES, MONTAGUE RHODES   (1862-1936)

PRIMARY

S. G. Lubbock. *A Memoir of M. R. James.* Cambridge: Cambridge
University Press, 1939. Pp. 87.

Pp. 49-87, A. F. Scholfield, ''List of his Writings.'' Primary.
Subject arrangement: Bible and Apocrypha; Manuscripts and
Books; History and Antiquities; Friends and Contemporaries;
Inscriptions; Miscellaneous. Chronological in each section.
Books: publisher, date, place, format. Periods: date, vol-
ume, pages.

A. F. Scholfield. ''Additions to a List of the Writings of Dr. M.
R. James.'' *Transactions of the Cambridge Bibliographical
Society* 2(1954-1958), 95.

Additions to Scholfield's list in Lubbock (above).

GENERAL

Batho & Dobrée.

JAMESON, MARGARET STORM   (1897-   )

Millett; Daiches; Temple & Tucker; WW 71.

JEANS, SIR JAMES HOPWOOD   (1877-1946)

PRIMARY

E. A. Milne. *Sir James Jeans A Biography. With a Memoir by S. C. Roberts.* Cambridge: Cambridge University Press, 1952. Pp. 176.

Pp. 167-171, bibliography. Primary. Arranged: Technical Books; Popular Books; Original Papers; Lectures. Chronological under each heading. Books: date, place, publisher, pages. Periods: volume, date, pages. Includes abstracts of Jean's unpublished lectures.

GENERAL

Daiches.

JEFFARES, ALEXANDER NORMAN   (1920-   )

WW 71.

JEFFRIES, G. M.: see GRAEME, BRUCE.

JELLICOE, PATRICIA ANN   (1927-   )

(Mrs. Roger Mayne).

Coleman & Tyler; Palmer & Dyson; WW 71.

187

JENKS, EDWARD   (1861-1939)

PRIMARY

R. W. Lee. [Bibliography of Jenks]. *Proceedings of the Bri-ish Academy* 26 (1940): 421-423.

Primary books. Chronological arrangement. Place, publisher, date; date of latest reprint or edition. Suggestions of loca-tions of periodical contributions.

JENNINGS, ELIZABETH JOAN   (1926-   )

Temple & Tucker; WW 71.

JEPSON, SELWYN   (-   )

WW 71; Hagen.

JEROME, JEROME KLAPFA   (1859-1927)

PRIMARY

Jerome K. Jerome. *My Life and Times.* London: Hodder and Stoughton Ltd., [1926]. Pp. 302.

No bibliography and no index, but much bibliographical infor-mation can be gained from this autobiography.

Alfred Moss. *Jerome K. Jerome. His Life and Work (from Pov-erty to the Knighthood of the People).* London: Selwyn and Blount Ltd., [1929]. Pp. 255.

No bibliography. Many references in text to Jerome's publi-cations. Index, pp. 251-255.

GENERAL

Batho & Dobrée; Temple & Tucker; Palmer & Dyson; NCBEL, III, 1062.

JESSE, FRYNIWYD MARSH TENNYSON   (1889-1958)

(Mrs. H. M. Harwood).

Millett; Daiches; WWW 51-60; Hagen.

JOAD, CYRIL EDWARD MITCHINSON   (1891-1953)

WWW 51-60.

JOB, THOMAS   (1900-1947)

Salem.

JOHNSON, LIONEL PIGOT   (1867-1902)

PRIMARY

Iain Fletcher, ed. *The Complete Poems of Lionel Johnson.*
London: Unicorn Press, 1953. Pp. 395. 1000 copies.

Pp. 289-294, ''Select Bibliography.'' Primary. Arranged:
MSS Sources; Printed Sources; Books with Contributions by
Johnson; Periodicals with Contributions by Johnson. Books:
editor, publisher, place, date, pages. Periods: date. Additional bibliographical information in Introduction, pp. xi-
xliv, and in Textual Notes, pp. 325-395. Secondary bibliography, pp. 292-294.

SECONDARY

Above, Fletcher, pp. 292-294.

GENERAL

Longaker & Bolles; Batho & Dobrée; NCBEL, III, 633-634.

JOHNSON, PAMELA HANSFORD   (1912-   )
  (Rt. Hon. Lady Snow).

PRIMARY

Isabel Quigly. *Pamela Hansford Johnson*. London: Longmans, Green and Co. (WTW 203), 1968. Pp. 48.

Pp. 47-48, bibliography of primary books. Chronological arrangement. Place, date, genre. Includes works written in collaboration with C. P. Snow. P. 48, secondary bibliography (four entries).

GENERAL

Temple & Tucker; WW 71; Hagen.

JOHNSTON, SIR HARRY HAMILTON   (1858-1927)

Batho & Dobrée; WWW 16-28.

JOHNSTON, WILLIAM DENIS   (1901-   )

PRIMARY

Kaspar Spinner. *Die Alte Dame Sagt: Nein! Irische Dramatiker. Lennox Robinson, Sean O'Casey. Denis Johnston.* Bern: Francke Verlag (Schweizer Anglistische Arbeiten 52), 1961. Pp. 210.

Pp. 208-209, bibliography. Primary selected. Arranged: Drama, Other Writings. Books: publisher, date. Plays: date of first performance. Pp. 209-210, general secondary bibliography, selected.

SECONDARY

Above, Spinner, pp. 209-210.

GENERAL

Daiches; Temple & Tucker; Salem; WW 71.

JONES, ALFRED ERNEST   (-1958)

WWW 51-60.

JONES, DAVID MICHAEL   (1895-   )

PRIMARY

Harman Grisewood, ed. *Epoch and Artist. Selected Writings by David Jones.* London: Faber & Faber, 1959. Pp. 320.

No bibliography. Many of Jones's contributions to books and periodicals are here collected with place of original publication identified. Useful.

Agenda, V, i-iii (1967). David Jones Special Issue.

Not seen.

GENERAL

Temple & Tucker; WW 71.

JONES, EMILY BEATRIX COURSOLLES   (1893-   )

Millett.

JONES, GLYN   (1905-   )

Temple & Tucker.

JONES, GWYN   (1907-   )

Temple & Tucker; WW 71.

JONES, SIR HENRY   (1852-1922)

NCBEL, III, 1540-1541.

JONES, HENRY ARTHUR   (1851-1929)

PRIMARY

Frank K. Walter. ''Reading List on Henry Arthur Jones.'' *Bulletin of Bibliography* 6 (1911): 273-275.

Primary, secondary selected. Arranged: Plays; Annotated List of Selected Non-Dramatic Works; Annotated List of Criticism of Jones. Alphabetical by title in each section. For each entry: place, publisher, date, price, reprints, subsequent editions; also brief quotation of criticism of each primary title and a list of reviews of that title.

Doris Arthur Jones. *The Life and Letters of Henry Arthur Jones.* London: Victor Gollancz Ltd., 1930. Pp. 448.

Pp. 411-431, bibliography. Primary. Form and genre arrangement. Books: publisher, place, date, Periods: date. For plays: details of first and subsequent performances: theatre, date, actors.

SECONDARY

Above, Walter.

GENERAL

Millett; Batho & Dobrée; Temple & Tucker; Coleman & Tyler; Adelman & Dworkin; Salem; NCBEL, III, 1164-1166.

JONES, JACK   (1884-1970)

PRIMARY

G. F. Adam.   *Three Contemporary Anglo-Welsh Novelists: Jack*

Jones, Rhys Davies, and Hilda Vaughan. Bern: A. Francke
A. G., (University of Bern Monograph, [1950]. Pp. 109.

Pp. 107-108, primary books. Chronological arrangement. Publisher, date.

GENERAL

WW 70.

JONES, THOMAS GWYNN   (1871-1949)

PRIMARY

Owen Williams. *A Bibliography of Thomas Gwynn Jones.* Wrexham: Principality Press, 1938. Pp. 53.

Not seen.

GENERAL

WWW 41-50.

JOYCE, JAMES   (1882-1941)

BIBLIOGRAPHIES OF BIBLIOGRAPHIES

Robert H. Deming. *A Bibliography of James Joyce Studies.*
Lawrence, Kansas: University of Kansas (Library Series No. 18), 1964. Pp. [viii], 180.

Pp. 1-4, "Bibliography of Exhibitions, Collections, Checklists and Bibliographies." Books: place, publisher, date. Periods: volume, pages, date. Brief annotations.

The most important listing of bibliographical information for material published before December, 1961.

Alan M. Cohn. "Joyce Bibliographies: A Survey." *American Book Collector* 15 (Summer, 1965): 11-16.

An essay on the history of Joyce bibliography to 1964. Bibliographies cited are listed on p. 16 (with information as for Deming, above); Cohn reproduces and supplements Deming's list.

See below, Beebe, Herring and Litz.

PRIMARY

John J. Slocum and Herbert Cahoon. *A Bibliography of James Joyce*. London: Rupert Hart-Davis (Soho Bibliography No. 5); New Haven: Yale University Press, 1953. Pp. [x], 195.

Primary first editions. Form arrangement. Books: transcribed TP, full collation, pagination, binding, date, price, number of copies, extremely full bibliographical, textual, and publishing notes. Periods: volume, pages, dates, annotations, reprintings. Includes unsigned writings; reviews by Joyce include author and title of book reviewed. Sections on Translations of Joyce's work (alphabetical listing by language, each language subdivided by form); Manuscripts; Musical Settings of Works by Joyce; Miscellany. Index. The definitive primary bibliography. Supplemental information given in Cohn and Kain, *James Joyce Quarterly*, below.

SECONDARY

See above, Deming, and Cohn, for titles of earlier checklists of secondary writings. Deming reprints most of the entries in these earlier works, dividing them by subject matter (General and Biographical; Reviews; Studies of Separate Works; and others). Each entry is annotated, and there is an index. Deming provides the basic secondary bibliography, being supplemented by the *James Joyce Quarterly* listings, below.

Alan M. Cohn and Richard M. Kain. "Supplemental James Joyce Checklist, 1962." *James Joyce Quarterly* 1 (Winter, 1964): 15-22.

Primary, secondary, and translations (excluding items listed in the PMLA annual bibliography). Books: place, publisher, date. Periods: volume, pages, date.

This checklist is continued in the following issues of the *James Joyce Quarterly* by Cohn and others: 2 (Fall, 1964): 50-60; 3 (Fall, 1965): 50-61; 3 (Winter, 1966): 141-153; 3 (Spring, 1966): 196-212; 4 (Winter, 1967): 120-130; 5 (Fall, 1967): 53-67; 6 (Spring, 1969): 242-261; continuing.

Maurice Beebe, Phillip F. Herring, Walton Litz. "Criticism of James Joyce: A Selected Checklist." *Modern Fiction Studies* 15 (Spring, 1969): 105-182.

Primary selected, secondary selected. Arranged: Primary Writings; Bibliographies; Biographical Material; General Studies; Studies of Individual Works (listed under primary titles). Books: place, publisher, date. Periods: volume, pages, date. Restrictions and principles of selection described on pp. 105-106.

Useful as a secondary bibliography complete in itself (particularly for the beginning student) and also for the additions it provides in its bibliography of bibliographies (pp. 108-109).

GENERAL

Millett; Longaker & Bolles; Daiches; Temple & Tucker; Coleman & Tyler; Adelman & Dworkin; Salem; Palmer & Dyson.

KAYE-SMITH, SHEILA   (1887-1956)

SECONDARY

Marie T. Tate. "Sheila Kaye-Smith." *English Literature in Transition* 6 (1963): 48-51.

Annotated.

GENERAL

Millett; Longaker & Bolles; Temple & Tucker.

KEITH, SIR ARTHUR   (1866-1955)
WWW 51-60.

KELLOW, KATHLEEN: see HIBBERT, ELEANOR.

KENDON, FRANK   (1893-1959)

WWW 51-60.

KENNEDY, MARGARET MOORE   (1896-1967)

(Lady Davies).

Millett; Daiches; Temple & Tucker; WW 67.

KENNY, COURTNEY STANHOPE   (1847-1930)

PRIMARY

H. D. Hazeltine. "List of Some of Courtney Stanhope Kenny's
Published Writings." *Proceedings of the British Academy*
18 (1932): 404-406.

Primary bibliography. Chronological arrangement. Books:
place, date. Periods: volume, date, pages. Includes reviews
with author and title of book reviewed.

KER, WILLIAM PATON   (1855-1923)

PRIMARY

J. H. P. Pafford. *W. P. Ker 1885-1923. A Bibliography.* London: University of London Press, Ltd., 1950. Pp. 72.

Pp. 11-47, primary bibliography. Chronological arrangement.
Books: place, date, pages, reviews. Periods: volume, pages,
date; reviews by Ker include title and author of book reviewed.
Pp. 48-57, secondary bibliography. Pp. 58-62, Miscellany, in-

cluding Iconography, Association Items, etc. Index.

Winifred Husbands, *Modern Language Review* 46 (1951): 298: "it [is] as complete as is humanly possible."

GENERAL

Batho & Dobrée; Temple & Tucker; NCBEL, III, 1440.

KERMODE, JOHN FRANK   (1919-   )

WW 71.

KEYES, SIDNEY ARTHUR KILWORTH   (1922-1943)

PRIMARY

Michael Meyer, ed. *The Collected Poems of Sidney Keyes.* London: Routledge, 1945. Pp. 124; Michael Meyer, ed. *Sidney Keyes. Minos of Crete. Plays and Stories with Selections from his Notebook and Letters and Some Early Unpublished Poems.* London: Routledge, 1948. Pp. 190.

No bibliographies; the introductory material in these two volumes provides miscellaneous bibliographical information.

John Guenther. *Sidney Keyes. A Biographical Inquiry.* London: London Magazine Edns, 1967. Pp. [223].

Bibliographical information in text, *passim.*

SECONDARY

Above, Guenther, *passim.*

GENERAL

Longaker & Bolles; Daiches.

KEYNES, SIR GEOFFREY LANGDON (1887-)

PRIMARY

W. R. LeFanu. "A List of the Writings of Sir Geoffrey Keynes, compiled by Permission from his own Register" in *Geoffrey Keynes Tributes on the Occasion of his Seventieth Birthday*. London: Rupert Hart-Davis for the Osler Club, 1961. Pp. 64.

Pp. 27-61, bibliography. Arranged under Surgery and General, with subdivisions based on subject matter. Books: publisher, date, subsequent editions. Periods: date, occasionally volume and pages. Includes unsigned reviews by Keynes with title and author of book reviewed.

GENERAL

WW 71.

KEYNES, JOHN MAYNARD, LORD KEYNES (1883-1946)

PRIMARY

Seymour E. Harris and Margarita Willfort. "Bibliography of Keyne's Writings" in Seymour E. Harris, ed., *The New Economics*. New York: A. A. Knopf, 1948. Pp. xxii, 686, ix.

Pp. 665-686, primary bibliography. Form and topic arrangement. Books: dates, translations with translators' names and language and date. Periods: date, pages. Reviews by Keynes include title and author of book reviewed. Includes items doubtfully attributed to Keynes. See pp. 58-61 for discussion of the primary bibliography and suggestions concerning the secondary bibliography.

GENERAL

Daiches.

KEYNES, JOHN NEVILLE   (1852-1949)

NCBEL, III, 1541.

KIDNER, ELAINE: see LANE, JANE.

KINGSMILL, HUGH   (1889-1949)

Pseudonym of Hugh Kingsmill Lunn.

WWW 41-50.

KINSELLA, THOMAS   (1928-   )

PRIMARY

[?John Rees Moore]. "Books by Thomas Kinsella." *Hollins Critic* 5 (October, 1968): 8-9.

Primary books, all English-language editions. Chronological arrangement. Place, publisher, date, price.

KIPLING, RUDYARD   (1865-1936)

PRIMARY

E. W. Martindell. *A Bibliography of the Works of Rudyard Kipling (1881-1923) A New Edition Much Enlarged Illustrated with 52 Plates.* London: John Lane The Bodley Head Ltd., 1923. Pp. [xviii], [222]. 700 copies.

Primary, secondary selected. Form arrangement. Books: transcribed TP, partial collation, abbreviated pagination, binding, date, contents occasionally with details of original printing, bibliographical notes. Brief account of collected editions. Uncollected periodical contributions: dates. Manuscripts, proofs, and author's working copies: varying details. Brief account of later editions. Index.

The first bibliography: most, but not all, of its information is given in Livingston (below).

Flora V. Livingston. *Bibliography of the Works of Rudyard Kipling.* New York: Edgar H. Wells and Co., 1927. Pp. xviii,
523. *Supplement to Bibliography of the Works of Rudyard
Kipling (1927).* Cambridge: Harvard University Press, 1938.
Pp. [xvi], 333.

Primary books and pamphlets. Chronological arrangement.
Transcribed TP without line bars; partial collation, brief
pagination, binding, date, contents with details of original
printing, bibliographical notes. *Supplement* arranged: Continuation of bibliography for 1926-1937; Additions and corrections to the 1927 Bibliography; Brief account of pirated
pamphlets and issues. Translations of primary writings:
original and translated title, place, publisher, date, translator; arranged under name of language. Titles of books
printed in Braille. Checklist of secondary criticism. Index
to Bibliography and Supplement.

Livingston has long been the standard Kipling bibliography;
see also comments on Stewart (below).

*Catalogue of the Works of Rudyard Kipling Exhibited at the
Grolier Club.* New York: Grolier Club, 1930. Pp. [xii], 201.
34 plates. 325 copies.

Primary selected, secondary selected.

A catalogue and not a complete bibliography which offers
much incidental information not given in Livingston and
Stewart.

James McG. Stewart. *Rudyard Kipling A Bibliographical Catalogue,* ed. A. W. Yeats. Toronto: Dalhousie University Press,
and University of Toronto Press, 1959. Pp. [xviii], [674].
750 copies.

Primary. Arranged: Major works; Other works; Appendices.
Chronological within each section. Transcribed TP, partial
collation, pagination, full details of bindings with variants;
date, subsequent editions, contents with details of original
printing. Appendices include: Items in Sales Catalogues; Uncollected Prose and Verse; Works in Anthologies and Readers;

Collected Sets; Musical Settings; Unauthorized editions. Index.

Adds many details to Livingston; particularly strong on accounts of editions later than the first British. R. J. Roberts, *Book Collector* 9 (Winter, 1960): 482: "the most comprehensive and detailed...invites acceptance as the standard bibliography of Kipling in succession to that of E. W. Martindell and Mrs. Livingston."

George Monteiro. "Rudyard Kipling: Early Printings in American Periodicals." *Papers of the Bibliographical Society of America* 61 (1967): 127-128.

Adds five items to Livingston and Stewart.

SECONDARY

Above, Martindell, pp. 193-203; Grolier Club, pp. 185-192; Livingston, *Supplement*, pp. 237-261.

Helmut E. Gerber and Edward Lauterbach, eds. "Rudyard Kipling: An Annotated Bibliography of Writings about Him." *English Fiction in Transition* 3, iii, iv, v (1960): 1-235.

Approximately 1630 items, annotated. Note description of limitations, 3: iii: 1-2, and references to other secondary sources. Books: place, publisher, date, pages. Periods: volume, pages, date. Supplements to this list appear in later issues of *English Fiction* (later *English Literature*) *in Transition;* see particularly 8, iii-iv (1965): 136-241.

Probably the most complete single checklist.

Reginald Engledon Harbord (successor to Roger L. Green), ed. *The Reader's Guide to Rudyard Kipling's Work.* The Kipling Society. Privately printed by Gibbs and Sons, Canterbury; issued unbound and unsewn in parts; limited to 100 copies. 1961-1965.

An enormous work, over two thousand pages long, written by and for members of the Kipling Society, providing detailed references found nowhere also. Helmut Gerber, *English Literature in Transition* 9 (1966): 49: "simply no other tool [is] as useful for close analyses of Kipling's work..."

GENERAL

Millett; Longaker & Bolles; Batho & Dobrée; Temple & Tucker; NCBEL, III, 1019-1032.

KIRKUP, JAMES FALCONER   (1923-   )

Daiches; WW 71.

KNIGHT, GEORGE WILSON   (1897-   )

PRIMARY

D. W. Jefferson, ed. *The Morality of Art: Essays Presented to G. Wilson Knight...* London: Routledge and Kegan Paul; New York: Barnes and Noble, 1969. Pp. xii, 237.

Pp. 222-231, John E. Van Domelen, "A Select List of the Published Writings of George Wilson Knight." Chronological arrangement. Books: place, publisher, date. Periods: volume, pages, date, title of book in which reprinted. Includes one unsigned writing in *TLS*.

GENERAL

Daiches; WW 71.

KNIGHTS, LIONEL CHARLES   (1906-   )

Daiches; WW 71.

KNOBLOCK, EDWARD   (1874-1945)

Palmer & Dyson; WWW 41-50.

KNOTT, FREDERICK   (1919-   )

Salem.

KNOX, EDMUND GEORGE VALPY   (1881-   )

WW 71.

KNOX, RT. REV. MSGR. RONALD ARBUTHNOTT   (1888-1957)

PRIMARY

Evelyn Waugh. *The Life of the Right Reverend Ronald Knox
Fellow of Trinity College, Oxford and Protonotary Apostolic
to His Holiness Pope Pius XII.* London: Chapman and Hall;
Boston: Little, Brown and Co., 1959. Pp. [358].

Pp. 336-338, "Chronological List of the chief published works
of Ronald Knox, not including the various editions of his trans-
lation of the Bible." Primary books only: place, publisher,
date. See text for additional writings, *passim.* Index.

GENERAL

WWW 51-60; Hagen.

KOESTLER, ARTHUR   (1905-   )

PRIMARY

Jenni Calder. *Chronicles of Conscience. A Study of George
Orwell and Arthur Koestler.* London: Secker and Warburg,
1968. Pp. 303.

Pp. 291-292, primary books. Genre arrangement. Publisher,
date. Pp. 293-294, brief selected secondary bibliography of
Koestler and Orwell.

SECONDARY

KOE

Above, Calder, pp. 293-294.

Peter Alfred Huber. *Arthur Koestler. Das Literarische Werk.*
Zürich: Fretz und Wasmuth Verlag A. G., 1962. Pp. 173.

Pp. 166-168, secondary bibliography.

GENERAL

Temple & Tucker; WW 71.

KOPS, BERNARD   (-   )

Coleman & Tyler.

KOTELIANSKY, SAMUEL SOLOMONOVICH   (1882-1955)

PRIMARY

George T. Zytaruk. "S. S. Koteliansky's Translations of Russian Works into English." *Bulletin of Bibliography* 25 (1967):
65-66.

Arrangement: alphabetical by author of work translated. Books:
place, publisher, date, pages. Periods: date, pages. Includes
names of collaborators; other notes. Introduction, p. 65, provides brief list of secondary criticism.

LANCASTER, OSBERT   (1908-   )

WW 71.

LANE, JANE   (-   )

Pseudonym of Elaine Kidner (Mrs. Andrew Dakers).

WW 71.

LANE, MARGARET   (1907-   )

(Countess of Huntingdon).

WW 71.

LANG, ANDREW   (1844-1912)

PRIMARY

C. M. Falconer. *Catalogue of a Library Chiefly the Writings of
Andrew Lang*. Dundee: Privately Published, 1898. Pp. 32.
25 copies.

A list of 495 items in Falconer's collection; the idiosyncratic
arrangement defies description. The collection is now a part
of the Darlington Collection in the Lilly Library, Indiana University (see below).

Roger Lancelyn Green. *Andrew Lang. A Critical Biography*.
Leicester: Edmund Ward, 1946. Pp. 265.

Pp. [241]-259, "A Short-Title Bibliography of the Works of
Andrew Lang." Primary selected. Form arrangement with
books listed chronologically and periodical contributions
under title of period. Books: date. Periods: date. Pp.[223]-
231: notes include primary and secondary entries not elsewhere listed. Pp. [236] - 240, secondary selected bibliography.

The most comprehensive checklist yet compiled, though not
complete.

Roger Lancelyn Green. "Andrew Lang--'The Greatest Bookman
of his Age' "; "Descriptions from the Darlington Collection
of Andrew Lang." *Indiana University Bookman* 7 (April, 1965):
10-72, 73-101.

An important essay on the Lang bibliography with special reference to the Darlington-Falconer Collection, followed by
descriptions as follows: titles of 12 MSS; descriptions of 25

rare or unique primary books and pamphlets. Transcribed TP, part collation, pagination, binding, date, number of copies, price, notes; chronological list of primary titles with dates; List of contributions to Encyclopedias.

Green's various writings together provide a fairly complete primary bibliography.

SECONDARY

Above, Green (1946), pp. [223]-231, [236]-240.

GENERAL

Batho & Dobrée; Temple & Tucker; NCBEL, III, 1440-1444.

LANGDON, DAVID   (1914-   )

WW 71.

LANKESTER, SIR EDWIN RAY   (1847-1929)

Batho & Dobrée; WWW 29-40.

LARKIN, PHILIP ARTHUR   (1922-   )

Temple & Tucker; WW 71.

LASKI, HAROLD JOSEPH   (1893-1950)

PRIMARY

Herbert A. Deane. *The Political Ideas of H. J. Laski.* New York: Columbia University Press, 1955. Pp. 370.

Pp. 346-357, bibliography. Primary, secondary. Genre arrangement: Books and essays by Laski; Editing; Translating; Introductions. Books: place, publisher, date. Periods: volume, date, pages.

Above, Deane, pp. 356-357.

GENERAL

Daiches.

LASKI, MARGHANITA   (1915-   )

(Mrs. J. E. Howard).

Temple & Tucker; WW 71.

LAVER, JAMES   (1899-   )

Millett; Temple & Tucker; WW 71.

LAVIN, MARY   (1912-   )

(Mrs. M. MacDonald Scott).

PRIMARY

Paul A. Doyle. "Mary Lavin: A Checklist." *Papers of the Bibliographical Society of America* 63 (1969): 317-321.

Primary. Genre and form arrangement; chronological thereunder. Books: place, publisher, date. Periods: volume, pages, date. Compiled with Miss Lavin's assistance.

GENERAL

WW 71.

LAWRENCE, DAVID HERBERT   (1885-1930)

PRIMARY

Edward D. McDonald. *A Bibliography of the Writings of D. H. Lawrence.* Philadelphia: Centaur Book Shop (Centaur Bibliographies No. 6), 1925. Pp. [154]. 500 copies. *The Writings of D. H. Lawrence, 1925-1930. A Bibliographical Supplement.* Philadelphia: Centaur Book Shop, 1931. [Not seen.] Reprinted in one volume (?Dawsons, 1970).

Primary first editions, British and American; secondary selected. Form arrangement. Primary books: transcribed TP, part collation, pagination, binding, date, contents, extensive bibliographical notes. Period contributions arranged by genre: dates, and titles of works in which collected. Pp. 131-145, secondary bibliography arranged by form. Books: place, date, publisher. Periods: date.

Most of the information in this first bibliography is reprinted in Roberts (below), but there are interesting notes here which should be consulted.

Warren Roberts. *A Bibliography of D. H. Lawrence.* London: Rupert Hart-Davis (Soho Bibliography No. 13), 1963. Pp. 399.

Primary first editions; secondary selected (books and pamphlets only). Form arrangement. Primary books: transcribed TP, part collation, binding, pagination, date, price, contents, number of copies of first printing, full bibliographical notes, some account of reprints and subsequent editions, list of reviews of the edition described. Translations of Lawrence listed under name of language: place, publisher, date, pages. List of MSS with brief description and location. Pp. 359-364, secondary bibliography.

The standard bibliography. Harry T. Moore, *Papers of the Bibliographical Society of America* 59 (1965): 75-77: "no serious studies of Lawrence from now on can be made without its help; the book is valuable for criticism as well as biography."

James G. Hepburn. "Note 241. D. H. Lawrence's Plays: An Annotated Bibliography," *Book Collector* 14 (Spring, 1965): 78-81.

Alphabetical list of play titles with dates of composition, of publication, and of production; reviews listed. Ample notes and list of 'lost' plays.

Information additional to Roberts.

SECONDARY

Above, McDonald; Roberts; Hepburn.

William White. *D. H. Lawrence: A Checklist, 1931-1950.* Detroit: Wayne University Press, 1950. Pp. 46. 350 copies. Reprinted from *Bulletin of Bibliography* 19 (1948-1949): 174-177, 209-211, 235-239.

Primary; secondary selected. One chronological list. Books: place, publisher, date, pages, reviews of the book. Periods: volume, pages, date.

Maurice Beebe and Anthony Tommasi. "Criticism of D. H. Lawrence: A Selected Checklist with an Index to Studies of Separate Works," *Modern Fiction Studies* 5 (Spring, 1959): 83-98.

Arranged: General Writings, alphabetical by author. Studies of Separate Works of Fiction, alphabetical list of primary titles with studies listed under each. Books: place, publisher, date. Periods: volume, pages, date.

Keith Sagar. *The Art of D. H. Lawrence.* Cambridge: University Press, 1966. Pp. [xii], [267].

Pp. 248-250, selected secondary books. Chronological arrangement. Author, title, publisher, date. Pp. 251-256, selected secondary bibliography, 1959-1965. Information varies.

Richard D. Beards with G. B. Crump. "D. H. Lawrence: Ten Years of Criticism, 1959-1968: A Checklist," *D. H. Lawrence Review* 1 (1968): 245-285.

A supplement to Beebe and Tommasi (above). Arranged: General, Poetry, Studies of Individual Works of Fiction (titles alphabetically arranged), Studies of Non-Fiction Prose, Studies of the Drama. In each section, alphabetical by author. Books: place, publisher, date. Periods: volume, date, pages. Occasional brief annotations.

This comprehensive secondary checklist is continued in subsequent issues of the *Review,* the same form being maintained: 3 (Spring, 1970): 70-79; 4 (Spring, 1971): 90-102. National secondary checklists, either in this form or in alphabetical by author arrangement, and with the same information, are also given in the *Review:* [Japan, 1951-1968] 2 (1969): 172-191; [Scandinavia, 1934-1968] 2 (1969): 275-277; [Germany, 1923-1970] 4 (1971): 210-220. Also see "Doctoral Dissertations on D. H. Lawrence 1931-1969: A Bibliography." 3 (1970): 80-86.

By consulting all of these items, one gains a fairly complete list of the writings about Lawrence. One should also note the announcement in 1971 by the Annotated Secondary Bibliography Series on English Literature in Transition, Helmut E. Gerber, general editor, Northern Illinois University Press, that James C. Cowan is preparing the volume on Lawrence for publication in the fall, 1974.

GENERAL

Millett; Longaker & Bolles; Daiches; Temple & Tucker; Coleman & Tyler; Adelman & Dworkin; Palmer & Dyson.

LAWRENCE, THOMAS EDWARD   (1888-1935)

PRIMARY

T. German-Reed. *Bibliographical Notes on T. E. Lawrence's Seven Pillars of Wisdom and Revolt in the Desert.* London: W. and G. Foyle, Ltd., 1928. Pp. 16. 375 copies.

G. [Terence Ian Fytton Armstrong]. *Annotations on Some Minor Writings of 'T. E. Lawrence.'* London: Eric Partridge Ltd., 1935. Pp. 28. 500 copies.

Although less informative than Duval (below), these two books provide bibliographical details not in Duval.

Elizabeth W. Duval. *T. E. Lawrence: A Bibliography.* New York: Arrow Editions, 1938. Pp. 95. 500 copies.

Primary writings. Form arrangement. Books: transcribed TP, part collation, pagination, binding, date, all editions, reprints including foreign, notes. Includes books in which Lawrence's letters are quoted. Index.

The standard bibliography.

SECONDARY

"A List of References by and on Col. T. E. Lawrence in the Imperial War Museum Library." London, 1952. Two mimeographed sheets. [British Museum Pressmark B. S. 50/2].

7 primary items; 24 secondary references. Author, title, publisher, date.

GENERAL

Millett; Longaker & Bolles; Daiches; Temple & Tucker.

LAWSON, HENRY ARCHIBALD   (1867-1922)

PRIMARY

George MacKaness. *An Annotated Bibliography of Henry Lawson.* Sydney: Angus and Robertson Ltd., 1951. Pp. [viii], [102].

Primary books. Chronological arrangement. Transcribed TP, part collation, pagination, binding, date, price, contents, subsequent editions and impressions with number of copies in each. Extensive annotations and quotations. Pp. 69-92, index of poems and stories locating the first publication and first reprinting of each. Pp. 93-96, miscellaneous primary writings. Pp. 97-98, secondary bibliography.

LAW

Above, MacKaness, pp. 97-98.

Denton Prout. *Henry Lawson. The Grey Dreamer.* London:
Angus and Robertson; Adelaide: Rigby Ltd., 1963. Pp. [306].

Pp. 301-304, secondary bibliography.

LEACOCK, STEPHEN BUTLER   (1869-1944)

PRIMARY

Gerhard R. Lomer. *Stephen Leacock. A Checklist and Index
of his Writings.* Ottawa: National Library of Canada, 1954.
Pp. 153.

Primary. Arranged: alphabetical checklist of books; alphabetical list of individual titles including all appearances in
print; alphabetical list of MSS. Books: place, publisher, date,
pages, height, contents, reprints and subsequent editions; occasional notes. Periods: volume, pages, date.

Ralph L. Curry. "Stephen Butler Leacock. A Check-List." *Bulletin of Bibliography* 22 (1958): 106-109.

Adds to and continues Lomer (above). Same information, arranged under: whole volumes; contributions; miscellaneous
writings; articles published through syndicated outlets; translations of Leacock.

GENERAL

Millett.

LEAVIS, FRANK RAYMOND   (1895-   )

PRIMARY

Donald F. McKenzie and M. P. Allum. *Frank Raymond Leavis.*

A Check-List. 1924-1964. London: Chatto and Windus; Hamden, Connecticut: Shoe String Press, 1966. Pp. 87.

Primary complete, secondary select. Primary: chronological arrangement. Books: place, publisher, date, pages, contents; includes all editions and most subsequent impressions. Periods: volume, pages, date; reviews by Leavis include title and author of book reviewed. Pp. 57-69, secondary bibliography, arranged: Reviews; Articles; Books. Index for primary titles.

TLS, No. 3364 (18 August 1966), p. 738: severely critical of lack of information and of organization; adds important secondary bibliography entries.

SECONDARY

Above, McKenzie-Allum, pp. 57-69.

GENERAL

Millett; Daiches; Temple & Tucker; WW 71.

LEDWIDGE, FRANCIS   (1891-1917)

PRIMARY

Henry Danielson. *Bibliographies of Modern Authors.* London: Bookman's Journal, 1921. Pp. [xii], [212].

Pp. 115-116, primary books. Chronological arrangement. Transcribed TP, part collation, pagination, binding, variants, miscellaneous bibliographical notes.

LEE, LAURIE   (1914-   )

Daiches; Temple & Tucker; WW 71.

LEE, SIR SIDNEY   (1859-1926)

NCBEL, III, 1657-1658.

LEE, VERNON   (1856-1935)

Pseudonym of Violet Paget.

PRIMARY

F. Elizabeth Libbey, *et al.* "Vernon Lee Papers" [at Colby College]. *Colby Library Quarterly*, Third Series, 1952.

Not seen.

Carl J. Weber. "An Interim Bibliography of Vernon Lee." *Colby Library Quarterly*, Third Series. 8 (November, 1952): 123-127.

Not seen.

Peter Gunn. *Vernon Lee. Violet Paget, 1856-1935.* London: Oxford University Press, 1964. Pp. [xii], 244.

Pp. 233-234, primary books, English first editions. Chronological arrangement. Place, publisher, date. Pp. 234-235, general secondary bibliography.

Of limited use, since the many periodical contributions are not included (some are mentioned, in passing, in the text).

GENERAL

Millett; Temple & Tucker; NCBEL, III, 1444-1446.

LEGALLIENNE, RICHARD   (1866-1947)

PRIMARY

R. J. C. Lingel. *A Bibliographical Checklist of the Writings of Richard LeGallienne.* Metuchen, New Jersey: Charles F. Heartman for the Americana Collector, 1926. Pp. 95. 151 copies.

Primary books, first editions. Chronological arrangement.
Transcribed TP, format, pagination, binding, occasional
brief notes. Index of names and titles. Pp. 7-21, ''Reminiscences by an Old Friend,'' by Temple Scott.

Richard Whittington-Egan and Geoffrey Smerdon. *The Quest
of the Golden Boy. The Life and Letters of Richard Le-
Gallienne.* London: The Unicorn Press, 1960. Pp. [xxiv],
580.

Pp. 553-561, ''A Catalogue of the Writings of Richard Le-
Gallienne.'' Primary books. Chronological arrangement.
Date, place, publisher, number of copies of limited editions.

Neither of these two entries provides a list of LeGallienne's
many periodical contributions, although its outlines are suggested in the text of the biography. Further unpublished primary writings (letters and a diary) are located by L. D. Jacobs,
''The Quest of the Golden Boy: Richard LeGallienne and
Some Unpublished Evidence,'' *English Literature in Transition* 10 (1967): 195-198.

GENERAL

Longaker & Bolles; NCBEL, III, 1063-1064.

LEHMANN, ROSAMOND NINA   (1904-   )

PRIMARY

Margaret T. Gustafson. ''Rosamond Lehmann: A Bibliography.''
Twentieth Century Literature 4 (1959): 143-147.

Primary, secondary selected. Genre arrangement. Books:
place, publisher, date. Periods: volume, pages, date. Includes translations of primary writings.

SECONDARY

Above, Gustafson, p. 147.

LEH

GENERAL

Millett; Longaker & Bolles; Daiches; Temple & Tucker; WW 71.

LEHMANN, RUDOLPH JOHN FREDERICK   (1907-   )

Daiches; Temple & Tucker; WW 71.

LESLIE, SIR JOHN RANDOLPH SHANE   (1885-   )

Millett; Temple & Tucker; WW 71.

LESSING, DORIS   (1919-   )

PRIMARY

Dorothy Brewster. *Doris Lessing*. New York: Twayne Publishers Inc. (TEAS 21), 1965. Pp. 172.

Pp. 165-170, "Selected Bibliography." Primary selected,
secondary selected. Genre and form arrangement. Books:
place, publisher, date (for both British and American edns).
Periods: date. Annotations and information about contents
of collections and reprintings of individual pieces, and about
unpublished plays. Reviews of primary books listed under
title of the appropriate book. A very useful checklist, superi-
or to others in this series.

Selma R. Burkom. "A Doris Lessing Checklist." *Critique* 11,
i (1968), 69-81.

Primary complete, secondary complete. Genre arrangement.
Books: place, publisher, date, all editions. Periods: volume,
pages, date. Contents listed for collections; reviews of
primary books listed under title of the appropriate book. The
most complete primary and secondary checklist.

SECONDARY

Above, Brewster and Burkom.

GENERAL

Temple & Tucker; WW 71.

LETTS, WINIFRED M.   (1882-   )

(Mrs. W. H. Verschoyle).

Longaker & Bolles; WW 71.

LEVERTOV, DENISE   (1923-   )

Temple & Tucker.

LEVEY, MICHAEL VINCENT   (1927-   )

WW 71.

LEVY, BENN WOLFE   (1900-   )

Daiches; Temple & Tucker; Salem; WW 71.

LEWIS, ALUN   (1915-1944)

PRIMARY

John Stuart Williams. "Alun Lewis. A Select Bibliography."
Anglo-Welsh Review 16 (Spring, 1967): 13-15.

Primary books. Chronological arrangement. Place, date,
publisher. Secondary bibliography arranged Articles and
Notices; Reviews.

SECONDARY

Above, Williams, pp. 14-15.

GENERAL

Longaker & Bolles; Daiches; Temple & Tucker.

LEWIS, CECIL DAY   (1904-   )

Pseudonym used: Nicholas Blake.

PRIMARY

Clifford Dyment. *Cecil Day Lewis*. London: Longmans, Green
and Co. (WTW 62), 1955. Pp. 48.

Pp. 46-48, bibliography. Primary books, including books edited by Lewis and books published under his pseudonym
Nicholas Blake. Chronological arrangement. Date, genre.

Geoffrey Handley-Taylor and Timothy D'Arch Smith. *C. Day-
Lewis. The Poet Laureate. A Bibliography*. Chicago and
London: St. James Press, 1968. Pp. xii, 42.

Primary books. Arranged: books and pamphlets by Lewis;
books with contributions by Lewis; detective stories published under pseudonym Nicholas Blake. For the first two
sections: transcribed TP without lineation bars, part collation, binding, date, price. For third section: date. Index.
Pp. ix-x give details of omissions.

TLS, No. 3489 (9 January 1969); p. 44: [As to] "the value
of the bibliography to students of Mr. Day-Lewis's work...
it must be roundly stated that it has none." Includes additional bibliographical information and corrects errors.

GENERAL

Millett; Longaker & Bolles; Temple & Tucker; WW 71; Hagen.

LEWIS, CLIVE STAPLES   (1898-1963)

PRIMARY

Jocelyn Gibb, ed. *Light on C. S. Lewis*. London: Geoffrey
Bles, 1965. Pp. 160.

Pp. 117-160, "A Bibliography of the Writings of C. S. Lewis,"
by Walter Hooper. Primary. Form and genre arrangement.
Books: place, publisher, date, reprints, subsequent editions.
Periods: volume, pages, date; title of volume in which collected, also revised titles. Includes reviews by Lewis with
author and title of book reviewed and published letters by
Lewis. Index of titles.

SECONDARY

Clyde S. Kilby. *The Christian World of C. S. Lewis*. Grand
Rapids: William B. Eardmans Publishing Co., 1964. Pp. 216.

Pp. 191-207, "Appendix." Précis of "five doctoral dissertations and five books devoted either wholly or in part to
Lewis" (p. 191). NB: Dabney A. Hart, "C. S. Lewis's De-
fense of Poesie," University of Wisconsin, 1959, which includes "a bibliography of Lewis's critical and imaginative
works and of criticisms in secondary sources. No one who
wishes to study Lewis seriously can afford to ignore this
bibliography" (p. 196).

GENERAL

Longaker & Bolles; Daiches; Temple & Tucker.

LEWIS, DOMINIC BEVAN WYNDHAM   (1894-1969)

Temple & Tucker.

LEWIS, PERCY WYNDHAM   (1884-1957)

PRIMARY

John Gawsworth [T. Fytton Armstrong], *Apes, Japes, and*

Hitlerism: A Study and Bibliography of Wyndham Lewis. London: Unicorn Press, 1932. Pp. 100.

Pp. 83-100, bibliography. Form arrangement. Transcribed TP, full collation, pagination, binding, price, notes.

Hugh Kenner. *Wyndham Lewis.* Norfolk, Connecticut: New Directions Books (Makers of Modern Literature Series), 1954. Pp. xv, 169.

Pp. 159-164, bibliography. Primary selected. Chronological arrangement. Date, place, publisher, annotations.

Wyndham Lewis and Vorticism. A Tate Gallery Exhibition, circulated by the Arts Council. London, [1956]. Pp. 24.

Pp. 11-17, catalogue of drawings and paintings; complete description and location.

Geoffrey Wagner. *Wyndham Lewis. A Portrait of the Artist as the Enemy.* London: Routledge and Kegan Paul, 1957. Pp. 363.

Pp. 315-336, "Checklist of the Writings of Wyndham Lewis." Primary, secondary selected. Chronological arrangement, May 1909 to November 1956. Place, publisher, date, occasional notes. Some authors and titles of books reviewed by Lewis are identified; translations of Lewis include translator's name. Pp. 336-348, secondary bibliography, excluding reviews of Lewis, some of them being mentioned in text, *passim.*

SECONDARY

Above, Wagner, pp. 336-348.

William H. Pritchard. *Wyndham Lewis.* New York: Twayne Publishers, Inc. (TEAS 65), 1968. Pp. 180.

Pp. 173-175, secondary bibliography. Alphabetical-by-author arrangement. Annotated.

GENERAL

Millett; Longaker & Bolles; Daiches; Temple & Tucker.

LIDDELL, JOHN ROBERT   (1908-   )

Temple & Tucker; WW 71.

LIDDELL HART, SIR BASIL HENRY   (1895-1970)

WW 70.

LINDSAY, JACK   (1900-   )

WW 71.

LINDSAY, NORMAN ALFRED WILLIAM   (1879-1969)

PRIMARY

George MacKaness. "Collecting Norman Lindsay." *American Book Collector* 7 (1956): i, 15-20; ii, 22-27; iii, 17-20.

Discursive essay mentioning many primary books, usually with place, publisher, format, binding, original and current prices. Much miscellaneous bibliographical information, including mention of secondary bibliography.

John Hetherington. *Norman Lindsay*. Melbourne: Lansdowne Press (AWTW), 1962. Pp. 48.

Pp. 47-48, primary books. Genre arrangement. Place, publisher, date. Includes selected secondary bibliography.

Harry F. Chaplin. *Norman Lindsay. His books, manuscripts and autograph letters in the library of, and annotated by, Harry F. Chaplin.* Sydney: Wentworth Press, 1969. Pp. vi, 90. Reproduced from typescript.

A checklist of primary material with extensive bibliographical annotations.

Together MacKaness, Hetherington, and Chaplin provide a fairly complete bibliography.

SECONDARY

Above, MacKaness and Hetherington.

LINDSAY, PHILIP   (1906-1958)

WWW 51-60.

LINKLATER, ERIC ROBERT RUSSELL   (1899-   )

Daiches; Temple & Tucker; WW 71.

LIVINGSTONE, SIR RICHARD WINN   (1880-1960)

WWW 51-60.

LLEWELYN, RICHARD   (-   )

Pseudonym of Richard Dafydd Vivian Lloyd.

WW 71.

LLOYD, RICHARD DAFYDD VIVIAN: see LLEWELYN, RICHARD.

LOCKE, WILLIAM JOHN   (1863-1930)

PRIMARY

Henry Danielson. "Bibliographies of Modern Authors. XVI. William J. Locke." *Bookman's Journal* 3 (1920-1921): 162, 183, 192, 214, 228, 245, 274, 286.

Primary books and pamphlets, 1895-1921. Chronological arrangement. Transcribed TP, part collation, pagination, binding, variants, bibliographical notes.

GENERAL

WWW 29-40.

LODGE, SIR OLIVER JOSEPH   (1851-1940)

PRIMARY

Theodore Besterman. *A Bibliography of Sir Oliver Lodge, F. R. S.* London: Humphrey Milford, Oxford University Press, 1935. Pp. xiv, 219.

Primary, secondary selected. Chronological arrangement. Books: transcribed TP without lineation bars, part collation, dates of reprints. Periods: volume, pages, date. Occasional annotations. Includes translations. Index.

SECONDARY

Above, Besterman, pp. 187-195.

LOFTS, NORAH   (1904-   )

(Mrs. Robert Jorisch).

WW 71; Hagen.

LOGUE, CHRISTOPHER   (1926-   )

Temple & Tucker.

LONG, MRS. GABRIELLE MARGARET VERE CAMPBELL
(1885-1952)
Pseudonyms used: Joseph Shearing, Marjorie Bowen,

Robert Paye, George R. Preedy, John Winch.

PRIMARY

Edward Wagenknecht. "Bowen, Preedy, Shearing & Co., A Note in Memory and a Check List." *Boston University Studies in English* 3 (1957): 181-189.

Pp. 186-189, check list of approximately 150 books: date, publisher; nom de plume under which published.

GENERAL

Hagen.

LONGFORD, COUNTESS OF: ELIZABETH PAKENHAM
(1906-   )

WW 71.

LONSDALE, FREDERICK   (1881-1954)

PRIMARY

Frances Donaldson. *Freddy Lonsdale.* London: William Heinemann Ltd., 1957. Pp. 257.

Pp. 247-249, bibliography, primary plays. Chronological arrangement. Date of first performance, theatre, number of performances. No information concerning publication.

GENERAL

Millett; Longaker & Bolles; Temple & Tucker; Salem.

LOWRY, H. D.   (1869-1906)

PRIMARY

A. J. A. Symons. *H. D. Lowry, 1869-1906.* London: Proof
Edition Unpublished, October, 1925. Pp. 8. 39 copies.
British Museum Pressmark 2785. cs. 14.

Primary books. Chronological arrangement. Transcribed TP,
part collation, pagination, binding, contents, number of copies,
British Museum Pressmark.

LOWRY, MALCOLM   (1909-1957)

PRIMARY

Maurice Nadeau, ed. *Malcolm Lowry.* Paris, *Les Lettres
Nouvelles* 5 (July-August, 1960). Pp. 208.

A special issue with eleven essays devoted to Lowry. Bibliographical references, *passim,* to primary and secondary material.

Malcolm Lowry. *Selected Letters.* Ed. Harvey Breit and M. B.
Lowry. Philadelphia: J. B. Lippincott Co., 1965. Pp. xx,
459.

References to published and unpublished writings, *passim,*
and particularly p. xiv.

A Malcolm Lowry Catalogue. With essays by Perle Epstein and
Richard Hauer Costa. New York: J. Howard Woolmer, 529 E.
85th St., 1968. Pp. 64.

Not seen.

Lawrence S. Thompson, *Papers of the Bibliographical Society
of America* 63 (1969): 148: "a dealer's price list...likely to
find a home in reference collections on English literature of
our time...very substantial corpus of Lowry pieces offered
here..."

SECONDARY

Above, Nadeau.

GENERAL

Temple & Tucker.

LUBBOCK, PERCY   (1879-1965)

Millett; Daiches; Temple & Tucker; WW 65.

LUCAS, EDWARD VERRALL   (1868-1938)

PRIMARY

Audrey Lucas. *E. V. Lucas: A Portrait*. London: Methuen and
Co., Ltd., 1939. Pp. xiii, 159.

Pp. 158-159, primary books. Topical arrangement includes
"Miscellaneous" and "Books Edited by Lucas." Titles
only.

GENERAL

Millett; Longaker & Bolles; Batho & Dobrée; Temple & Tucker;
NCBEL, III, 1099.

LUCAS, FRANK LAURENCE   (1894-1967)

Millett; Daiches; Temple & Tucker; WW 67.

LUCIE-SMITH, JOHN EDWARD MCKENZIE   (1933-   )

WW 71.

LUDOVICI, ANTHONY M.   (1882-   )

WW 71.

LUNN, SIR ARNOLD (1888-)

WW 71.

LUNN, HUGH KINGSMILL: see KINGSMILL, HUGH.

LUTYENS, MARY (1908-)

(Mrs. J. G. Links).

WW 71.

LYLE, ROB (1920-)

Temple & Tucker.

LYND, ROBERT (1879-1949)

Millett; Longaker & Bolles; Temple & Tucker.

LYND, SYLVIA (1888-1952)

(Mrs. Robert Lynd).

WWW 51-60.

LYON, LILIAN HELEN BOWES (1895-1949)

Longaker & Bolles; Temple & Tucker.

MAC--: *also see* MC--.

MACAULAY, GEORGE CAMPBELL (1852-1915)

NCBEL, III, 1658.

MACAULAY, DAME ROSE   (1881-1958)

PRIMARY

Alice R. Bensen. *Rose Macaulay*. New York: Twayne Publishers, Inc. (TEAS 85), 1969. Pp. 184.

Pp. 175-176, primary books. Genre arrangement. British
and American first editions. Place, publisher, date. Pp.
177-178, secondary bibliography, selected. Alphabetical
by author arrangement, annotated. Also see text, *passim*,
and notes for an additional 78 reviews of Dame Rose's
books.

A basic checklist; there is no published list of the extensive journalism and periodical contributions.

SECONDARY

Above, Bensen, pp. 177-178, also notes and text.

"Rose Macaulay." *English Fiction* (later *English Literature*)
in Transition 3, i (1960): 31; 3, ii (1960): 51; 4, i (1961): 25;
5, i (1962): 44; 6, i (1963): 52; 6, ii (1963): 108; 6 (1963):
235; 8 (1965): 119-121.

This continuing list of secondary studies, annotated, provides
the most up-to-date account of studies of Dame Rose.

GENERAL

Millett; Longaker & Bolles; Daiches; Temple & Tucker.

MACBETH, GEORGE MANN   (1932-   )

WW 71.

MACCARTHY, SIR DESMOND   (1878-1952)

Millett; Daiches; Temple & Tucker.

MACDIARMID, HUGH: see GRIEVE, CHRISTOPHER MURRAY.

MAC DONAGH, THOMAS   (1878-1916)

PRIMARY

Patrick Sarsfield O'Hegarty. "Bibliographies of 1916 and the Irish Revolution. No. 2. Thomas Mac Donagh." *Dublin Magazine* 7 (January-March, 1932): 26-29. (Also issued as a pamphlet).

Primary books. Chronological arrangement. Transcribed TP, part collation, pagination, binding, variant bindings, bibliographical notes.

Edd Winfield Parks and Aileen Wells Parks. *Thomas Mac Donagh. The Man, The Patriot, The Writer.* Athens: University of Georgia Press, 1967. Pp. xiv, 151.

Pp. 139-141, primary bibliography. Form arrangement. Books: place, publisher, year. Periods: volume, pages, date; reviews by Mac Donagh include title and author of book reviewed. Locates MSS.

O'Hegarty gives bibliographical details, and the Parks, inclusive lists; together they provide an ample bibliography.

SECONDARY

Above, Parks-Parks, pp. 142-145.

MACDOUGALL, ROGER   (1910-   )

Temple & Tucker.

229

MACHEN, ARTHUR LLEWELYN JONES   (1863-1947)

PRIMARY

Henry Danielson. *Arthur Machen. A Bibliography with Notes by Arthur Machen.* London: Henry Danielson, 1923. Pp. 59. 500 copies.

    Primary books. Chronological arrangement. Transcribed TP, part collation, pagination, binding, illustrator, full bibliographical notes.

    Information additional to that in Goldstone and Sweetser (below).

Adrian Goldstone and Wesley Sweetser. *A Bibliography of Arthur Machen.* Austin: University of Texas Press, 1965. Pp. 180. 500 copies.

    Primary, secondary. Form arrangement. Books: transcribed TP, part collation, binding, date, price, contents with account of previous publication for each, later editions, notes. Pp. 68-73, translations by Machen. Pp. 86-144, Machen's periodical contributions, listed under alphabetically arranged periodical titles: volume, pages, date.

    S. A. Reynolds, *Book Collector* 15 (1966): 229-230: "Much less entertaining but far more informative [than Danielson's bibliography] ...a really useful bibliography."

SECONDARY

Above, Goldstone-Sweetser, pp. 146-164.

Wesley Sweetser. "Arthur Machen. A Bibliography of Writings about Him." *English Literature in Transition* 11 (1968): 1-33.

    Annotated. Mainly post-1965 additions to Goldstone and Sweetser.

GENERAL

Millett; Batho & Dobrée; Temple & Tucker.

MACINNES, COLIN   (1914-   )

Temple & Tucker; WW 71.

MACINNES, HELEN CLARK   (1907-   )

WW 71; Hagen.

MACKAIL, DENNIS GEORGE   (1892-   )

WW 71; Hagen.

MACKAIL, JOHN WILLIAM   (1859-1945)

Batho & Dobrée; Temple & Tucker.

MACKENZIE, AGNES MURE   (1891-1955)

Daiches; WWW 51-60.

MACKENZIE, SIR EDWARD MONTAGUE COMPTON   (1883-   )

PRIMARY

Henry Danielson. *Bibliographies of Modern Authors.* London:
Bookman's Journal, 1921. Pp. [xii], [212].

Pp. 119-124, primary books, 1907-1921. Chronological arrangement. Transcribed TP, part collation, pagination, binding, variants, miscellaneous bibliographical notes.

Leo Robertson. *Compton MacKenzie. An Appraisal of his Literary Work.* London: Richards Press, 1954. Pp. 230.

Pp. 229-230, primary books. Chronological arrangement. Date.

Kenneth Young. *Compton MacKenzie*. London: Longmans, Green and Co. (WTW 202), 1968. Pp. 32.

Pp. 29-32, primary books. Chronological arrangement. Date, genre. Includes list of "Children's Short Stories." P. 32, secondary bibliography (12 entries).

P. 29: "A bibliography...is being prepared by Mr. Eugene Edge III for the University of Texas. The University has most of Sir Compton's manuscripts."

SECONDARY

Above, Young, p. 32.

Helmut Gerber. "Compton MacKenzie." *English Fiction in Transition* 1 (Winter, 1957): 29-30.

GENERAL

Millett; Longaker & Bolles; Daiches; Temple & Tucker; WW 71.

MACLEAN, ALISTAIR   (1922-   )

WW 71; Hagen.

MACLEOD, JOSEPH TODD GORDON   (1903-   )

WW 71.

MACLEOD, FIONA: see SHARP, WILLIAM.

MACLIAMMÓIR, MICHÉAL   (1899-   )

WW 71.

MACMECHAN, ARCHIBALD M'KELLAR   (1862-1933)

   Millett.

MACMULLAN, CHARLES WALDEN KIRKPATRICK: see MUNRO,
CHARLES KIRKPATRICK.

MACNEICE, LOUIS   (1907-1963)

PRIMARY

E. R. Dodds, ed. *The Collected Poems of Louis MacNeice*.
London: Faber and Faber, 1966; New York: Oxford University Press, 1967. Pp. xviii, 575.

   No bibliography. See Contents (pp. v-xiii) for titles of
   earlier collections with lists of poems therein and dates of
   composition; Appendix I (pp. 560-561) lists poems in earlier
   volumes excluded from this collection; Appendix II (p. 562)
   lists variant titles of poems. Index of titles.

Elton Edward Smith. *Louis MacNeice*. New York: Twayne
Publishers Inc. (TEAS 99), 1970. Pp. 232.

   Pp. 215-218, selected primary bibliography. Form and
   genre arrangement. Books: place, publisher, date. Periods:
   volume, pages, date. Pp. 218-224, secondary bibliography.
   Annotated. Includes unpublished dissertations.

William T. McKinnon. "Louis MacNeice: A Bibliography."
Bulletin of Bibliography 27 (1970): 51-52, 48, 79-84.

   Primary selected, secondary selected. Form and genre arrangement, each section chronologically arranged. Primary
   books: place, publisher, date, British and American editions.
   Periods: volume, pages, date. Includes reviews by MacNeice
   with author and title of book reviewed. Pp. 80-82, secondary
   bibliography. Reviews of primary books listed under title of
   book reviewed. Pp. 82-84, location of MSS and corrected
   proofs, description of main collections with suggestions of

233

sources of additional items.

Although admittedly not complete, this appears to be the best available checklist.

SECONDARY

Above, Smith, pp. 218-224, also notes, pp. 207-213, for additional entries; McKinnon, pp. 80-82.

GENERAL

Longaker & Bolles; Daiches; Temple & Tucker; Coleman & Tyler.

MAC SWINEY, TERENCE JOSEPH   (1879-1920)

PRIMARY

Patrick Sarsfield O'Hegarty. "Bibliographies of 1916 and the Irish Revolution. X. Terence Mac Swiney." *Dublin Magazine* 11 (October-December, 1936): 74-76.

Primary books. Chronological arrangement. Transcribed TP, part collation, pagination, binding, bibliographical and occasionally biographical notes.

MADGE, CHARLES HENRY   (1912-   )

Daiches; Temple & Tucker; WW 71.

MAGEE, WILLIAM KIRKPATRICK: see EGLINTON, JOHN.

MAIS, STUART PETRE BRODIE   (1885-   )

WW 71.

MALET, LUCAS   (1852-1931)

    Pseudonym of Mary St. Leger Kingsley (later Mrs. William
Harrison).

    NCBEL, III, 1066.

MALINOWSKI, BRONISLAW KASPER   (1884-1942)

    WWW 41-50.

MALLESON, WILLIAM MILES   (1888-1969)

    WW 68.

MALLOCK, WILLIAM HURRELL   (1849-1923)

PRIMARY

    Charles C. Nickerson. "A Bibliography of the Novels of W.
H. Mallock." *English Literature in Transition* 6 (1963): 190-
198.

    Primary books. Chronological arrangement. Transcribed TP,
full collation, pagination, binding, date, price, full notes.
Brief account of subsequent editions.

GENERAL

    NCBEL, III, 1066-1067.

MANKOWITZ, WOLF   (1924-   )

    WW 71.

MANN, WILLIAM SOMERVELL   (1924-   )

    WW 71.

MAN

MANNHEIM, KARL   (1893-1947)

WWW 41-50.

MANNIN, ETHEL   (1900-   )

WW 71.

MANNING, OLIVIA   (-   )

(Mrs. R. D. Smith).

Daiches; Temple & Tucker; WW 71.

MANSFIELD, KATHERINE   (1888-1923)

Pseudonym of Kathleen Mansfield Beauchamp (later Mrs. J. Middleton Murry).

PRIMARY

Ruth Elvish Mantz. *The Critical Bibliography of Katherine Mansfield*. Introduction by J. M. Murry. London: Constable and Co., Ltd., 1931. Pp. xx, 204. 1000 copies.

Primary (pp. 27-105); secondary complete. Form arrangement. Books: transcribed TP, full collation, pagination, binding, date, price, subsequent editions and reprints (no descriptions of these). Contents listed with full account of previous publications. Periods: volume, pages, date. Includes uncollected periodical contributions; also lists periodicals to which Mansfield contributed. Secondary bibliography arranged under title of primary work studied. Various prefaces, biographical notes, appendices.

P. H. Muir, *Book Collector's Quarterly*, No. 5 (January-March, 1932), pp. 89-91: praise for the bibliography, which "almost serves as a model of its kind."

SECONDARY

Above, Mantz, pp. 109-127.

G. N. Morris. *Mansfieldiana. A Brief Katherine Mansfield Bib-liography.* Wellington: Beltane Book Bureau (New Zealand Collector's Monograph No. 3), 1948. Pp. vi, 9.

> Short-title list, parochial in scope, with many notes, includ-ing (pp. 6-9) books and articles not elsewhere listed.

Sylvia Berkman. *Katherine Mansfield. A Critical Study.* New Haven: Yale University Press, 1951. Pp. 246.

> Pp. 231-236, Bibliography. Arranged: books by Mansfield; reference works; articles and reviews.

Marvin Magalaner. *The Fiction of Katherine Mansfield.* Car-bondale: Southern Illinois University Press, 1971. Pp. [xii], 148.

> Pp. 142-145, secondary bibliography. Notes, pp. 133-140, provide additional entries.

GENERAL

Millett; Longaker & Bolles; Daiches; Temple & Tucker.

MANVELL, ARNOLD ROGER   (1909-   )

WW 71.

MARKIEVICZ, CONSTANCE GORE-BOOTH, COUNTESS DE
(1868-1927)

PRIMARY

Patrick Sarsfield O'Hegarty. "Bibliographies of 1916 and the Irish Revolution. VIII. Constance Gore-Booth, Countess de Markievicz." *Dublin Magazine* 11 (July-September, 1936): 57-59.

Primary books. Chronological arrangement. Transcribed TP, part collation, pagination, binding, bibliographical notes.

Jacqueline Van Voris. *Constance de Markievicz in the Cause of Ireland*. Amherst: University of Massachusetts Press, 1967. Pp. 384.

Pp. 361-363, primary bibliography. Chronological arrangement. Includes periodical contributions and unpublished writings. Dates for each item. A much more comprehensive listing than that in O'Hegarty, above.

SECONDARY

Above, Voris, pp. 353-361.

Anne Marreco. *The Rebel Countess. The Life and Times of Constance Markievicz*. London: Weidenfeld and Nicolson; Philadelphia: Chilton Books, 1967. Pp. [xiv], 330. Reprinted London: Corgi Books, 1969. Pp. 319.

[Philadelphia edition] Pp. 307-309, general bibliography: books only: author, title, date, place. Pp. 311-317, notes with specific references to secondary sources. Index.

MARLOW, LOUIS   (1881-1966)

Pseudonym of Louis Umfreville Wilkinson.

WW 65.

MARRIOTT, CHARLES   (1869-1957)

Temple & Tucker.

MARSH, SIR EDWARD HOWARD   (1872-1953)

PRIMARY

Christopher Hassall. *Edward Marsh. Patron of the Arts. A Biography.* London: Longmans. Pp. 732.

No bibliography. Index. The beginning point of bibliographical study of Marsh.

See above, BROOKE, RUPERT: John Schroder. *A Catalogue of Books and Manuscripts by Rupert Brooke, Edward Marsh and Christopher Hassall; and* HASSALL, CHRISTOPHER: *Ambrosia and Small Beer. The Record of a Correspondence between Edward Marsh and Christopher Hassall,* for additional bibliographical information.

GENERAL

Temple & Tucker.

MARSH, DAME NGAIO   (1899-   )

WW 71; Hagen.

MARSHALL, ALFRED   (1842-1924)

PRIMARY

John Maynard Keynes. "Bibliographical List of the Writings of Alfred Marshall." *Economic Journal* 34 (1924): 627-637.

Primary ("nearly, but not quite, complete, only a few items of minor importance being omitted" [p. 627]). Chronological arrangement. Books: publisher, date, pages, subsequent editions, number of copies. Periods: date or volume or pages (information varies). Includes Letters to the *Times*. Annotations or else chapter or section headings.

MARSHALL, ARCHIBALD   (1866-1934)

PRIMARY

"Bibliographies of Modern Authors: Archibald Marshall." *London Mercury* 2 (1920): 741.

Primary books, 1899-1920. Chronological arrangement. Publisher, year.

GENERAL

WWW 29-40.

MARTIN, BASIL KINGSLEY   (1897-1969)

WW 69.

MARTIN, DAVID   (1915-   )

(Né Ludwig Detsinyi).

Hetherington.

MARTIN, VIOLET FLORENCE   (1862-1915)

See: SOMERVILLE, EDITH ANNA Œnone.

MARTINDALE, CYRIL CHARLIE, S. J.   (1878-1963)

PRIMARY

Edmund Felix Sutcliffe. *Bibliography of the English Province of the Society of Jesus, 1773-1953.* London: Manresa Press, 1957. Pp. xii, 247.

Not seen.

Philip Caraman. *Cyril Charlie Martindale: A Biography.* London: Longmans, 1967. Pp. [xvi], 244.

P. 240, brief mention of omissions of primary writings in the list given by Sutcliffe (above).

MARTYN, EDWARD (1859-1923)

Coleman & Tyler; Adelman & Dworkin; NCBEL, III, 1939.

MASEFIELD, JOHN (1878-1967)

PRIMARY

Charles H. Simmons. *A Bibliography of John Masefield*. New York: Columbia University Press; London: Oxford University Press, 1930. Pp. xii, [1 leaf], 171. 800 copies.

Primary first editions, secondary selected. Form arrangement. Transcribed TP, full collation, binding, pagination, date, number of copies; contents with place and date of previous publication. Textual and bibliographical notes. Uncollected contributions to books and periodicals arranged alphabetically by titles. Books: transcribed TP, date, size, pages. Periods: place, date. Pp. 141-142, list of earlier bibliographies providing information not given in Simmons. Index of titles and names.

Drew (below), p. 188: "accurate, extensive, and attractively organized and presented."

Fraser Bragg Drew. "Some Contributions to the Bibliography of John Masefield." *Papers of the Bibliographical Society of America* 53 (1959): 188-196, 262-267.

Pp. 188-196: list of 318 book reviews by Masefield in the *Manchester Guardian:* date, title of review. Pp. 262-267: corrections and additions to Simmons.

Geoffrey Handley-Taylor. *John Masefield, O. M. The Queen's Poet Laureate. A Bibliography and Eighty-First Birthday Tribute*. London: Cranbrook Tower Press, 1960. Pp. 96. 999 copies.

241

Primary books, secondary books. Chronological arrangement for primary material; alphabetical for secondary. Primary books: date, place, publisher, number of copies, partial account of subsequent editions and reprints; miscellaneous notes. Pp. 19-24, brief account of seven collections of primary writings.

SECONDARY

Above, Simmons, pp. 141-153; Handley-Taylor, pp. 71-73.

Clarence E. Sherman. "John Masefield. A Contribution toward a Bibliography." *Bulletin of Bibliography* 8 (1915): 158-160.

Includes many early periodical reviews of Masefield.

GENERAL

Millett; Longaker & Bolles; Batho & Dobrée; Daiches; Temple & Tucker; Coleman & Tyler; Salem.

MASON, ALFRED EDWARD WOODLEY   (1865-1948)

PRIMARY

Roger Lancelyn Green. *A. E. W. Mason.* London: Max Parrish, 1952. Pp. 272.

Pp. 267-268, primary bibliography. Genre and form arrangement. Dates. Additional items are suggested in text, *passim*.

GENERAL

Temple & Tucker; Hagen.

MASSINGHAM, HAROLD JOHN   (1888-1952)

WWW 51-60.

MASTERS, JOHN   (1914-   )

Temple & Tucker; WW 71.

MAUGHAM, ROBIN CECIL ROMER, LORD MAUGHAM
                                                 (1916-   )

WW 71.

MAUGHAM, WILLIAM SOMERSET   (1874-1965)

PRIMARY

Raymond Mander and Joe Mitchenson, *Theatrical Companion to Maugham*. London: Rockliff, 1955. Pp. [xii], [308].

> Pp. 299-302, published plays: titles, place, publisher, date. Important details of performances, *passim*.

Raymond Toole Stott. *The Writings of W. S. Maugham. A Bibliography*. London: Bertram Rota, 1956. Pp. 136. Subsequently issued by Nicholas Vane Ltd. (London), along with *Supplement (1961) to The Writings of W. S. Maugham (1956)*. [London, Nicholas Vane Ltd.], 1961. Pp. 20.

> Primary first editions. Form arrangement. Transcribed TP, full collation, pagination, binding, date, number of copies, descriptions of selected later editions and issues; extensive bibliographical notes. Periods: chronological arrangement: dates, occasional notes. Index of titles. *Supplement* provides additions, also secondary bibliography.

> The basic bibliography, but not complete. Klaus Jonas, *Book Collector* 6 (Spring, 1957): 86-88: praises with qualifications "this welcome work" and provides additions to it.

J. Terry Bender. *A Comprehensive Exhibition of the Writings of W. S. Maugham*. [May-August, 1958]. Stanford: Stanford University Library, 1958. 1000 copies. Pages unnumbered.

Includes important association material, locates MSS, and provides additions to Stott.

W. H. Henry, Jr. *A French Bibliography of W. S. Maugham. A List of his works published in France, his contributions to French periodicals, the Swiss, Belgian, and French criticism of his books, plays, and films.* Charlottesville: Bibliographical Society of the University of Virginia, 1967. Pp. [viii], 133.

Primary and secondary bibliography, providing complete bibliographical information for all aspects of French criticism and appreciation of Maugham. Note Table of Contents, pp. v-vii, and Index of Names and Titles, pp. 127-133.

See below, Sanders, pp. 3-8.

SECONDARY

See above, Mander and Mitchenson, *passim;* Stott (1956), pp. 131-132, (1961), pp. 11-18; Bender, *passim;* Henry, *passim.*

Charles Sanders, ed. *W. S. Maugham An Annotated Bibliography of Writings about Him.* DeKalb, Illinois: Northern Illinois University Press, 1970. Pp. x, 436.

Pp. 3-8, primary books. Genre arrangement. Place and date of British and American editions, contents of collections. Pp. 14-381, secondary bibliography. Chronological arrangement. Books: place, publisher, date. Periods: volume, pages, date. Précis of each of the 2355 entries (1897-1968). Indices of authors, of titles of secondary works, of periodicals and newspapers, of foreign languages, and of primary titles. Includes (especially pp. v-viii) references to earlier primary and secondary bibliographies listing additional material.

The beginning point for locating studies and reviews of Maugham.

Edward Halim Mikhail. "Somerset Maugham and the Theatre." *Bulletin of Bibliography* 27 (1970): 42-48.

Arranged: Bibliographies, Books, Periodicals, Reviews, Unpublished Material. Alphabetical by author or title in each section. Books: place, publisher, date. Periods: volume, pages, date.

The selectivity and arrangement of this specialized check-list make it a valuable addition to Sanders.

GENERAL

Millett; Longaker & Bolles; Daiches; Temple & Tucker; Coleman & Tyler; Adelman & Dworkin; Salem; Palmer & Dyson.

MAVOR, OSBORNE HENRY: see BRIDIE, JAMES.

MAYNE, ETHEL COLBURN   (187?-1941)

Millett; Daiches; WWW 41-50.

MAYNE, RUTHERFORD   (1878-   )

Pseudonym of Samuel Waddell.

NCBEL, III, 1941-

MC--: also see MAC--.

MCCAIG, NORMAN   (1910-   )

Daiches; Temple & Tucker.

MCCRACKEN, ESTHER   (1902-   )

WW 71.

MCDOUGALL, WILLIAM   (1871-1938

PRIMARY

Anthony Lewin Robinson. *William McDougall, M. B., D. Sc.,
F. R. S. A Bibliography. Together with a Brief Outline of
his Life.* Foreword by Helge Lundholm. Durham, North
Carolina: Duke University Press, 1943. Pp. [xiv], 54.

Primary, secondary selected. Form arrangement (incon-
sistent). Books: publisher, place, date, pages, height in
cm., subsequent editions. Periods: volume, pages, date,
annotations. Reviews and discussions of primary writings
listed under the primary title. Additional secondary bibliography, alphabetically arranged, pp. 38-41. P. 42, English
and American editions of primary books: publisher, date.
Index.

MCEVOY, CHARLES ALFRED   (1879-1929)

Millett.

MCFEE, WILLIAM   (1881-1966)

PRIMARY

James T. Babb. *A Bibliography of the Writings of William
McFee with an Introduction and Notes by William McFee.*
Garden City, New York: Doubleday, Doran and Co., Inc.,
1931. Pp. [xxvi], [127]. 360 copies.

Primary, secondary selected. Form arrangement. Books:
transcribed TP, part collation, pagination, binding, date,
number of copies, price, variants, reprints or subsequent
editions, bibliographical notes. For each title, note by
McFee concerning composition and publication. Periods:
date (includes only uncollected writings). Pp. 109-112,
secondary bibliography, excluding reviews. Index.

Book Collector's Quarterly, No. 8 (December, 1932), p. 60:

"comprehensive and excellent study."

Harold Sinclair. "William McFee: A Checklist Bibliography."
Reading and Collecting, 1, vi (May, 1937): 6.

Primary books, including books with contributions by McFee.
Place, date, binding, notes. Information additional to Babb.

SECONDARY

Above, Babb, pp. 109-112.

GENERAL

Longaker & Bolles.

MCKENNA, STEPHEN   (1888-1967)

Daiches; WW 67.

MCKERROW, RONALD BRUNLEES   (1872-1940)

PRIMARY

F. C. Francis. "A List of the Writings of Ronald Brunlees
McKerrow." *Library*, 4th Series, 21 (1940-1941): 228-263.

Primary bibliography. Chronological arrangement. Books:
place, publisher, date, pages. Periods: volume, pages, date.
Reviews by McKerrow include author and title, place of publication, and date, of books reviewed. Includes letters by
and periodicals edited by McKerrow. Occasional annotations.

SECONDARY

Above, Francis, p. 263: brief list of obituary notices.

MCLAREN, MORAY   (1901-   )

WW 71.

MCMANUS, CHARLOTTE ELIZABETH   (1853-1944)

PRIMARY

Patrick Sarsfield O'Hegarty. "L. McManus. Obituary." *Dublin Magazine* 20 (January-March, 1945): 68.

Primary books listed in text. Publisher, year, occasionally brief annotations.

MCNEILE, HERMAN CYRIL: see SAPPER.

MCTAGGART, JOHN MCTAGGART ELLIS   (1866-1925)

Batho & Dobrée.

MÉGROZ, RODOLPHE LOUIS   (1891-1968)

WW 1967.

MENEN, AUBREY   (1912-   )

Temple & Tucker.

MERCER, CECIL WILLIAM: see YATES, DORNFORD.

MERRICK, LEONARD   (1864-1938)

PRIMARY

Henry Danielson. *Bibliographies of Modern Authors*. London: Bookman's Journal, 1921. Pp. [xii], [212].

Pp. 159-166, primary books. Chronological arrangement. Transcribed TP, part collation, pagination, binding, variants, miscellaneous bibliographical notes.

The Works of Leonard Merrick. London: Hodder and Stoughton, 1918-1922. 14 volumes.

A fairly complete collection, each volume having a critical introduction by various authors.

SECONDARY

"Leonard Merrick." *English Fiction in Transition* 1, i (1957): 32; 1, ii (1958): 33; 3, i (1960): 32.

Miscellaneous references to secondary writings.

GENERAL

Millett; Batho & Dobrée; NCBEL, III, 1068-1069.

MEW, CHARLOTTE MARY (1870-1928)

PRIMARY

Charlotte Mew. *Collected Poems,* ed. Alida Monro. London: Gerald Duckworth and Co., Ltd., 1953. Pp. 80.

No bibliography, but the biographical memoir by Monro provides bibliographical information and suggestions.

T. E. M. Boll. "The Mystery of Charlotte Mew and May Sinclair: An Inquiry." *Bulletin of the New York Public Library* 74 (1970): 445-453.

An important essay on Mew, indicating sources of both primary and secondary writings, and explaining some of the covert references in Monro's memoir (above).

GENERAL

Millett; Longaker & Bolles; Daiches; Temple & Tucker.

MEYER, KUNO   (1859-1919)

NCBEL, III, 1894.

MEYERSTEIN, EDWARD HARRY WILLIAM   (1889-1952)

PRIMARY

E. H. W. Meyerstein. Poet and Novelist. A Bibliography.
Bristol: Bristol Public Libraries, 1938. One printed sheet,
folded.

Primary books. Genre arrangement. Title, date, publisher.

E. H. W. Meyerstein. *Some Poems*, ed. Maurice Wollman.
London: Neville Spearman, 1960. Pp. 168.

Pp. 167-168, chronological list of primary books. Arranged:
lyrical poetry; narrative and dramatic poetry; translations.
Title, year.

GENERAL

Temple & Tucker.

MEYNELL, ALICE CHRISTIANA THOMPSON   (1847-1922)

(Mrs. Wilfrid Meynell).

PRIMARY

C. A. and H. W. Stonehill. *Bibliographies of Modern Authors*
(Second Series). London: John Castle, 1925. Pp. [xiv],
162. 750 copies.

Pp. 79-125, primary bibliography. Form arrangement (but
mainly books). Transcribed TP, full collation, pagination,
binding, price, number of copies, variants, notes.

Anne Kimball Tuell. *Mrs. Meynell and Her Literary Generation.*
New York: E. P. Dutton and Co., 1925. Pp. 286.

Pp. 259-271, "Bibliographical Notes." Primary selected. Form and genre arrangement. Place, publisher, date. Essays in collections listed with date and place of original publication. Includes short list of essays not reprinted. Limitations of the bibliography described, p. 259.

Sir Francis Meynell. *Alice Meynell, 1847-1922. Catalogue of the Centenary Exhibition.* London: National Book League, [1947]. Pp. 45.

Includes books, MSS, letters, portraits. Information varies; generally for books: place, publisher, date.

Terence L. Connolly, S. J., ed. *Alice Meynell Centenary Tribute.* Boston: Bruce Humphries, Inc., 1948. Pp. 72.

Pp. 41-72, "A Short-Title List of Poetry, Essays, Miscellaneous Works, Anthologies, Translations, Editings, and Introductions with Data on some of the volumes in the complete collection at Boston College." Chronological arrangement under each of the above divisions. Place, publisher, date, number of copies, binding.

These four bibliographies together provide a fairly complete list of primary writings, although there are many unsigned or pseudonymous writings which can likely never be identified.

GENERAL

Millett; Longaker & Bolles; Batho & Dobrée; Temple & Tucker; NCBEL, III, 638-639.

MEYNELL, SIR FRANCIS   (1891-   )

PRIMARY

Francis Meynell. *My Lives.* London: Bodley Head, 1971. Pp. 331.

Autobiography. Not seen.

GENERAL

WW 71.

MEYNELL, VIOLA   (1886-1956)

(Mrs. John Dallyn).

Millett; Temple & Tucker; WWW 51-60.

MEYNELL, WILFRID   (1852-1948)

WWW 41-50.

MIDDLETON, EDGARR   (1894-1939)

WWW 29-40.

MIDDLETON, RICHARD BARHAM   (1882-1911)

PRIMARY

Henry Danielson. *Bibliographies of Modern Authors.* London:
Bookman's Journal, 1921. Pp. [xii], [212].

Pp. 171-172, primary books. Chronological arrangement.
Transcribed TP, part collation, pagination, binding, variants,
miscellaneous bibliographical notes.

GENERAL

Batho & Dobrée.

MIDDLETON, STANLEY   (1919-   )

WW 71.

MILLIN, SARAH GERTRUDE LIEBSON   (1889-1968)

PRIMARY

Morag Whyte. *The Works of Sarah Gertrude Millin. Bibliography.*
Cape Town: University of Cape Town, School of Librarianship, 1952. Pp. 6, 21. (Mimeographed sheets).

Primary, secondary. Genre and form arrangement. Books:
place, publisher, date. Periods: volume, pages, date. Reviews listed under title of book reviewed; other secondary
material listed alphabetically by author.

J. P. L. Snymain. *The Works of Sarah Gertrude Millin.* South
Africa: Central News Agency, Ltd., 1955. Pp. 216.

No bibliography; references in text add to the list given by
Whyte.

SECONDARY

Above, Whyte.

GENERAL

Millett.

MILNE, ALLAN ALEXANDER   (1882-1956)

PRIMARY

Montrose J. Moses and Oscar J. Campbell, eds. *Dramas of
Modernism and Their Forerunners.* Boston: Little, Brown
and Co., 1941. Pp. xvi, 946.

Pp. 923-924, 941, bibliography. Primary selected, secondary
selected. One alphabetical by author list. Books: place,
publisher, date. Periods: volume, pages, date. Criticism of
specific books or plays listed under the appropriate title.
Mainly concerned with Milne as dramatist.

John R. Payne. "Four Children's Books by A. A. Milne."
Studies in Bibliography 23 (1970): 127-139.

Primary books. Chronological arrangement. Transcribed
TP, full collation, pagination, description of paper and of
illustrations, binding, variants, subsequent editions and
reprints, number of copies, detailed bibliographical notes.
Includes suggestions of sources of other primary writings.
Although these two items do not provide complete lists of
Milne's writings, they are the starting points for making such
a list.

SECONDARY

Above, Moses and Campbell.

GENERAL

Millett; Longaker & Bolles; Temple & Tucker; Adelman &
Dworkin; Salem; Palmer & Dyson.

MINNEY, RUBEIGH JAMES   (1895-   )

WW 71.

MITCHELL, GLADYS MAUDE WINIFRED   (1901-   )

WW 71; Hagen.

MITCHELL, JAMES LESLIE   (1901-1935)

Pseudonym used: Lewis Grassic Gibbon.

PRIMARY

Geoffrey Wagner. "James Leslie Mitchell/Lewis Grassic Gibbon. A Chronological Checklist of his Writings." *Bibliotheck*
[Library Association, University of Glasgow] 1 (Autumn,
1956), 3-21.

Not seen.

W. R. Aitken. "Further Notes on the Bibliography of James Leslie Mitchell/Lewis Grassic Gibbon." *Bibliotheck* 1 (Winter, 1956), 34-35.

Not seen.

Ian S. Munro. *Leslie Mitchell: Lewis Grassic Gibbon.* Edinburgh and London: Oliver and Boyd, 1966. Pp. 224.

Pp. 223-224, bibliography. Form and genre arrangement. Place, date. Secondary bibliography in footnotes, *passim.*

SECONDARY

Above, Munro, footnotes, *passim.*

GENERAL

Daiches.

MITCHELL, MARY   (1892-   )

Hetherington.

MITCHISON, NAOMI MARGARET HALDANE, LADY MITCHISON.
                                            (1897-   )

Millett; Daiches; Temple & Tucker; WW 71.

MITFORD, HON. NANCY   (1904-   )

Daiches; Temple & Tucker; WW 71.

MONCRIEFF, CHARLES KENNETH SCOTT   (1889-1930)

PRIMARY

J. M. Scott Moncrieff and L. W. Lunn, eds. *C. K. Scott Mon-crieff. Memories and Letters.* London: Chapman and Hall, 1931. Pp. 242.

No bibliography, but on p. [ii] a list of titles translated by Moncrieff, while the letters themselves point to some of his periodical contributions and other literary work.

MONKHOUSE, ALLAN NOBLE   (1858-1936)

Millett; Longaker & Bolles; Batho & Dobrée; Temple & Tucker.

MONRO, HAROLD EDWARD   (1879-1932)

PRIMARY

Joy Grant. *Harold Monro and the Poetry Bookshop.* London: Routledge and Kegan Paul, 1967. Pp. x, 286.

Pp. 276-279, bibliography. Primary books, secondary selected. Arranged: published works (including books, pamphlets, periodicals edited by Monro); unpublished works (including brief account of three main collections of MSS); selected criticism and reminiscences of Monro. Publisher, place, date. Additional primary and secondary bibliography in footnotes.

GENERAL

Millett; Longaker & Bolles; Batho & Dobrée; Daiches; Temple & Tucker.

MONSARRAT, NICHOLAS JOHN TURNEY   (1910-   )

Temple & Tucker; WW 71.

MONTAGUE, CHARLES EDWARD   (1867-1928)

PRIMARY

Margaret Stapleton. "A Bibliography of Writings by and about
Charles Edward Montague." *Bulletin of Bibliography* 16
(1938-1939): 135-136, 157-158.

Primary, secondary selected. Form arrangement. Books:
place, publisher, later editions, brief description of contents. Periods: volume, pages, date. "Miscellaneous Writings" gives contents of books listed alphabetically by title
with place of first publication. P. 158, secondary bibliography. Arranged alphabetically by author with reviews listed
under title of book reviewed.

GENERAL

Millett; Longaker & Bolles.

MOORE, DORIS LANGLEY   (-   )

WW 71.

MOORE, GEORGE   (1852-1933)

PRIMARY

Jean C. Noël. *George Moore. L'homme et l'œuvre (1852-1933).*
Paris: Marcel Didier (Etudes Anglaises No. 24), 1966. Pp.
706.

Pp. 555-647, bibliography. Primary, secondary selected.
Form and genre arrangement. Primary books: transcribed TP,
part collation, binding, pagination, occasional notes. Periods:
volume, dates, pages. Pp. 604-647, secondary bibliography.
Arranged by topic and by language, including many general
references. [In French].

While Gilcher (below) provides the more authoritative primary
bibliography, Noël is a useful cross-check and often helpful.

Edwin Gilcher. *A Bibliography of George Moore*. DeKalb, Illinois: Northern Illinois University Press, 1970. Pp. xiv, 274.

Primary bibliography. Form arrangement. Books (new editions): transcribed TP, full collation, price, pagination, binding, contents, full notes. Other primary books: place, publisher, date, notes. Periods: chronologically arranged, dates, notes on inclusion of item in later writings or collections; author and title of books reviewed by Moore identified; unsigned writings by Moore identified. Translations of Moore listed under language in which translated. Index.

A model of bibliographic completeness. See pp. ix-xiv for Gilcher's statement of bibliographical principles and pp. 243-246 for his acknowledgement of assistance, both providing clues to the secondary bibliography and to further research.

SECONDARY

Above, Noël, pp. 604-647.

Helmut E. Gerber. "George Moore: An Annotated Bibliography of Writings about Him." *English Fiction in Transition* 2, ii (1959): 1-91.

Alphabetical by author arrangement. Books: place, publisher, date. Periods: volume, pages, date. Annotations.

This basic checklist of secondary writings is supplemented in almost every issue of *English Fiction* (later *English Literature*) *in Transition*, particularly lengthy or otherwise important installments being as follows: 1, i (1957): 32-35; 3, ii (1960): 34-46; 4, ii (1961): 30-42; 4, iii (1961): 52-53; 5, iv (1962): 33-35; 14 (1971): 75-83.

Through the efforts of Noël, Gilcher, and Gerber, Moore has received almost as much bibliographical attention as he would have considered his due.

GENERAL

Millett; Longaker & Bolles; Batho & Dobrée; Temple & Tucker; NCBEL, III, 1014-1019.

MOORE, GEORGE EDWARD   (1873-1958)

PRIMARY

Emerson Buchanan and G. E. Moore. "Bibliography of the Writings of G. E. Moore to November, 1942." In *The Philosophy of G. E. Moore,* ed. Paul Arthur Schilp. Evanston and Chicago: Northwestern University Press (Library of Living Philosophers, IV), 1942. Pp. 717.

Pp. 681-689, bibliography. Primary, secondary selected. Chronological arrangement. Books: place, publisher, date, pages, subsequent editions, translations, reprints; reviews of primary writings listed under primary title. Periods: volume, pages, date.

GENERAL

Batho & Dobrée.

MOORE, NICHOLAS   (1918-   )

Daiches; Temple & Tucker.

MOORE, THOMAS STURGE   (1870-1944)

PRIMARY

Frederick L. Gwynn. *Sturge Moore and the Life of Art.* Lawrence: Kansas University Press, 1951. Pp. 159.

Pp. 125-135, bibliography. Primary, secondary selected. Chronological arrangement, with years subdivided: Prose and Verse. Books: publisher, date, reviews of the book. Periods: volume, pages, date. Chronological list of "Printed Wood-Engravings." Pp. 134-135, secondary bibliography.

MOO

GENERAL

Millett; Longaker & Bolles; Daiches; Batho & Dobrée; Temple & Tucker.

MOOREHEAD, ALAN MCCRAE   (1910-   )

Hetherington; WW 71.

MORAES, DOM   (1938-   )

WW 71.

MORGAN, CHARLES LANGBRIDGE   (1894-1957)

PRIMARY

Gilbert H. Fabes. *The First Editions of A. E. Coppard, A. P. Herbert, and Charles Morgan, with Values and Bibliographical Points*. London: Myers and Co., 1933. Pp. 154.

Transcribed TP, binding, variants, value in sterling. A book for dealers or collectors.

Henry Charles Duffin. *The Novels and Plays of Charles Morgan*. London: Bowes and Bowes, 1959. Pp. 221.

No bibliography; index lists Morgan's novels and plays. There appears to be no account of Morgan's journalism.

GENERAL

Millett; Longaker & Bolles; Daiches; Temple & Tucker; Adelman & Dworkin.

MORGAN, CONWY LLOYD   (1852-1936)

Batho & Dobrée; WWW 29-40.

MORLEY, ROBERT   (1908-   )

Salem; WW 71.

MORRISON, ARTHUR   (1863-1945)

PRIMARY

Jocelyn Bell. "A Study of Arthur Morrison" in *Essays and Studies 1952* (NS 5), ed. Arundell Esdaile for The English Association. London: John Murray, 1952. Pp. 77-89.

A survey of Morrison's literary œuve which provides titles and dates for his books and suggestions for locating his other writings.

Vincent Brome. *Four Realist Novelists*. London: Longmans, Green, and Company (WTW 183), 1963. Pp. 36.

P. 33, primary books. Place, date, genre. P. 36, general secondary bibliography, selected.

SECONDARY

Above, Brome, p. 36.

Helmut E. Gerber. "Arthur Morrison." *English Fiction in Transition* 1, i (1957): 35; 4, ii (1961): 58; 4, iii (1961): 53.

A total of five entries, annotated.

GENERAL

Batho & Dobrée; WWW 41-50; NCBEL, III, 1069-1070; Hagen.

MORRISON, NANCY AGNES BRYSSON   (-   )

Daiches.

MORTIMER, JOHN CLIFFORD   (1923-   )

  WW 71.

MORTON, HENRY CANOVA VOLLAM   (1892-   )

  WW 71.

MORTON, JOHN CAMERON ANDRIEU BINGHAM MICHAEL
                                             (1893-   )

  WW 71.

MOTTRAM, RALPH HALE   (1883-   )

PRIMARY

Gilbert H. Fabes. *The First Editions of Ralph Hale Mottram*.
London: Myers and Co., 1934. Pp. 128. 300 copies.

Primary books, including books with contributions by Mottram. Chronological arrangement. Transcribed TP, full
collation, pagination, binding, notes.

GENERAL

Millett; Longaker & Bolles; Daiches; Temple & Tucker; WW 71.

MOULT, THOMAS   (-   )

  WW 71.

MUGGERIDGE, MALCOLM   (1903-   )

  WW 71; Hagen.

MUIR, EDWIN   (1887-1959)

PRIMARY

Elgin W. Mellown. *Bibliography of the Writings of Edwin Muir.*
University: University of Alabama Press, 1964; Reprinted
with corrections and additions, London: Nicholas Vane Ltd.,
1966. Pp. 144. 1964 edition reissued with Mellown's
*Supplement to the Bibliography ...Incorporating Additional
Entries Compiled by Peter Hoy.* University: University of
Alabama Press, [1971]. Pp. 28.

Primary bibliography, complete. Form arrangement. Books:
transcribed TP, part collation, pagination, binding, date,
price, miscellaneous notes, contents. Periods: volume,
pages, date; some reviews by Muir include author and title
of book reviewed. Index of titles provides history of individual publication. London edition includes selected secondary criticism with reviews listed under book titles, also
additional primary bibliography. *Supplement* arranged in the
form of the 1964 edition.

With the *Supplement* this bibliography provides a virtually
complete list of the primary writings.

SECONDARY

Above, Mellown, (1966), pp. 138-144.

Peter C. Hoy and Elgin W. Mellown. *A Checklist of Writings
about Edwin Muir.* Troy, New York: Whitston Publishing
Co., Inc., 1971. Pp. [iv], 80.

Form arrangement, including list of previous primary and
secondary bibliographies. Brief annotations identify type
of criticism.

GENERAL

Millett; Daiches; Temple & Tucker.

MUIR, KENNETH   (1907-   )

Daiches; WW 71.

MULGAN, JOHN   (1911-1945)

PRIMARY

P. W. Day. *John Mulgan*. New York: Twayne Publishers, Inc.
(TWAS 58), 1968. Pp. 151.

Pp. 145-146, primary bibliography. Form arrangement. Books:
place, publisher, date. Pp. 146-148, secondary bibliography,
annotated.

MUNBY, ALAN NOEL LATIMER   (1913-   )

WW 71.

MUNRO, CHARLES KIRKPATRICK   (1889-   )

Pseudonym of Charles Walden Kirkpatrick Macmullan.

Millett; Daiches; Temple & Tucker; Salem; WW 71.

MUNRO, HECTOR HUGH   (1870-1916)
Pseudonym used: Saki.
PRIMARY

George James Spears. *The Satire of Saki*. New York: Espo-
sition Press, 1963. Pp. 127.

Pp. [123] -127, primary selected, secondary selected bibliography. Genre arrangement. Books: place, publisher, date,
pages, brief critical annotations and bibliographical evaluations. Periods: volume, pages, date. Includes reviews of
primary books.

While the secondary bibliography is limited, it includes works omitted by Gillen (below); and the primary bibliography gives details not in Gillen.

Charles H. Gillen. *Hector Hugh Munro (Saki)*. New York: Twayne Publishers (TEAS 102), 1969. Pp. 178.

Pp. 171-172, primary books: Place, publisher, date. Pp. 172-175, secondary bibliography. Arranged: alphabetical by author. Periods: volume, pages, date. Each entry annotated. Other secondary references in notes, pp. 161-169.

Spears and Gillen together provide a starting point for, but not, the definitive bibliography. It appears that no one has ever listed the journalism.

SECONDARY

Above, Spears and Gillen.

Robert Drake, "Saki: Some Problems and a Bibliography," *English Fiction in Transition* 5 (1962): 12-26. [See later issues of *English Fiction* (later *English Literature*) *in Transition* for continuation by various compilers].

Annotations.

GENERAL

Millett; Longaker & Bolles; Batho & Dobrée; Temple & Tucker.

MURDOCH, JEAN IRIS   (1919-   )

(Mrs. J. O. Bayley).

PRIMARY

R. L. Widmann. "An Iris Murdoch Checklist," *Critique* 10, i (1968): 17-29.

Primary, secondary. Form arrangement. Primary books:

place, publisher, date, all editions including translations, reviews. Secondary books: place, date. Periods: volume, pages, date.

The most informative list of primary writings to 1966.

Ann Culley, with John Feaster. "Criticism of Iris Murdoch: A Selected Checklist," *Modern Fiction Studies* 15 (1969): 449-457.

Primary selected, secondary selected. Arranged: general studies, criticism of individual novels (under title of novel); primary writings subdivided novels, critical works and essays, interviews. Books: place, publisher, date. Periods: volume, pages, date.

Supplements the primary bibliography in Widmann which provides more details; the secondary bibliography in Culley is more complete than that in Widmann or Wolfe.

William M. Murray. "A Note on the Iris Murdoch Manuscripts in the University of Iowa Libraries," *Modern Fiction Studies* 15 (1969): 445-448.

Brief description of the eight MSS in Iowa.

SECONDARY

Above, Widmann and Culley.

Peter Wolfe. *The Disciplined Heart: Iris Murdoch and Her Novels*. Columbia: University of Missouri Press, 1966. Pp. [xii], 220.

Pp. 217-220, secondary bibliography. Alphabetical by author arrangement. Books: place, date. Periods: volume, pages, date.

GENERAL

Temple & Tucker; WW 71.

MURRAY, GEORGE GILBERT AIMÉ   (1866-1957)

PRIMARY

"Bibliographies of Modern Authors: George Gilbert Aimé Murray"
London Mercury 3 (1921): 326-327.

Primary books. Genre arrangement. Publisher, date, notes.

J. A. K. Thomson and A. J. Toynbee, eds. *Essays in Honour
of Gilbert Murray.* London: Allen and Unwin Ltd., 1936. Pp.
[310].

Pp. [309-310], primary books published by Allen and Unwin.

Gilbert Murray. *An Unfinished Autobiography*, ed. Jean Smith
and Arnold Toynbee. London: Allen and Unwin Ltd., 1960.
Pp. [228].

Pp. [227-228], primary books published by Allen and Unwin;
see "Introduction" by E. R. Dodds (pp. 13-19) for references
to other titles.

GENERAL

Millett; Longaker & Bolles; Temple & Tucker.

MURRAY, THOMAS CORNELIUS   (1873-1959)

Millett; Adelman & Dworkin; Salem; NCBEL, III, 1944-1945.

MURRY, JOHN MIDDLETON   (1889-1957)

PRIMARY

Philip Mairet. *John Middleton Murry.* London: Longmans, Green
and Co. (WTW 102), 1958. Pp. 40.

Pp. 37-40, bibliography of primary books. Chronological arrangement. Place, date, genre; occasionally contents of col-

lections with notes on previous periodical publication.

F. A. Lea. *The Life of John Middleton Murry*. London: Methuen and Co., 1959. Pp. 378.

Pp. 355-356, bibliography of primary books. Chronological arrangement. Publisher, date, occasionally subsequent editions. Pp. 356-357, secondary bibliography, books. Publisher, date, brief annotations.

Ernest G. Griffin. *John Middleton Murry*. New York: Twayne Publishers, Inc. (TEAS 72), 1969. Pp. 182.

Pp. 173-175, primary writings. Books, British and American editions, chronologically arranged: place, publisher, year, subsequent editions. Periodical contributions: ten uncollected items: volume, pages, date. Pp. 175-177, secondary bibliography. Annotated. Other primary and secondary references in notes, pp. 159-172, and suggestions of Murry's periodical contributions in Chronology, pp. [15]-[18].

There appears to be no published list of Murry's extensive journalism and periodical contributions.

GENERAL

Millett; Longaker & Bolles; Daiches; Temple & Tucker.

MYERS, LEOPOLD HAMILTON   (1881-1944)

PRIMARY

Geoffrey Herman Bantock. *L. H. Myers. A Critical Study.* Leicester: University College, and London: Jonathan Cape, 1956. Pp. [x], 157.

Little or no bibliographical information as such, yet titles and dates of Myers' books are given, along with letters both to and from him referring to his writings.

GENERAL

Millett; Daiches; Temple & Tucker.

NAIPAUL, VIDIADHAR SURAJPRASAD   (1932-   )

WW 71.

NAMIER, SIR LEWIS BERNSTEIN   (1888-1960)

PRIMARY

Sir Lewis Namier. *Collected Essays*. London: Hamish Hamilton. I (1958); II (1962).

Each volume gives the bibliographical history of each essay included, as well as a list of books by Namier.

Julia Namier. *Lewis Namier. A Biography*. London: Oxford University Press, 1971.

Not seen. J. H. Plumb, *Observer*, 16 May 1971, p. 32: "this will remain the basic study."

GENERAL

Daiches; WWW 51-60.

NASH, PAUL   (1889-1946)

See BOTTOMLEY, GORDON.

NEALE, SIR JOHN ERNEST   (1890-   )

Daiches; WW 71.

NESBIT, EDITH   (1858-1924)

(Mrs. Hubert Bland, later Mrs. Tucker).

PRIMARY

Doris Langley Moore. *E. Nesbit. A Biography.* (Revised with New Material). Philadelphia and New York: Chilton Books, 1966. Pp. [xxxiii], [315].

Pp. 302-306, bibliography. Primary books, first English editions. Chronological arrangement. Place, publisher, year, format, occasionally pages, and occasionally names of illustrators. Anthologies and periodicals are excluded from this list, but many of them are mentioned in the text, *passim*, as are secondary criticisms and references to Hubert Bland's literary career.

GENERAL

Batho & Dobrée; WWW 16-28; NCBEL, III, 641-642.

NEVINSON, HENRY WOODD   (1856-1941)

PRIMARY

Henry W. Nevinson. *Visions and Memories*, ed. Evelyn Sharp. London: Oxford University Press, 1944. Pp. 199.

P. 188, bibliography. Primary books. Genre arrangement. Dates. See p. vi for selected list of periodicals to which Nevinson contributed.

GENERAL

Millett.

NEWBOLT, SIR HENRY JOHN   (1862-1938)

PRIMARY

"Bibliographies of Modern Authors: Sir Henry John Newbolt." *London Mercury* 2 (1920): 115.

Primary books, 1892-1918. Publisher, date, brief notes.

Margaret Newbolt, ed. *The Later Life and Letters of Sir Henry Newbolt*. London: Faber and Faber, 1942. Pp. 426.

Pp. 413-414, "A Short Bibliography." Primary books. Publisher, date. References to writings not included in this bibliography will be found in the text, *passim;* and also in Newbolt's memoirs, *My World in My Time*. London: Faber and Faber, 1932. Pp. 321.

GENERAL

Millett; Longaker & Bolles; Temple & Tucker; NCBEL, III, 642-643.

NEWBY, PERCY HOWARD   (1918-   )

Daiches; Temple & Tucker; WW 71; Hagen.

NEWMAN, ERNEST   (1868-1959)

PRIMARY

Herbert Van Thal, ed. *Fanfare for Ernest Newman*. London: Arthur Barker, 1955. Pp. 192.

P. 192, checklist. Titles and dates of original writings; also translations and works edited or introduced by Newman.

Vera Newman. *Ernest Newman. A Memoir by his Wife*. London: Putnam, 1963. Pp. [x], 278.

References to primary writings, including weekly journalism, *passim*. Index.

GENERAL

Millett; WWW 51-60.

NICHOLS, JOHN BEVERLEY (1899-   )

Temple & Tucker; WW 71; Hagen.

NICHOLS, ROBERT MALISE BOWYER (1893-1944)

PRIMARY

Robert Nichols. *Robert Nichols*. London: Ernest Benn Ltd. (Augustan Books of Poetry), 1932. Pp. [32].

P. [32], bibliography. Primary books, first editions. Genre arrangement. Publisher, date.

John Gawsworth. *Ten Contemporaries. Notes Toward their Definitive Bibliography* [First Series]. London: Ernest Benn Ltd., 1932. Pp. 224.

Pp. 118-131, primary books, first editions, 1915-1932. Chronological arrangement. Transcribed TP, full collation, pagination, binding, date, bibliographical notes.

Montrose J. Moses and Oscar J. Campbell, eds. *Dramas of Modernism and Their Forerunners*. Boston: Little, Brown and Co., 1941. Pp. xvi, 946.

Pp. 925, 941, bibliography. Primary selected, secondary selected. One alphabetical list. Books: place, publisher, date. Periods: volume, pages, date. Studies or reviews of *Wings over Europe* listed thereunder.

No complete list of all of Nichol's writings is available.

SECONDARY

Above, Moses and Campbell.

GENERAL

Millett; Longaker & Bolles; Temple & Tucker; Salem.

NICHOLSON, NORMAN CORNTHWAITE   (1914-   )

Daiches; Temple & Tucker; WW 71.

NICOLL, JOHN RAMSAY ALLARDYCE   (1894-   )

WW 71.

NICOLSON, HON. SIR HAROLD GEORGE   (1886-1968)

Millett; Daiches; Temple & Tucker; WW 68.

NORWAY, N. S.: see SHUTE, NEVIL.

NOVELLO, IVOR   (1893-1951)

WWW 51-60.

NOYES, ALFRED   (1880-1958)

PRIMARY

Walter C. Jerrold. *Alfred Noyes*. London: Harold Shaylor (Modern Writers Series, ed. Thomas Moult), 1930. Pp. 251.

Pp. 247-251, bibliography of primary books, including books edited or introduced by Noyes. Place, publisher, date.

Catherine Merrick Neale. "Contemporary Catholic Authors: Alfred Noyes, Litteratur." *Catholic Library World* 13 (October, 1941): 3-8.

Not seen.

James E. Tobin. "Alfred Noyes: A Corrected Bibliography." *Catholic Library World* 15 (March, 1944): 181-184, 189.

NOY

Revisions to Neale (above). Not seen.

GENERAL

Millett; Longaker & Bolles; Batho & Dobrée; Temple & Tucker.

O'BRIEN, CONOR CRUISE   (1917-   )

WW 71.

O'BRIEN, FLORENCE ROMA MUIR WILSON: see WILSON, ROMER.

O'BRIEN, KATE   (1897-   )

Daiches; WW 71.

O'BYRNE, DERMOT: see BAX, SIR ARNOLD.

O'CASEY, SEAN   (1884-1964)

PRIMARY

I. M. Levidova and V. M. Parchevskaia. *Sean O'Casey Biblio-graphic Guide*. Moscow: Kniga Publishing House (Writers of Foreign Countries Series), 1964. Pp. [100]. In Russian.

Primary complete, secondary complete. Form and genre arrangement. Books: place, publisher, date, reprints, subsequent editions; translations listed separately. Periods: pages, date. Secondary bibliography includes reviews; brief annotations.

Particularly strong on O'Casey's Russian publications.

William A. Armstrong. *Sean O'Casey*. London: Longmans, Green and Co. (WTW 198), 1967. Pp. 39.

Pp. 35-39, bibliography. Primary; secondary books. Chronological arrangement. Books: place, date, genre, occasional
annotations. Periods: dates.

Not complete--but easy to use.

Ronald Ayling, ed. *Sean O'Casey*. *Modern Judgements*. London: Macmillan (Modern Judgements Series), 1969. Pp. 274.

Pp. 261-269, bibliography. Primary books, secondary selected. Genre arrangement. Books: date, place, publisher
(both British and American editions). Periods: volume, date,
pages. Annotations.

An easy-to-use list with helpful evaluations; see also comments in the "Introduction," pp. 11-41. NB, p. 270: Ayling
and Michael J. Durkan are compiling a primary bibliography.
Bernard Benstock, *Sean O'Casey*. Lewisburg: Bucknell
University Press (Irish Writers Series), 1970: Ayling provides
"the best and most current bibliography of secondary material"
(p. 122).

SECONDARY

Otto Brandstädter, "Ein O'Casey-Bibliographie." *Zeitschrift
fur Anglistik and Amerikanistik* [Berlin], 2 (1954), 240-254.

Pp. 244-254, secondary bibliography. Books arranged alphabetically by author (place, publisher, date). Periodicals arranged chronologically (volume, pages, date).

Armstrong, p. 35: "...detailed, but not always accurate."

Charles A. Carpenter, "Sean O'Casey Studies Through 1964."
Modern Drama, 10 (1967): 17-23.

Alphabetical-by-author arrangement. Books: place, date,
Periods: date, volume, pages.

Comprehensive list through 1964.

Above, Levidova and Parchevskaia; Ayling, pp. 263-269.

GENERAL

Millett; Longaker & Bolles; Daiches; Temple & Tucker; Coleman & Tyler; Adelman & Dworkin; Salem; Palmer & Dyson.

O'CONNOR, FRANK   (1903-1966)

Pseudonym of Michael O'Donovan.

PRIMARY

Gerry Brenner. "Frank O'Connor, 1903-1966: A Bibliography." *West Coast Review* 2, ii (1967): 55-64.

Pp. 55-62, primary bibliography. Form and genre arrangement. Books: place, publisher, year; contents with place, date, pages, of original publication (but not contents of verse collections). Periods: dates, pages. Includes unpublished plays, occasional annotations; recordings. Pp. 62-64, secondary bibliography. Includes book reviews listed under title of book reviewed.

GENERAL

Temple & Tucker.

O'DONOVAN, MICHAEL: *see* O'CONNOR, FRANK.

O'DUFFY, EIMAR ULTAN   (1893-1935)

PRIMARY

Alf MacLochlainn. "Eimar O'Duffy. A Bibliographical Biography." *Irish Book*, 1 (Winter, 1959-1960): 37-46.

Essay with bibliographical information in text. For books, usually date, notice of later editions, publisher; some account of contributions to periodicals.

GENERAL

WWW 29-40; Hagen.

O'FAOLAIN, SEAN   (1900-   )

PRIMARY

Maurice Harmon. *Sean O'Faolain. A Critical Introduction.*
Notre Dame and London: University of Notre Dame Press,
1967. Pp. xix, 221.

> Pp. 203-213, bibliography. Primary. Form arrangement.
> Books: place, publisher, date. Periods: volume, pages,
> date. Pp. 216-217, secondary bibliography.

Paul A. Doyle. *Sean O'Faolain.* New York: Twayne Publishers, Inc. (TEAS 70), 1968. Pp. 156.

> Pp. 143-147, primary bibliography. Chronological arrange-
> ment. Books: place, publisher, date; includes both British
> and American editions. Periods: volume, pages, date, anno-
> tations. Pp. 148-152, secondary bibliography. Additional
> primary and secondary bibliography in notes, pp. 131-141.

> Doyle provides a more complete list of titles (especially of
> primary periodical contributions) than does Harmon and also
> gives additional information about editions and a longer secon-
> dary bibliography; yet Harmon includes entries which Doyle
> omits; and both should be consulted.

SECONDARY

Above, Harmon, pp. 216-217; Doyle, pp. 148-152, 131-141.

GENERAL

Millett; Daiches; Temple & Tucker; WW 71.

O'FLAHERTY, LIAM   (1896-   )

PRIMARY

John Gawsworth. *Ten Contemporaries. Notes Toward Their Definitive Bibliography. (Second Series)*. London: Joiner and Steele, 1933. Pp. 240. 1000 copies.

Pp. 144-160, primary first editions, 1923-1932. Chronological arrangement. Transcribed TP, full collation, pagination, binding, date, bibliographical notes.

Paul A. Doyle. "A Liam O'Flaherty Checklist." *Twentieth Century Literature* 13 (1967): 49-51.

Primary, secondary selected. Form and genre arrangement. Books: place, date. Periods: volume, pages, date. P. 51, secondary bibliography; alphabetical by author arrangement.

Gawsworth provides bibliographical details about first editions to 1932; while Doyle supplements the list without providing details.

SECONDARY

Above, Doyle, p. 51.

GENERAL

Millett; Daiches; Temple & Tucker; WW 71.

O'GRADY, STANDISH   (1846-1928)

PRIMARY

Patrick Sarsfield O'Hegarty. *A Bibliography of Books written by Standish O'Grady*. Dublin: For the author, 1930. Pp. 8. 25 copies. [Reprint of "Bibliographies of Irish Authors. No. 2. Standish O'Grady." *Dublin Magazine* 5 (April-June, 1930): 49-56].

Primary books. Chronological arrangement. Transcribed TP, part collation, pagination, binding, date, bibliographical notes.

John R. McKenna. "The Standish O'Grady Collection at Colby College: A Check List," *Colby Library Quarterly*, 4 (1958): 291-303.

Not seen.

Phillip L. Marcus. *Standish O'Grady*. Lewisburg: Bucknell University Press (Irish Writers Series), 1970. Pp. 92.

Pp. 90-91, primary books. Chronological arrangement. Place, publisher, date, all editions. Pp. 91-92, secondary selected. Information as for primary.

There appears to be no account of O'Grady's journalism and contributions to periodicals.

SECONDARY

Above, Marcus, pp. 91-92.

GENERAL

NCBEL, III, 1892-1894.

O'HANRAHAN, MICHAEL   (-1916)

PRIMARY

Patrick Sarsfield O'Hegarty. "Bibliographies of 1916 and the Irish Revolution. IX. Micheál O'Hannracháin." *Dublin Magazine* 11 (July-September, 1936): 59.

Primary books. Chronological arrangement. Transcribed TP, part collation, pagination, binding, bibliographical notes.

O'HIGGINS, KEVIN CHRISTOPHER   (1892-1927)

PRIMARY

Patrick Sarsfield O'Hegarty. "Bibliographies of 1916 and the

279

Irish Revolution. XIV. Kevin O'Higgins." *Dublin Magazine* 12 (January-March, 1937): 67.

Primary books. Chronological arrangement. Transcribed TP, part collation, pagination, binding, bibliographical and biographical notes.

O'KELLY, SEUMAS   (1881-1918)

PRIMARY

Patrick Sarsfield O'Hegarty. "Bibliographies of 1916 and the Irish Revolution. IV. Seumas O'Kelly." *Dublin Magazine* 9 (October-December, 1934): 47-51.

Primary books. Chronological arrangement. Transcribed TP, part collation, pagination, binding, bibliographical notes.

OLIVER, F. S.   (1864-1934)

Daiches.

OLIVER, GEORGE: see ONIONS, OLIVER.

OLIVIER, EDITH   (-   )

Millett.

OMAN, CAROLA MARY ANIMA   (1897-   )

(Lady Lenanton).

Millett; WW 71.

OMAN, SIR CHARLES WILLIAM CHADWICK   (1860-1946)

Batho & Dobrée; WWW 41-50.

ONIONS, CHARLES TALBUT   (1873-1965)

PRIMARY

A List of the Published Writings of Charles Talbut Onions.
Oxford: Clarendon Press, 1948. Pp. 18.

Not seen.

GENERAL

WW 65.

ONIONS, OLIVER   (1873-1961)

Pseudonym of George Oliver.

PRIMARY

John Gawsworth. Ten Contemporaries. Notes Toward Their
Definitive Bibliography. (Second Series). London: Joiner
and Steele, 1933. Pp. 240. 1000 copies.

Pp. 170-188, primary first editions, 1900-1931. Chronological
arrangement. Transcribed TP, full collation, pagination,
binding, date, bibliographical notes. Pp. 167-169, list of
collections of primary books and MSS.

Apparently the only primary bibliography. NB: a complete
collection (as of 1931) was given to the Widener Library,
Harvard, by Randolph Edgar.

SECONDARY

(Although English Literature in Transition lists Onions as an
author whose works will be listed by its compilers, by summer, 1971, no material relating to him had been published).

GENERAL

Millett; Daiches; Temple & Tucker.

OPPENHEIM, EDWARD PHILLIPS   (1866-1946)

PRIMARY

Hulings C. Brown. "Oppenheim and his Ninety Novels." *Boston Evening Transcript.* 5 May 1923.

　　Primary books. British and American titles, publisher, date, genre, nom de plume under which published.

Grant Overton. *Cargoes for Crusoes.* New York: D. Appleton and Co., 1924. Pp. 416.

　　Pp. 138-141, bibliography. Primary books. Chronological arrangement. British and American titles, nom de plume under which published, date. Secondary bibliography, pp. 126-138; also see text, *passim.*

Robert Standish. *The Prince of Storytellers. The Life of E. Phillips Oppenheim.* London: Peter Davies, 1957. Pp. 253.

　　Pp. 247-253, "1887-1943. The Harvest of Fifty-six Years' Writing." Primary books. Genre arrangement. British and American titles, date. P. 247, note concerning contributions to periodicals and American piracies.

SECONDARY

Above, Overton.

GENERAL

Hagen.

ORAGE, ALFRED RICHARD   (1873-1934)

PRIMARY

Wallace Martin. *'The New Age' under Orage. Chapters in English Cultural History.* Manchester: Manchester University Press; New York: Barnes and Noble, Inc., 1967. Pp. [xiv], 303.

Although there is no bibliography, there are bibliographical footnotes; and this excellent study must provide the start for any bibliographical work relating to Orage until Prof. Martin publishes his bibliography, first announced in *English Literature in Transition* 6 (1963): 237.

GENERAL

Millett.

ORIGO, IRIS CUTTING (1902-   )

(Marchesa Iris Origo).

WW 71.

O'RIORDAN, CONAL HOLMES O'CONNELL (1874-1950)

Millett; Longaker & Bolles; WWW 41-50; CBEL, III, 1065.

ORWELL, GEORGE (1903-1950)

Pseudonym of Eric Blair.

PRIMARY

Zoltan G. Zeke and William White. "Orwelliana." *Bulletin of Bibliography* 23 (1961): 110-114, 140-144, 166-168.

Primary. Genre arrangement, chronological in each section. Books: title, place, publisher, year, pages, subsequent editions, name used. Periods: volume, pages, date; reviews include title and author of book reviewed. Pp. 140-144, secondary bibliography. Form arrangement. Reviews of Orwell listed under title of book. Pp. 166-168, continuation of reviews; p. 168, addenda to all sections.

M. Jennifer McDowell. "George Orwell: Bibliographical Addenda." *Bulletin of Bibliography* 23 (1963): 224-229; 24 (1963): 19-24, 36-40.

Pp. 224-229, additional primary bibliography; also letters of reply to Orwell in periodicals. Pp. 19-24, 36-40, additional secondary bibliography and supplemental addenda for all sections.

Ian R. Willison and Ian Angus. "George Orwell: Bibliographical Addenda." *Bulletin of Bibliography* 24 (1965): 180-187.

Additional primary bibliography and letters of reply.

George Orwell. *The Collected Essays, Journalism and Letters of George Orwell*, ed. Sonia Orwell and Ian Angus. London: Secker and Warburg; New York: Harcourt, Brace and World, 1968. Four volumes.

Chronologically arranged primary material. Important bibliographical footnotes, *passim*, indicate date and place of publication of essays and reviews, the latter including author and title of book reviewed. Other information.

SECONDARY

Above, Zeke and White; McDowell; Willison and Angus.

Robert A. Lee. *Orwell's Fiction*. Notre Dame and London: University of Notre Dame Press, 1969. Pp. [xviii], 188.

Selected secondary bibliography, pp. 180-183; also in notes, pp. 163-178. Books: place, date. Periods: volume, date, pages.

GENERAL

Longaker & Bolles; Daiches; Temple & Tucker.

OSBORNE, JOHN JAMES   (1929-   )

PRIMARY

Alan Carter. *John Osborne*. Edinburgh: Oliver and Boyd
(Biography and Criticism, 14), 1969. Pp. [x], 194.

P. 187, primary bibliography. Form arrangement. Books:
place, publisher, date. Periods: date. Pp. 187-191, secondary bibliography. P. 184, list of first performances of
plays: dates, theatre, director, star.

Simon Trussler. *The Plays of John Osborne. An Assessment.*
London: Victor Gollancz Ltd., 1969. Pp. 252.

Pp. 247-249, primary bibliography. Form arrangement. Books:
date. Periods: volume, date, pages, reprints. Secondary bibliography, pp. 249-252. Pp. 235-246, detailed accounts of
first performances.

Trussler gives more details than Carter; he is also the author
of the WTW pamphlet, *John Osborne*. London: Longmans,
Green and Co. (WTW 213), 1969. Pp. 32. Bibliography, pp.
31-32, primary books, secondary selected. Dates, places,
genres.

SECONDARY

Above, Carter, pp. 187-191; Trussler, pp. 249-252.

Shirley Jean Bailey. "John Osborne: A Bibliography," *Twentieth Century Literature* 7 (October, 1961): 118-120.

A useful list of reviews of the plays listed under title of the
play.

GENERAL

Temple & Tucker; Coleman & Tyler; Adelman & Dworkin, Salem;

OSB

Palmer & Dyson; WW 71.

OSTLERE, GORDON: see GORDON, RICHARD.

O'SULLIVAN, SEUMAS   (1878-1958)

Pseudonym of James Sullivan Starkey.

PRIMARY

Michael Joseph MacManus. "Bibliographies of Irish Authors. No. 3. Seumas O'Sullivan." *Dublin Magazine* 5 (July-September, 1930): 47-50.

Primary books. Chronological arrangement. Transcribed TP, part collation, pagination, binding, bibliographical notes.

GENERAL

Longaker & Bolles; WWW 51-60.

O'SULLIVAN, VINCENT   (1872-1940)

PRIMARY

George Sims. "Some Uncollected Authors. XV. Vincent O' Sullivan." *Book Collector* 6 (1957): 395-402.

Primary. Arranged: Books; Contributions to Books. Chronological in both sections. Transcribed TP, format, binding, date; also date of first American edition. Bibliographical notes.

OULD, HERMAN   (1885-1951)

WWW 51-60.

OWEN, ALUN DAVIES   (1926-   )

Coleman & Tyler; WW 71.

OWEN, WILFRED   (1893-1918)

PRIMARY

Joseph Cohen. ''Wilfred Owen: Fresher Fields than Flanders.''
English Literature in Transition 7 (1964): 1-7.

An important essay on the various publications of Owen's
writings.

William White. *Wilfred Owen (1893-1918): A Bibliography.*
Kent: Kent State University Press (Serif Series, 1), 1967.
Pp. 41.

Primary, secondary. Form arrangement. Books: place,
publisher, pages, contents, subsequent editions and reprints. Periods: volume, pages, date. Includes translations of Owen's poems. Reviews of primary books listed under title of book.

SECONDARY

Above, White, pp. 25-37, biography and general criticism; pp.
38-41, reviews.

GENERAL

Millett; Longaker & Bolles; Daiches; Temple & Tucker.

OXENHAM, ELSIE JEANETTE   (-1960)

WWW 51-60.

PACKER, JOY   (1905-   )
  (Lady Packer).
  WW 71; Hagen.

PAGET, VIOLET: see LEE, VERNON.

PAINTER, GEORGE DUNCAN   (1914-   )
  WW 71.

PAKENHAM, ELIZABETH: see LONGFORD, COUNTESS OF.

PALMER, HERBERT EDWARD   (1880-1961)

PRIMARY

John Gawsworth. *Ten Contemporaries. Notes Toward their
  Definitive Bibliography* [First Series]. London: Ernest Benn
  Ltd., 1932. Pp. 224.

  Pp. 141-148, primary first editions, 1918-1931. Chronological
  arrangement. Transcribed TP, full collation, pagination, binding, date, bibliographical notes; occasionally number of copies.

GENERAL

Daiches; WW 60.

PALMER, JOHN LESLIE   (1885-1944)

  Pseudonyms used: Francis Beeding, Christopher Haddon; and,
  with Hilary St. George Saunders, David Pilgrim.

PRIMARY

Hilary St. George Saunders, "John Palmer, 1885-1944, A
  Memoir." *In* David Pilgrim, *The Emperor's Servant*. London:

Macmillan and Co., 1946. Pp. 124.

Pp. ix-xxxiv, essay account of Palmer's literary activities. No actual list of writings.

GENERAL

Millett; Hagen.

PALMER, LEONARD ROBERT   (1906-   )

   WW 71.

PARGETER, EDITH   (1913-   )

   WW 71; Hagen.

PARKER, LOUIS N.   (1852-1944)

   Salem; WWW 41-50.

PARKER, THOMAS MAYNARD   (1906-   )

   WW 71.

PARKES, JAMES WILLIAM   (1896-   )

   WW 71.

PARKINSON, CYRIL NORTHCOTE   (1909-   )

   WW 71.

PAR

PARRY, SIR CHARLES HUBERT HASTINGS   (1848-1918)

   NCBEL, III, 1449.

PARTRIDGE, ERIC HONEYWOOD   (1894-   )

   WW 71.

PASCAL, ROY   (1904-   )

   WW 71.

PASSFIELD, SYDNEY WEBB, LORD: see WEBB, BEATRIX POTTER.

PAUL, CEDAR   (-   )

      Née Gertrude Mary Davenport.

   WW 71.

PAUL, LESLIE ALLEN   (1905-   )

   WW 71.

PAUL, MAURICE EDEN   (1865-1944)

   WWW 41-50.

PAYE, ROBERT : see LONG, MRS. GABRIELLE.

PAYNE, ERNEST ALEXANDER   (1902-   )

   WW 71.

PEACH, LAWRENCE DU GARDE   (1890-   )

WW 71

PEAKE, MERVYN   (1911-1968)

PRIMARY

G. A. J. Farmer. "Mervyn Peake, Book Illustrator, and a
Checklist of his Works." *Australian Library Journal* 8 (July,
1959): 134-137.

Not seen.

GENERAL

WW 69.

PEARSE, PADRAIC HENRY   (1879-1916)

PRIMARY

Patrick Sarsfield O'Hegarty. "Bibliographies of 1916 and the
Irish Revolution. I. Padraic Henry Pearse." *Dublin Magazine* 6 (July-September, 1931): 44-49.

Primary books. Chronological arrangement. Transcribed
TP, part collation, pagination, binding, bibliographical notes;
occasionally textual notes and description of contents.

PEARSON, HESKETH   (1887-1964)

PRIMARY

Hesketh Pearson by Himself. New York: Harper and Row, 1965.
Pp. xiv, 331.

P. [ii], list of primary books. Other bibliographical information in text, *passim.* Index. The British edition (London:
Heinemann, 1965. Pp. [viii], 358), includes two preliminary
chapters omitted from the American edition.

GENERAL

WW 64.

PEARSON, KARL   (1857-1936)

PRIMARY

E. S. Pearson. *Karl Pearson. An Appreciation of Some Aspects of his Life and Work.* Cambridge: University Press, 1938. Pp. viii, 170.

Pp. 127-132, selected primary bibliography. Books: place, publisher, date. Periods: volume, date, pages.

GENERAL

Batho & Dobrée; NCBEL, III, 1577.

PEROWNE, STEWART HENRY   (1901-   )

WW 71.

PETRIE, SIR CHARLES ALEXANDER   (1895-   )

WW 71.

PETRIE, SIR WILLIAM MATTHEW FLINDERS   (1853-1942)

Batho & Dobrée; WWW 41-50.

PEVSNER, SIR NIKOLAUS BERHARD LEON   (1902-   )

PRIMARY

John H. Barr. *Sir Nikolaus Pevsner: A Bibliography.* Charlottesville: University of Virginia Press (American Association of Architectural Bibliographers, Papers, Vol. VII), 1970. Pp. xi, 98.

Not seen. Praised for high standard of bibliography by *TLS*, 23 July 1971, p. 869: "exhaustive lists of [Pevsner's] books, of the reviews they were given, of his contributions to periodicals and of book reviews written by him."

GENERAL

WW 71.

PHILLIPS, JOHN BERTRAM   (1906-   )

WW 71.

PHILLIPS, STEPHEN   (1868-1915)

PRIMARY

Edward Everett Hale, Jr. *Dramatists of Today*. London: George Bell and Sons, 1906. Pp. 236.

P. 220, plays by Phillips: title, theatre and date of first performances in England, America, and on the Continent. Brief annotations.

Clara A. Milliken. "Reading List on Modern Dramatists: Stephen Phillips." *Bulletin of Bibliography* 5 (1907): 51.

Primary books. Alphabetical arrangement. Date, place, publisher, pages, format, price, précis; reviews. Secondary criticism arranged alphabetically by author: date, pages.

GENERAL

Longaker & Bolles; Batho & Dobrée; Temple & Tucker; Salem; NCBEL, III, 1194-1196.

PHILLPOTTS, EDEN   (1862-1960)

PRIMARY

Percival Hinton. *Eden Phillpotts. A Bibliography of First Editions*. Birmingham: Greville Worthington, 1931. Pp. 164. 350 copies.

Primary books, 1888-1931. Chronological arrangement. Transcribed TP, full collation, pagination, binding, number of copies, bibliographical notes. P. v, important note on periodical contributions excluded and their location; pp. x-xiii, chronological list of book titles; pp. xiv-xvi, books classified by subject matter. P. 158, books with contributions by Phillpotts: author or editor, year, title of contribution. Pp. 159-161, chronological list of American first editions. Index.

Book Collector's Quarterly, No. 5 (January-March, 1932), p. 111: "one of the best printed bibliographies ever produced."

Waveney Girvan. *Eden Phillpotts. An Assessment and a Tribute*. London: Hutchinson, 1953. Pp. 159.

Pp. 153-159, English first editions, 1888-1953. Chronological arrangement. Publisher, genre.

Girvan supplements Hinton's list of book titles, but even Hinton and Girvan together do not provide a complete primary list.

Percival F. Hinton. "Note 226. A Ghost Laid." *Book Collector* 13 (1964): 350-351.

Notes on a spurious edition.

GENERAL

Millett; Temple & Tucker; Hagen.

PHILLPOTTS, MARY ADELAIDE EDEN   (-   )
   (Mrs. Nicholas Ross).

WW 71.

PICKTHALL, MARMADUKE WILLIAM   (1875-1936)

PRIMARY

Anne Fremantle. *Loyal Enemy*. London: Hutchinson and Co.,
   1938. Pp. 448.

   A biography with many references, *passim*, to primary books
   and other writings. Index of names, only.

GENERAL

Millett.

PILGRIM, DAVID: see PALMER, JOHN LESLIE.

PILKINGTON, ROGER WINDLE   (1915-   )

WW 71.

PINE, LESLIE GILBERT   (1907-   )

WW 71.

PINERO, SIR ARTHUR WING   (1855-1934)

PRIMARY

H. Hamilton Fyfe. *Arthur Wing Pinero. Playwright. A Study*.
   London: Greening and Co., Ltd., 1902. Pp. 250.

   Pp. 232-250, plays by Pinero, 1877-1901. Title, theatre and
   date of first performance, cast. No information concerning
   publications.

Edward Everett Hale, Jr. *Dramatists of Today*. London: George Bell and Sons, 1906. Pp. 236.

Pp. 212-227, plays by Pinero, 1877-1904. Title, theatre and date of first performance in England, in America, and on the Continent. Brief annotations.

Frank K. Walter. "Reading List on Arthur Wing Pinero." *Bulletin of Bibliography* 6 (1912): 298-300.

Primary books. Alphabetical arrangement. Place, publisher, format, pages, price, précis; reviews. Secondary bibliography arranged alphabetically by author: volume, pages, date, brief annotations.

Wilbur Dwight Dunkel. *Sir Arthur Wing Pinero. A Critical Biography with Letters*. Chicago: University of Chicago Press, 1941. Pp. 142.

Pp. 137-138: cogent discussion of sources of primary and secondary bibliography.

SECONDARY

Above, Walter, Dunkel.

GENERAL

Millett; Longaker & Bolles; Batho & Dobrée; Temple & Tucker; Coleman & Tyler; Adelman & Dworkin; Salem; Palmer & Dyson; NCBEL, III, 1166-1169.

PINTER, HAROLD   (1930-   )

PRIMARY

Martin Esslin. *The Peopled Wound: The Work of Harold Pinter*. Garden City, New York: Doubleday and Co., Inc., 1970. Pp. [xii], 270.

Pp. 255-261, primary bibliography. Arranged: Plays, Other

Writings, Interviews, and Translations. Books: British and American editions, place, publisher, date (NB: p. 255, important note concerning textual changes in different editions). Periods: date. Translations listed under name of language (13 different languages listed). Pp. 262-265, secondary bibliography selected, excluding reviews. Form arrangement.

The best primary bibliography, and a basic list of secondary studies.

SECONDARY

Lois G. Gordon. "Pigeonholing Pinter: A Bibliography," *Theatre Documentation* 1 (Fall, 1968): 3-20.

Arranged in two parts: alphabetical by author list of studies, and alphabetical list of primary writings with reviews listed under each. Books: place, date. Periods: volume, pages, date. Précis of contents of each study.

An extremely helpful checklist, clearly set forth.

David S. Palmer. "A Harold Pinter Checklist." *Twentieth Century Literature* 16 (1970): 287-297.

Primary, secondary. Secondary bibliography arranged: General criticism (alphabetical by author); Reviews (under title of work criticized); Miscellaneous. Books: place, date. Periods: volume, pages, date.

GENERAL

Temple & Tucker; Coleman & Tyler; Adelman & Dworkin; Salem; Palmer & Dyson; WW 71.

PINTO, VIVIAN DE SOLA   (1895-1969)

Daiches; WW 69.

PITTER, RUTH   (1897-   )

Longaker & Bolles; Daiches; Temple & Tucker; WW 71.

PLAIDY, JEAN: see HIBBERT, ELEANOR.

PLOMER, WILLIAM CHARLES FRANKLYN   (1903-   )

Millett; Daiches; Temple & Tucker; WW 71.

PLUMB, JOHN HAROLD   (1911-   )

WW 71.

PLUNKETT, EDWARD JOHN MORETON DRAX, LORD DUNSANY:
see DUNSANY.

PLUNKETT, JOSEPH MARY   (1887-1916)

PRIMARY

Patrick Sarsfield O'Hegarty. "Bibliographies of 1916 and the
Irish Revolution. III. Joseph Mary Plunkett." *Dublin Magazine* 7 (January-March, 1932): 30.

Primary books. Chronological arrangement. Transcribed TP,
part collation, pagination, binding, bibliographical notes.

POLLARD, ALBERT FREDERICK   (1869-1948)

Batho & Dobrée; WWW 41-50.

POLLARD, ALFRED WILLIAM   (1859-1944)

PRIMARY

Gwendolyn Murphy. *A Select Bibliography of Alfred William*

Pollard, ed. H. Thomas. Oxford: For the Subscribers, 1938. Pp. 69. 260 copies.

Pp. 21-66, bibliography. Primary. Chronological arrangement. Books: part collation, publisher, place, date, annotations (mainly by Pollard). Periods: volume, pages, date; reviews by Pollard include author and title of book reviewed.

POLLARD, HENRY GRAHAM   (1903-   )

WW 71.

POPE, DUDLEY BERNARD EGERTON   (1925-   )

WW 71.

POPE-HENNESSY, JAMES   (1916-   )

WW 71.

POPE-HENNESSY, JOHN WYNDHAM   (1913-   )

WW 71.

PORTER, HAL   (1917-   )

PRIMARY

Janette Helen Finch. *Bibliography of Hal Porter.* Adelaide: Libraries Board of South Australia (Bibliographies of Australian Writers), 1966. Pp. [vii], [27].

Primary, secondary. Form arrangement. Books: place, publisher, date. Periods: volume, pages, date. Reviews listed under title of work reviewed. Includes sections on biography, unpublished primary writings, and illustrators. Index of names and titles.

SECONDARY

Above, Finch, *passim.*

GENERAL

Hetherington.

POSTGATE, RAYMOND WILLIAM   (1896-   )

WW 71; Hagen.

POTOCKI, GEOFFREY WLADISLAS VAILE   (1903-   )

?Count De Montalk.

PRIMARY

A Letter from Richard Aldington, and a Summary Bibliography of Count Potocki's Published Works. Draguignan (Var), France: Melissa Press, [1961], [1963].   Four leaves.

P. IV $_r$, primary books. Place, date (1927-1947).

Rigby Graham. "A Tentative Checklist of the Work of Geoffrey Count Potocki." *Private Libraries* 8 (1967): 23-26.

Primary writings. Chronological arrangement. Date, place, publisher, annotations.

POTTER, DENNIS CHRISTOPHER GEORGE   (1935-   )

WW 71.

POTTER, HELEN BEATRIX   (1866-1943)

(Mrs. William Heelis).

PRIMARY

Jane Quinby. *Beatrix Potter: A Bibliographical Checklist.*
New York: The Author, 1954. 250 copies.

Not seen.

Marcus Crouch. *Beatrix Potter.* London: Bodley Head
(Bodley Head Monograph), 1960. P. 19: Quinby's "work is
clearly incomplete... [but] ...it is indispensable."

Leslie Linder. *Beatrix Potter, 1866-1943, Centenary Catalogue,
1966.* London: National Book League, [1966]. Pp. 109.

Not seen.

Described in the essay by Laurie Deval, *Book Collector* 15
(1966): 454-459.

-- *A History of the Writings of Beatrix Potter including Unpublished Work.* London and New York: Frederick Warne and
Co. Ltd., 1971. Pp. xxvi, 446.

Essays on all aspects of all primary writings, published and
unpublished, arranged under headings: Letters to Children;
Peter Rabbit Books; Painting Books; Plays; Music Books;
Fairy Caravan; Sister Anne; Wag-by-Wall; Tale of the Faith-
ful Dove; Miscellaneous Writings including journalism and
election work. Appendices provide tabulated information for
books and illustrations, including part collation, date, number
of copies in first edition, price. Lavish illustrations, many
of MSS here first reproduced. Text of many writings also provided. Index.

TLS, No. 3610 (7 May 1971): 535: "a most detailed and careful examination of the provenance of Beatrix Potter's written
work, and a valauble contribution to the bibliography of her
published books...With the publication of this massive com-
pilation, Beatrix Potter becomes almost the best documented
writer of the century."

POTTER, SIMEON   (1898-   )

WW 71.

POTTER, STEPHEN   (1900-1969)

Daiches; Temple & Tucker; WW 69.

POWELL, ANTHONY DYMOKE   (1905-   )

PRIMARY

Bernard Bergonzi. *L. P. Hartley and Anthony Powell.* London: Longmans, Green and Co. (WTW 144), 1962. Pp. 40.

P. 40, bibliography of primary books, first editions. Date, genre. Brief secondary bibliography.

GENERAL

Daiches; Temple & Tucker; WW 71.

POWELL, JOHN ENOCH   (1912-   )

WW 71.

POWER, WILLIAM   (1873-1951)

WWW 51-60.

POWICKE, SIR FREDERICK MAURICE   (1879-1963)

WW 63.

POWYS, JOHN COWPER   (1872-1963)

PRIMARY

Lloyd Emerson Siberell. *A Bibliography of the First Editions of John Cowper Powys.* Cincinnatti: Ailanthus Press, 1934. Pp. 53. 350 copies.

Primary first editions. Form arrangement. Transcribed TP, part collation, pagination, binding, date, bibliographical notes. P. 49, titles of books with introductions by Powys. Pp. 50-52, articles by Powys: chronological arrangement. Dates; poems are identified.

R. C. Churchill. *The Powys Brothers*. London: Longmans, Green and Co. (WTW 150), 1962. Pp. 40.

Pp. 32-34, primary books. Date, place, genre, miscellaneous notes.

Derek Langbridge. *John Cowper Powys. A Record of Achievement*. London: Library Association, 1966. Pp. 256.

Pp. 74-229, bibliography. Primary, secondary. Chronological arrangement, with works by Powys on verso (books: place, publisher, date, pages, quotations; and periods: volume, date, pages), and on the facing recto, reviews of, comments about, and reprints of Powys. Pp. 233-256, indices.

An accurate and virtually complete list, arranged so eccentrically as to prevent one's using it (see comments of R. J. Roberts, *Book Collector* 17 [1968]: 103).

Arthur J. Anderson. "John Cowper Powys: A Bibliography." *Bulletin of Bibliography* 25 (1967): 73-78, 94.

Primary, secondary selected. Chronological arrangement in both parts. Books: place, publisher, date. Periods: volume, date, pages. Excludes reviews of Powys.

Less informative than Langbridge, but much simpler to use.

SECONDARY

Above, Churchill, pp. 39-40; Langridge, *passim*; Anderson, pp. 77-78, 94.

GENERAL

Millett; Daiches; Longaker & Bolles; Temple & Tucker.

POWYS, LLEWELLYN   (1884-1939)

PRIMARY

A Catalogue of the Llewellyn Powys Manuscripts. Hurst, Berks,
G. F. Sims (Rare Books), n.d. [ca. 1953].

200 plus items in this bookseller's catalogue.

Kenneth Hopkins, ed. *Llewellyn Powys.* New York: Horizon
Press, 1961. Pp. 318.

Pp. 311-316, "A Check List of Books by Llewellyn Powys."
Publisher, place, date, short description of contents. Sep-
arate entry for each edition. Pp. 317-318, books relating to
Powys.

R. C. Churchill. *The Powys Brothers.* London: Longmans,
Green and Co. (WTW 150), 1962. Pp. 40.

Pp. 34-36, primary books. Date, place, genre, miscellaneous
notes.

SECONDARY

Above, Hopkins, pp. 317-318; Churchill, pp. 39-40.

GENERAL

Millett; Daiches; Longaker & Bolles.

POWYS, THEODORE FRANCIS   (1875-1953)

PRIMARY

Henry Coombes. *Theodore Francis Powys.* London: Barrie
and Rockliff, 1960. Pp. 173.

Pp. 167-169, primary books. Place, publisher, date.

R. C. Churchill. *The Powys Brothers*. London: Longmans, Green and Co. (WTW 150), 1962. Pp. 40.

Pp. 36-38, primary books. Date, place, genre, miscellaneous notes.

Peter Riley. *A Bibliography of Theodore Francis Powys*. Hastings: R. A. Brimmell, 1967. Pp. 72.

Primary first editions, secondary selected. Form arrangement. Transcribed TP, full collation, pagination, binding, date, price, list of later editions, contents, bibliographical and textual notes. Includes lists of uncollected contributions to periodicals and anthologies. Pp. 68-69, literary studies of Powys, excluding reviews.

The standard bibliography. R. J. Roberts, *Book Collector* 17 (1968): 103: "virtues of orthodoxy...sensible and competent."

SECONDARY

Above, Riley, pp. 68-69.

GENERAL

Millett; Longaker & Bolles; Daiches; Temple & Tucker.

PREEDY, GEORGE R.: see LONG, MRS. GABRIELLE.

PRESCOTT, HILDA FRANCES MARGARET   (1896-   )

WW 71; Hagen.

PRESLAND, JOHN   (-   )

(Mrs. Gladys Bendit).
WW 71.

PRESS, JOHN BRYANT   (1920-   )

WW 71.

PRICHARD, KATHARINE SUSANNAH   (1883-[deceased])

(Mrs. H. V. H. Throssell).

PRIMARY

Katharine S. Prichard. *Child of the Hurricane. An Autobiography*. London: Angus and Robertson, 1964. Pp. 266.

P. [ii], list of primary books. Genre arrangement. Dates. Bibliographical information in text, *passim*.

Henrietta Frances York Drake-Brockman. *Katherine S. Prichard*. Melbourne: Oxford University Press (AWTW), 1967. Pp. 56.

Pp. 55-56, bibliography. Primary books, secondary selected. Genre arrangement. Books: place, publisher, date. Period: volume, date.

SECONDARY

Above, Drake-Brockman, p. 56.

GENERAL

Millett; Hetherington; WW 70.

PRIESTLEY, JOHN BOYNTON   (1894-   )

PRIMARY

Ivor Brown. *J. B. Priestley*. London: Longmans, Green and Co.

(WTW 84), 1957. Pp. 39.

Pp. 35-39, bibliography of primary books. Genre arrangement. Date, occasionally contents.

Ladislaus Löb. *Mensch und Gesellschaft bei J. B. Priestley.* Bern: Francke Verlag (Schweizer Anglistische Arbeiten 53), 1962. Pp. [iv], 222.

Pp. 215-220, bibliography of primary books, first editions. Genre arrangement. Place, publisher, date. Pp. 220-221, secondary bibliography, excluding reviews.

Lucetta J. Teagarden. "The J. B. Priestley Collection" [at the University of Texas]. *Library Chronicle of the University of Texas 7*, iii (1963): 27-32.

A descriptive essay of this extensive collection. Reference is made here to the following bibliographies (not seen):

A. E. Day. "J. B. Priestley: An Interim Bibliography." Unpublished typescript. Copy in University of Texas Library.

Lucetta J. Teagarden. *J. B. Priestley. An Exhibition of Books and Manuscripts.* Austin: University of Texas, 1963. Pp. 34. 1500 copies.

Described as "a selective descriptive list, not a complete bibliography" (p. 27).

SECONDARY

Above, Löb, pp. 220-221.

Gareth L. Evans. *J. B. Priestley--The Dramatist.* London: Heinemann, 1964. Pp. 230.

Pp. 226-227, secondary bibliography.

GENERAL

Millett; Longaker & Bolles; Daiches; Temple & Tucker; Coleman

& Tyler; Adelman & Dworkin; Salem; Palmer & Dyson; WW 71.

PRINCE, FRANK TEMPLETON   (1912-   )

Daiches; Temple & Tucker; WW 71.

PRINGLE-PATTISON, ANDREW SETH: see SETH, ANDREW.

PRITCHETT, VICTOR SAWDON   (1900-   )

Daiches; Temple & Tucker; WW 71.

PRITT, DENIS NOWELL   (1887-   )

WW 71.

PUDNEY, JOHN SLEIGH   (1909-   )

Longaker & Bolles; Temple & Tucker; WW 71.

PUGH, EDWIN   (1874-1930)

PRIMARY

Theophilus E. M. Boll. *The Works of Edwin Pugh (1874-1930)*.
Philadelphia: University of Pennsylvania Dissertation, 1934.
Pp. 104.

P. [97], bibliography. Primary books, English editions.
Genre arrangement. Publisher, date, reprints.

Vincent Brome. *Four Realist Novelists*. London: Longmans,
Green and Co. (WTW 183), 1965. Pp. 36.

Pp. 33-34, primary books. Date, place, genre.

QUENNELL, PETER COURTNEY   (1905-   )

Millett; Daiches; Temple & Tucker; WW 71.

QUILLER-COUCH, SIR ARTHUR THOMAS   (1863-1944)

PRIMARY

"Bibliographies of Modern Authors. Sir Arthur Thomas Quiller-Couch." *London Mercury* 4 (1921): 532-533.

Primary books, 1881-1920. Chronological arrangement. Publisher, year, brief notes.

Fred Brittain. *Arthur Quiller-Couch. A Biographical Study of Q.* Cambridge: University Press, 1947. Pp. 174.

Pp. 159-166, "Chronological List of Q's Publications, including a selection from his contributions to periodical . literature." Books: date, genre. Periods: date. Also mention of Q's contributions to books.

GENERAL

Millett; Longaker & Bolles; Batho & Dobrée; Temple & Tucker; NCBEL, III, 1071-1073.

QUIRK, CHARLES RANDOLPH   (1920-   )

WW 71.

RACKHAM, ARTHUR   (1867-1939)

PRIMARY

Frederick Coykendall. *Arthur Rackham. A List of Books Illustrated by Him.* New York: Privately Printed, 1922. Pp. 22. 175 copies.

Pp. 15-22, list of titles with author, date, place, publisher.

Sarah Briggs Latimore and Grace Clark Haskell. *Arthur Rackham A Bibliography.* Los Angeles: Suttonhouse, 1936. Pp. 112. 550 copies. Reprinted: New York: Burt Franklin, 1970.

Primary bibliography. Form arrangement. Books: Transcribed TP, binding, description of Rackham's illustration, bibliographical notes. Periods: date, author and title of work illustrated, description of illustrations.

Roland Baughman, *Book Collector* 10 (Summer, 1961):236: "the definitive bibliography of Rackham..." But see Dorothy Colman's review in *Reading and Collecting* 1 (December, 1936): 11, 24, for corrections of errors and numerous additional items.

Bertram Rota, "The Printed Work of Arthur Rackham," in Derek Hudson, *Arthur Rackham.* London: William Heinemann Ltd.; New York: Charles Scribner's Sons, 1960 [also available as separate offprint]. Pp. 181.

Pp. 164-181, bibliography. A simplified listing of all items in Latimore and Haskell, with a number of additional items.

Latimore and Haskell provide the most details, while Rota must be checked for his complete list of illustrations.

RAFFALOVICH, MARK ANDRÉ   (1864-1934)

PRIMARY

Father Brocard Sewell, ed. *Two Friends, John Gray and André Raffalovich. Essays Biographical and Critical.* Aylesford: St. Albert's Press, 1963. Pp. 193.

Pp. 188-189, "Checklist of Raffalovich," by Alan Anderson. Primary. Form, place, publisher, date. Secondary bibliography in text, *passim*.

RAINE, KATHLEEN JESSIE   (1908-   )

Daiches; Temple & Tucker; WW 71.

RALEIGH, SIR WALTER ALEXANDER   (1861-1922)

PRIMARY

Lady Raleigh, ed. *The Letters of Sir Walter Raleigh (1879-1922)*. London: Methuen and Co., Ltd., 1926. 2nd edition enlarged. Two volumes.

II, 557-562, primary bibliography of books and contributions to books and periodicals, excluding reviews by Sir Walter. Chronological arrangement. Books: publisher, date. Period: date.

GENERAL

Batho & Dobrée; NCBEL, III, 1449-1450.

RAMSAY, SIR WILLIAM MITCHELL   (1851-1939)

Batho & Dobrée; WWW 29-40; NCBEL, III, 1614.

RANSOME, ARTHUR MICHELL   (1884-1967)

PRIMARY

Anthony Rota. "Some Uncollected Authors. XXI. Arthur Ransome." *Book Collector* 8 (1959): 289-293.

Primary first editions. Publisher, date, format, binding. Occasional miscellaneous notes.

Hugh Shelley. *Arthur Ransome*. London: Bodley Head (Bodley Head Monograph), 1960. Pp. 72.

Pp. 71-72, primary bibliography. Books: dates. Books translated by, edited by, or with contributions by Ransome (''not exhaustive''): main author or editor, date, identification of Ransome's contribution.

RATTIGAN, TERENCE MERVYN   (1911-   )

Daiches; Temple & Tucker; Coleman & Tyler; Adelman & Dworkin; Salem; Palmer & Dyson; WW 71.

RAVEN, SIMON ARTHUR NOEL   (1927-   )

WW 71; Hagen.

RAY, CYRIL   (1908-   )

WW 71.

RAYMOND, ERNEST   (1888-   )

WW 71; Hagen.

READ, SIR HERBERT EDWARD   (1893-1968)

PRIMARY

Francis Berry. *Herbert Read*. London: Longmans, Green and Co. (WTW 45), 1961. Pp. 43.

Pp. 41-43, bibliography of primary books. Place, date, genre.

Henry Treece, ed. *Herbert Read: An Introduction to his Work by Various Hands*. London: Faber and Faber, 1944. Pp. 120.

Pp. 116-120, bibliography of primary books, first editions. Chronological arrangement. Transcribed TP, place, publisher, date, size in inches.

Robin Skelton, ed. *Herbert Read: A Memorial Synposium.*
London: Methuen and Co., Ltd., 1970. Pp. 264.

Pp. 192-258, ''A Checklist of the Herbert Read Archive in
the McPherson Library of the University of Victoria'' [based
upon Read's private papers], by Howard Gerwing. Primary.
Form arrangement. Books, arranged alphabetically by title:
place, publisher, date, pages, contents, subsequent editions,
miscellaneous notes. Lists of unique typescripts and manuscripts by Read with suggestions concerning place of publication; lists of letters to Read (with name of writer, number
of letters, holograph or type) and by him.

Not the definitive bibliography, but with Treece (above) the
start toward it.

GENERAL

Millett; Daiches; Longaker & Bolles; Temple & Tucker.

REED, DOUGLAS   (1895-   )

WW 71.

REED, HENRY   (1914-   )

WW 71.

REEVES, JAMES   (1909-   )

WW 71.

REID, FORREST   (1875-1947)

PRIMARY

Russell Burlingham. *Forrest Reid A Portrait and a Study.*
London: Faber and Faber, 1953. Pp. 259.

Pp. 227-250, primary, secondary bibliography. Form arrangement. Books: date, place, publisher, part collation, dedication,
price, binding, contents listed with details of previous publication. Bibliographical and textual notes include references
to reprints. Periods: volume, pages, dates, title of book in
which reprinted. Pp. 249-250, secondary bibliography.

*Forrest Reid. An Exhibition of Books and Manuscripts held in
the Museum and Art Gallery, Belfast.* September, 1953. City
and County Borough of Belfast, 1954. Pp. xxxv. 200 copies.

Checklist of Reid's printed work in this collection. Arranged:
Books; Contributions to Books and Periodicals; Letters;
Other Items. Locates Reid's manuscripts and letters.

SECONDARY

Above, Burlingham, pp. 249-250.

GENERAL

Daiches; Temple & Tucker.

REITLINGER, GERALD ROBERTS   (1900-   )

WW 71.

RENAULT, MARY   (1905-   )

Pseudonym of Mary Challans.

PRIMARY

Peter Wolfe. *Mary Renault.* New York: Twayne Publishers,
Inc. (TEAS 98), 1969. Pp. 198.

Pp. 193-194, "Selected Bibliography." Primary, secondary.
Books: place, publisher, date. Periods: volume, date, pages.
Additional secondary criticism in text, *passim.*

GENERAL

WW 71.

RHYS, KEIDRYCH   (1915-   )

WW 71.

RICHARDS, DENIS GEORGE   (1910-   )

WW 71.

RICHARDS, IVOR ARMSTRONG   (1893-   )

PRIMARY

Jerome P. Schiller. *I. A. Richards' Theory of Literature.* New
  Haven and London: Yale University Press, 1969. Pp. [xiv],
  189.

Pp. 177-180, primary bibliography. Form arrangement, alphabetical by title in each section. Books: place, publisher,
  date. Periods: volume, date, pages. Pp. 180-184, secondary
  bibliography. Form arrangement, alphabetical by author in
  each section. Information as for primary.

SECONDARY

Above, Schiller, pp. 180-184.

GENERAL

Millett; Daiches; Temple & Tucker; WW 71.

RICHARDSON, DOROTHY MILLER   (1882-1957)

(Mrs. Alan Odle).

PRIMARY

John Gawsworth. *Ten Contemporaries. Notes Toward their Definitive Bibliography (Second Series)*. London: Joiner and Steele, 1933. Pp. 240. 1000 copies.

Pp. 199-207, primary books, first editions, 1913-1932. Chronological arrangement. Transcribed TP, full collation, pagination, binding, occasional bibliographical notes. Includes books translated by Richardson.

Joseph Prescott, "A Preliminary Checklist of the Periodical Publications of Dorothy M. Richardson" in A. Dayle Wallace and Woodburn O. Ross, eds. *Studies in Honor of John Wilcox*. Detroit: Wayne State University Press, 1958. Pp. xiv, 269.

Pp. 219-225, primary periodical contributions. Chronological arrangement. Volume, date, pages, genre.

Caesar R. Blake. *Dorothy Richardson*. Ann Arbor: University of Michigan Press, 1960. Pp. 208.

Pp. 201-202, primary selected bibliography. Books: place, publisher, date. Periods: volume, pages, date. Pp. 202-207, secondary bibliography.

Gloria Glikin. "Checklist of Writings by Dorothy M. Richardson." *English Literature in Transition* 8 (1965): 1-11.

Primary. Genre arrangement. Books: place, publisher, date, notes on later editions and reprints. Periods: volume, pages, date.

The most complete primary bibliography.

SECONDARY

Above, Blake, pp. 202-207.

Gloria Glikin. "Dorothy M. Richardson: An Annotated Bibliography of Writings about Her." *English Literature in Transition* 8 (1965): 12-35; 14 (1971): 84-88.

ING

Alphabetical by author arrangement; annotated.

GENERAL

Millett; Longaker & Bolles; Daiches; Temple & Tucker.

RICHARDSON, HENRY HANDEL   (1870-1946)

Pseudonym of Mrs. J. G. Robertson, née Henrietta Ethel Florence Lindesay Richardson.

PRIMARY

Maria S. Haynes. "Henry Handel Richardson (Mrs. John G. Robertson)." *Bulletin of Bibliography* 21 (1955): 130-135.

Primary, secondary. Form and genre arrangement. Primary books: place, publisher, date, reprints, subsequent editions and translations with name of tramslator. Reviews and critical writings listed under each book title; many annotations for the secondary material. Primary periodicals: date, details of reprinting. Primary divisions include original songs and translations by Richardson. Secondary books: place, publisher, date, pages. Secondary periodicals: date, pages. Secondary divisions include general references, biographical references, and dissertations. P. 135, list of MSS in National Library, Canberra.

The most complete primary bibliography.

SECONDARY

Above, Haynes, *passim.*

Verna D. Wittrock. "Henry Handel Richardson: An Annotated Bibliography of Writings about Her," *English Literature in Transition* 7 (1964): 146-187.

The most complete secondary bibliography.

GENERAL

Daiches; Millett.

RICHARDSON, JOANNA   (-   )

WW 71.

RICKWORD, JOHN EDGELL   (1898-   )

Millett; Temple & Tucker.

RIDGE, WILLIAM PETT   (1860-1930)

PRIMARY

Vincent Brome. *Four Realist Novelists*. London: Longmans, Green and Co. (WTW 183), 1956. Pp. 36.

> Pp. 35-36, bibliography. Primary books. Chronological arrangement. Date, place, genre. P. 36, brief secondary bibliography.

SECONDARY

Above, Brome, p. 36.

GENERAL

Millett; Batho & Dobrée.

RIDLER, ANNE BARBARA BRADBY   (1912-   )

(Mrs. Vivian Ridler).

Daiches; Temple & Tucker; WW 71.

RIEU, EMILE VICTOR   (1887-   )

WW 71.

RITCHIE-CALDER, PETER RITCHIE, LORD RITCHIE-CALDER
(1906-   )

WW 71.

ROBERTS, CARL ERIC BECHHOFER   (1894-1949)

Pseudonym used: Ephesian.

WWW 41-50.

ROBERTS, CECIL EDRIC MORNINGTON   (1892-   )

WW 71.

ROBERTS, SIR CHARLES GEORGE DOUGLAS   (1860-1943)

PRIMARY

James Cappon. *Charles George Douglas Roberts*. Toronto:
Ryerson Press (Makers of Canadian Literature Series), 1925.
Pp. 148.

Pp. 127-148, bibliography. Primary books. Genre arrangement. Place, publisher, date, part collation, binding. Miscellaneous notes include mention of later editions and reprints. Pp. 142-144, secondary bibliography.

E. M. Pomeroy. *Sir Charles George Douglas Roberts. A Biography*. Toronto: Ryerson Press, 1943. Pp. 371.

Pp. 359-364, bibliography. Primary books. Genre arrangement. Date, place, publisher. Details for English, Canadian,
and American editions.

SECONDARY

Above, Cappon, pp. 142-144.

Millett.

ROBERTS, MICHAEL   (1902-1949)

PRIMARY

T. W. Eason and R. Hamilton. *A Portrait of Michael Roberts*.
Chelsea: College of S. Mark and S. John, 1949. Pp. 72.

    Pp. 65-72, "Select Bibliography of the Published Writings
of Michael Roberts," by R. Hamilton. Primary first editions.
Genre arrangement. Books: publisher, date. Periods: volume, pages. Reviews by Roberts include title and author of
book reviewed. P. 65, important note on limitations of bibliography.

Michael Roberts. *Collected Poems*. With Introductory Memoir
by Janet Roberts. London: Faber and Faber, 1958. Pp. 226.

    Bibliographical information additional to Hamilton (above) is
given on pp. 7-8, 13-40.

GENERAL

Daiches; Temple & Tucker.

ROBERTS, MORLEY CHARLES   (1857-1942)

PRIMARY

Storm Jameson. "Morley Roberts: The Last of the True Victorians." *Library Chronicle* (University of Pennsylvania)
27 (1961): 93-127.

    A biographical appreciation, followed on pp. 124-125 by
"Check-List" of primary books. Genre arrangement. Title
and date. Pp. 125-127, description and location by Jameson
and T. E. M. Boll of primary and secondary MSS, letters, .

and association items.

GENERAL

Millett; WWW 41-50.

ROBERTSON, EDITH ANNE   (1883-   )

WW 71.

ROBERTSON, JOHN MACKINNON   (1856-1933)

NCBEL, III, 1450-1451.

ROBINSON, ESMÉ STUART LENNOX   (1886-1958)

PRIMARY

Kaspar Spinner. *Die Alte Dame Sagt: Nein! Drei Irische Drama-tiker. Lennox Robinson. Sean O'Casey. Denis Johnston.* Bern: Francke Verlag (Schweizer Anglistische Arbeiten 52), 1961. Pp. 210.

Pp. 207-208, bibliography of primary books. Genre arrangement. Publisher, date; date of first performance for plays.

Michael J. O'Neill. *Lennox Robinson.* New York: Twayne Publishers, Inc. (TEAS 9), 1964. Pp. 192.

Pp. [15]-[21], chronological table includes primary books and plays: date, theatre of first performance or publisher. Pp. 181-184, annotated secondary bibliography arranged alphabetically by author. Books: place, publisher, date. Periods: volume, pages, date.

SECONDARY

Above, O'Neill, pp. 181-184.

GENERAL

Millett; Longaker & Bolles; Temple & Tucker; Salem; NCBEL, III, 1943.

ROBINSON, JOHN ARTHUR THOMAS   (1919-   )

WW 71.

RODGERS, WILLIAM ROBERT   (1909-1969)

PRIMARY

Darcy O'Brien. *W. R. Rodgers (1909-1969)*. Lewisburg: Bucknell University Press (Irish Writers Series), 1970. Pp. 103.

P. 103, primary books, British and American first editions. Place, publisher, date, other information concerning unpublished primary writings. Also see "Chronology," pp. 11-12, and text, *passim*, for suggestions of primary periodical contributions and secondary bibliography.

GENERAL

Daiches; Temple & Tucker.

ROLFE, FREDERICK WILLIAM   (1860-1913)

?Baron Corvo.

PRIMARY

George Frederick Sims. *A Catalogue of Letters, Manuscript Papers and Books of Frederick Rolfe* (Baron Corvo). Harrow: Sims (Booksellers), 1949. Pp. 24. 600 copies.

Extensive descriptions of 88 items.

Cecil Woolf. *A Bibliography of Frederick Rolfe Baron Corvo.*

London: Rupert Hart-Davis (Soho Bibliography No. 7), 1957. Pp. 136. Revised edition, 1970. Pp. 196. [Not seen].

Primary. Form arrangement. Transcribed TP, part collation, pagination, binding, date, all British and foreign editions; extensive bibliographical and textual notes. Books with contributions by Rolfe described like first editions. Periods: date, pages, notes. Chronology of Rolfe's writings. Index.

The authoritative bibliography praised by all reviewers.

Cecil Woolf and Timothy d'Arch Smith. *Frederick William Rolfe, Baron Corvo. A Catalogue.* Marylebone Central Public Library Exhibition, October 19 - November 12, 1960. Seven mimeographed sheets (eleven sides).

Catalogue of the Centenary exhibition, listing many association items.

Cecil Woolf. *A Corvo Library.* London: C. Woolf, 1965. Pp. 23.

Detailed description of Rabbi Bertram Korn's collection offered for sale by Woolf.

SECONDARY

Above, Woolf and Smith.

Robert John Bayer. "About Rolfe." *Reading and Collecting* 1 (February, 1937): 6.

Books and periodicals about Rolfe. Place, Date. Brief annotations.

GENERAL

Batho & Dobrée; Temple & Tucker.

ROLLESTON, THOMAS WILLIAM HAZEN   (1857-1920)

NCBEL, III, 1909.

ROLT, LIONEL THOMAS CASWALL   (1910-   )

WW 71.

ROS, AMANDA MCKITTRICK   (1861-1939)

PRIMARY

Jack Loudan. *O Rare Amanda! The Life of Amanda McKittrick Ros*. London: Chatto and Windus, 1954. Pp. 200.

Pp. 195-200, bibliography by T. Stanley Mercer. Primary books. Chronological arrangement. Transcribed TP, part collation, binding, date, variant bindings, bibliographical notes, subsequent editions.

ROSE, CHRISTINE BROOKE-   (1923-   )

(Mrs. Jerzy Peterkiewicz).

Temple & Tucker; Bufkin; WW 71.

ROSENBERG, ISAAC   (1890-1918)

PRIMARY

Gordon Bottomley and Denys Harding, eds. *The Collected Poems of Isaac Rosenberg*. London: Chatto and Windus, 1949. Pp. 240.

Pp. 1-2, description of primary books: date, publisher, place, pages. Important omissions and errors in this volume are listed by Joseph Cohen, "Isaac Rosenberg: The Poet's Progress in Print." *English Literature in Transition* 6 (1963), 142-146.

Jon Silkin and Maurice de Sausmarez, eds. *Isaac Rosenberg, 1890-1918. A Catalogue of an Exhibition held at Leeds University May-June, 1959, together with the text of unpublished material.* Leeds: University of Leeds with Partridge Press, 1959. Pp. 36.

Best checklist of Rosenberg's writings and other artistic activities. Arranged: pp. 4-20, texts of unpublished writings; pp. 21-23, poetry MSS; p. 24, MSS letters; p. 25, printed works; pp. 26-27, association material; pp. 28-36, paintings and drawings by Rosenberg.

GENERAL

Longaker & Bolles; Daiches; Temple & Tucker.

ROSS, ALAN   (1922-   )

Temple & Tucker; WW 71.

ROSS, MARTIN: see SOMERVILLE, EDITH ANNA ŒNONE.

ROSS, SIR RONALD   (1857-1932)

PRIMARY

Rodolphe L. Mégroz. *Ronald Ross, Discoverer and Creator.* London: Allen and Unwin, 1931. Pp. 282.

Pp. 263-273, bibliography. Arranged: Medical; Related Material by Others; Mathematics; Literature. Books: publisher, place, date, brief annotations.

John Gawsworth. *Ten Contemporaries. Notes Toward their Definitive Bibliography* [First Series]. London: Benn, 1931. Pp. 224.

Pp. 158-165, "The Literary Work of Sir Ronald Ross." Primary first editions, selected, 1883-1928. Chronological arrangement. Transcribed TP, full collation, pagination, binding, date, bibliographical and textual notes.

ROTHA, PAUL   (1907-   )

WW 71.

ROTHENSTEIN, SIR JOHN KNEWSTUB MAURICE   (1901-   )

WW 71.

ROWSE, ARTHUR LESLIE   (1903-   )

Daiches; Temple & Tucker; WW 71.

ROYDE-SMITH, NAOMI GWLADYS   (-1964)

(Mrs. Ernest Milton).

Millett; Temple & Tucker; WW 64; Hagen.

RUHEN, OLAF   (1911-   )

Hetherington.

RUSSELL, BERTRAND ARTHUR WILLIAM, LORD RUSSELL
(1872-1970)

PRIMARY

Gertrude Jacob. "Bertrand Russell. An Essay toward a Bibliography." *Bulletin of Bibliography* 13 (1929): 198-199; 14 (1930); 28-30.

Primary, secondary selected. Form and subject arrangement. Books: place, publisher, date, pages, brief annotations.

Periods: volume, date, pages. Reviews by Russell include title and author of book reviewed. Pp. 29-30, secondary bibliography. Continued by Ruja (below).

Harry Ruja. "Bertrand Russell. A Classified Bibliography, 1929-1967." *Bulletin of Bibliography* 25 (1968): 182-190, 192; 26 (1969): 29-32.

Information and arrangement as in Jacob (above), except that reviews of Russell's books are included in the primary title entry.

Lester E. Denonn. "Bibliography of the Writings of Bertrand Russell to 1962" in Paul Arthur Schilp, ed., *The Philosophy of Bertrand Russell*. New York: Harper and Row (Harper Torchbooks, The Academy Library), 1963. Two volumes.

II, 746-825, bibliography. Pp. 746-789, writings to 1944; pp. 790-811, writings 1944-1962; pp. 812-825, addenda and revisions. Primary. Chronological arrangement. Books: publisher, place, date, pages, contents, reprints and subsequent editions. Periods: volume, pages, date. Reviews by Russell include author and title of book reviewed.

Jacob, Ruja, and Denonn together provide a complete list of the primary writings to 1967; there appears to be no complete list for the last three years of Russell's life.

SECONDARY

Above, Jacob, pp. 29-30; Ruja, *passim*.

Alan Dorward. *Bertrand Russell. A Short Guide to his Philosophy*. London: Longmans, Green and Co. (Supplement to British Book News No. 10), 1951. Pp. 44.

P. 40, books about Russell.

GENERAL

Millett; Daiches; Batho & Dobrée; Temple & Tucker; WW 70.

RUSSELL, GEORGE WILLIAM (Æ) (1867-1935)

PRIMARY

Alan Denson. *Printed Writings by George William Russell (Æ) A Bibliography with some notes on his pictures and portraits.* Evanston, Illinois: Northwestern University Press, 1961. Pp. [256], plus additional 4 pp. "Corrigenda and Addenda" (issued separately).

Primary, secondary selected. Form arrangement. Primary books: transcribed TP, part collation, pagination, binding, date, price, variants and reprints, occasionally number of copies and contents with details of earlier publication; numerous notes, especially in reference to specific copies. Periodicals arranged alphabetically by title, Russell's contribution being listed chronologically under each title: volume, pages, date, various notes. Divisions of material include: Letters and MSS; Oral Evidence to Parliamentary Committees; Public Sales; Books Dedicated to Æ; Portraits by Æ; Printed Reproductions; and others. Also essays concerning Æ; chronology of his life; chronology of main publications; index.

M. O. N. Walsh, *Irish Book* 2 (Spring, 1963): 63-64: "There can be no doubting Mr. Denson's accuracy and comprehensiveness..."

SECONDARY

Above, Denson, pp. 182-205.

GENERAL

Millett; Longaker & Bolles; Temple & Tucker; NCBEL, III, 1912-1916.

RYAN, WILLIAM PATRICK (1867-1942)

PRIMARY

Patrick Sarsfield O'Hegarty. "Obituary." *Dublin Magazine*
18 (July-September, 1943): 72-73.

P. 73, primary books. Chronological arrangement. Date.

SACKVILLE-WEST, EDWARD CHARLES, LORD SACKVILLE
(1901-1965)

Millett; Daiches; Temple & Tucker; WW 65.

SACKVILLE-WEST, VICTORIA MARY   (1892-1962)

(Lady Nicolson).

PRIMARY

Florence Boochever. "A Selected List of Writings by and
about Victoria Sackville-West." *Bulletin of Bibliography*
16 (1938): 93-94, 113-115.

Primary first editions (either British or American, but not
both), secondary selected. Genre arrangement. Books:
place, publisher, date, pages, précis. Periods: volume,
pages, date, précis. P. 115, secondary bibliography.

An incomplete list. There appears to be no published
list of the primary writings, 1938-1962.

GENERAL

Millett; Longaker & Bolles; Daiches; Temple & Tucker.

SADLEIR, MICHAEL THOMAS HARVEY   (1888-1957)

PRIMARY

Simon Nowell-Smith. "Michael Sadleir A Handlist," *Library,*

5th Series, 13 (June, 1958): 132-138.

Primary selected. Two chronological sections: works wholly by Sadleir; selected list of his contributions to books and periodicals, including unsigned reviews by him in the *TLS*. British first and revised editions only (unless American edition is first). Books: date, brief identification or note on con-tents, occasionally place and publisher. Periods: dates. Reviews by Sadleir include title and author of book reviewed.

GENERAL

Daiches; WWW 51-60.

SAINTSBURY, GEORGE EDWARD BATEMAN   (1845-1933)

PRIMARY

John W. Oliver, ed. *George Saintsbury. A Last Vintage.* London: Methuen and Co., Ltd., 1950. Pp. 255.

Pp. 244-255, "A Saintsbury Bibliography," by W. M. Parker. Primary books. Arranged: Literary Histories; Biographical and Critical Works; Miscellaneous (including Translations); Introductions; Prefaces; Edited Matter. Publisher, date, occasional notes concerning reprints.

Leuba (below), p. 120: "a fairly complete check list."

Walter Leuba. *George Saintsbury.* New York: Twayne Publishers, Inc. (TEAS 56), 1967. Pp. 129.

Pp. 120-122, primary books and pamphlets (51). Chrono-logical arrangement. Place, publisher, date. Pp. 122-126, annotated secondary bibliography. Alphabetical by author. Books: as for primary. Periods: volume, date, pages. Additional primary and secondary references in notes, pp. 105-119. P. 120, evaluation of previous bibliographies.

SECONDARY

Above, Leuba, pp. 105-119, 122-126.

GENERAL

Longaker & Bolles; Batho & Dobrée; Temple & Tucker; NCBEL, III, 1451-1453.

SAKI: see MUNRO, HECTOR HUGH.

SALMON, ARTHUR LESLIE   (1865-[deceased])

PRIMARY

Arthur Leslie Salmon. London: Ernest Benn Ltd. (Augustan Books of Poetry), 1932. Pp. 32.

P. 31, bibliography of primary books. Genre arrangement. Publisher, date, price.

SANSOM, WILLIAM   (1912-   )

Daiches; WW 71.

SAPPER   (1888-1937)

Pseudonym of Herman Cyril McNeile.

PRIMARY

Richard Usborne. *Clubland Heroes.* London: Constable, 1953. Pp. 217.

Some details of the primary writings can be obtained from pp. 143-202.

GENERAL

WWW 29-40; Hagen.

SASSOON, SIEGFRIED LORAINE (1886-1967)

PRIMARY

Geoffrey Keynes. *A Bibliography of Siegfried Sassoon*. London : Rupert Hart-Davis (Soho Bibliography No. 10), 1962. Pp. [200].

Primary complete. Form arrangement. Books: transcribed TP, full collation, pagination, binding, date, price, subsequent editions, translations, reprints, contents, number of copies, full notes. Periods: volume, pages, date, references to later publication. Reviews by Sassoon include title and author of book reviewed. Indices of titles and of first lines locate all publications of individual pieces. Includes many unsigned and pseudonymous writings by Sassoon.

R. J. Roberts, *Book Collector* 11 (1962): 518: "a definitive bibliography"; offers corrections and additions.

David Farmer. "Addenda to Keyne's *Bibliography of Siegfried Sassoon*." *Papers of the Bibliographical Society of America* 63 (1969): 310-317.

Important additions and corrections.

SECONDARY

Michael Thorpe. *Siegfried Sassoon. A Critical Study*. Leiden: Leiden University Press; London: Oxford University Press, 1966. Pp. [xi], 318.

Pp. 301-302, secondary bibliography. Alphabetical-by-author arrangement. Books: place, publisher, date, annotations. Periods: date. Additional secondary bibliography in notes, *passim*.

GENERAL

Millett; Longaker & Bolles; Daiches; Temple & Tucker.

332

SAUNDERS, HILARY ST. GEORGE: *see* PALMER, JOHN LESLIE.

SAURAT, DENIS   (1890-1958)

  WWW 51-60.

SAVAGE, DEREK STANLEY   (1917-   )

  Temple & Tucker.

SAVI, ETHEL WINIFRED BRYNING   (-1954)

  (Mrs. J. A. Savi).

  WWW 51-60.

SAVILLE, LEONARD MALCOLM   (1901-   )

  WW 71.

SAYERS, DOROTHY LEIGH   (1893-1957)

  (Mrs. Atherton Fleming).

PRIMARY

James Sandoe. "Contribution toward a Bibliography of Dorothy L. Sayers." *Bulletin of Bibliography* 18 (1944): 76-81.

Primary first editions, British and American. Genre and form arrangement. Books: place, publisher, date, bibliographical notes, contents. Periods: volume, date, pages.

The best available checklist of writings to 1943.

Dorothy L. Sayers. *The Poetry of Search and the Poetry of Statement and Other Posthumous Essays on Literature,*

Religion and Language. London: Victor Gollancz Ltd., 1963. Pp. [287].

P. [287], list of original sources or places where these 12 essays were published or delivered.

Dorothy L. Sayers, ed. Roderick Jellema. *Christian Letters to a Post-Christian World. A Selection of Essays*. Grand Rapids: William B. Eerdmans Publishing Company, 1969. Pp. [xiv], 236.

Pp. vii-xiii, "Introduction," and p. [iv] provide some bibliographical assistance.

These two posthumous collections appear to provide all of the available bibliographical information for the later primary writings.

GENERAL

Daiches; WWW 51-60; Temple & Tucker; Hagen.

SCARFE, FRANCIS HAROLD   (1911-   )

Longaker & Bolles; Daiches; Temple & Tucker; WW 71.

SCHIFF, SYDNEY ALFRED: see HUDSON, STEPHEN.

SCHILLER, FERDINAND CANNING SCOTT   (1864-1937)

Batho & Dobrée; WWW 29-40.

SCHREINER, OLIVE   (1865-1920)

(Mrs. S. Cron Cronwright).

NCBEL, III, 1077.

SCOTT, ALEXANDER (1920-   )

Daiches.

SCOTT, CHARLES PRESTWICH (1846-1932)

PRIMARY

J. L. Hammond. *C. P. Scott of the Manchester Guardian.*
London: G. Bell and Sons, Ltd., 1934. Pp. 365.

This biography, although without bibliography, provides
the background information for any bibliographical investigation. But one should note the editorial comment in *C. P.
Scott, 1846-1932. The Making of The Manchester Guardian.*
London: Frederick Muller, Ltd., 1946. Pp. 252, to the effect
that "Scott wrote hardly anything under his own name or out-
side the columns of his paper. Almost all his work is buried
in newspaper files..." (p. 160).

SCOTT, GEOFFREY (1886-1928)

Daiches.

SCOTT, JOHN DICK (1917-   )

Daiches; WW 71.

SCOTT, TOM (1918-   )

Daiches.

SEAMAN, SIR OWEN (1861-1936)

Millett; Batho & Dobrée; WWW 29-40.

SEA

SEARLE, RONALD WILLIAM FORDHAM   (1920-   )

WW 71.

SEDGWICK, ANNE DOUGLAS   (1873-1935)

(Mrs. Basil de Selincourt).

WWW 29-40.

SELDON TRUSS, LESLIE   (1892-   )

WW 71.

SETH, ANDREW   (1856-1931)

(After 1898: Andrew Seth Pringle-Pattison).

Batho & Dobrée; WWW 29-40; NCBEL, III, 1579-1580.

SEYMOUR, BEATRICE KEAN STAPLETON   (-1955)

(Mrs. William Kean Seymour).

Millett; WWW 51-60.

SEYMOUR, WILLIAM KEAN   (1887-   )

WW 71.

SHAFFER, PETER LEVIN   (1926-   )

Coleman & Tyler; Adelman & Dworkin; Salem; WW 71; Hagen.

SHAIRP, ALEXANDER MORDAUNT   (1887-1939)

Salem.

SHANKS, EDWARD BUXTON   (1892-1953)

Millett; Longaker & Bolles; Daiches; Temple & Tucker.

SHARP, WILLIAM   (1855-1905)

Pseudonym used: Fiona MacLeod.

PRIMARY

Elizabeth A. Sharp. *William Sharp (Fiona MacLeod) A Memoir.*
New York: Duffield and Co.; London: Heineman, 1912. 2nd
Edition. Two volumes.

II, 359-446, primary bibliography. Form arrangement, chronological within each section. In all parts, entries arranged
under Sharp or MacLeod, according to name used on first publication. Books: place, publisher, date, format, pages, contents, details of subsequent issues or editions. Periods:
dates. Bibliographical notes.

Flavia Alaya (below), p. 217: " [This] list of Sharp's published works...though omitting some titles and containing a
few errors, is the most exhaustive bibliography available."

SECONDARY

Sharp, above, pp. 446-450, chronological list.

Flavia Alaya. *William Sharp--"Fiona MacLeod" 1855-1905.*
Cambridge: Harvard University Press, 1970. Pp. [xiv], 261.

Pp. 217-220, selected primary bibliography. Pp. 221-224,
general bibliography of secondary works; also see Notes, pp.
225-249, for further secondary references.

GENERAL

Batho & Dobrée; NCBEL, III, 1064-1066.

SHAW, GEORGE BERNARD   (1856-1950)

PRIMARY

Geoffrey H. Wells. *A Bibliography of the Books and Pamphlets
of George Bernard Shaw.* London: Bookman's Journal, 1928.
Pp. 46. [Reprinted from *Bookman's Journal* 11 (March, 1925);
12 (April, 1925).]

Primary books. Chronological arrangement (two lists: books
by Shaw and books with contributions by Shaw). Books:
transcribed TP, part collation, pagination, binding, date,
bibliographical notes. Books with contributions: title,
place, publisher, date, page numbers, identification of
Shaw's contribution.

An early work, designed mainly for the collector of first editions.

C. Lewis Broad and Violet M. Broad. *Dictionary to the Plays
and Novels of Bernard Shaw, with Bibliography of his Works
and of the Literature concerning him with a Record of the
principal Shavian Play Productions.* London: A. and C. Black;
New York: Macmillan Co., 1929. Pp. [xii], [231].

Primary selected, secondary selected. Form arrangement.
Pp. 87-100, Chronological list of primary books: date, British and American publishers, very brief annotations. Pp.
101-112, chronological lists of other writings and of reported
speeches: dates and titles of periodicals in which published.
Pp. 209-231, Play productions: alphabetical by title, including place, date, cast. Pp. 114-131, secondary criticism.

Useful mainly to the general reader.

Sir Maurice Holmes. *Some Bibliographical Notes on the Novels
of G. B. Shaw.* London: Dulau and Co., 1929. Pp. [20].
500 copies.

An essay on the bibliographical "points" of the four novels; pp. 17-[20], descriptions: transcribed TP, full collation, binding, pagination, notes.

F. E. Loewenstein. *The Rehearsal Copies of Bernard Shaw's Plays.* London: Reinhardt and Evans, 1950. Pp. 36.

Primary bibliography of the play-rehersal-copies or "First-prints." Chronological arrangement. Transcribed TP, part collation, binding, date, extensive bibliographical, textual, and historical notes. P. 36, alphabetical index of titles.

Alfred C. Ward. *Bernard Shaw.* London: Longmans, Green and Co., Ltd. (WTW 1), 1951. Pp. 56.

Pp. 41-56, bibliography and indices. Arranged: First Perform-ances of Principal Plays (date, place, theatre); Primary Books (date, genre, contents); Indices of Plays, Prefaces, and Es-says with titles of volumes in which collected.

Particularly useful for the listing of contents and locating of individual pieces.

Shaw Bulletin, I-II (1951-1959); title changed to *Shaw Review,* III (1960)- to date.

Almost every issue contains "A Continuing Check-List of Shaviana" by various editors; Part I lists "Works by Shaw" with title, place, publisher, date, notes and annotations.

A basic source of primary and secondary bibliographical in-formation.

Lawrence C. Keough. "George Bernard Shaw, 1946-1955: A Selected Bibliography." *Bulletin of Bibliography* 22 (1959): 224-226; 23 (1960), 20-24, 36-41.

Primary and secondary. Genre arrangement. Books: place, publisher, date. Periodicals: date, volume and page numbers. Secondary, alphabetical by author under general topics.

R. F. Bosworth. "Shaw Recordings at the B. B. C.," *Shaw Review* 7 (May, 1964): 42-46.

An essay in which ten recordings are described: title, date, length, B. B. C. number, quotations.

SECONDARY

Above, Broad and Broad, pp. 114-131; *Shaw Bulletin* (later *Review*): in each issue, "A Continuing Check-list of Shaviana": Part II, Books and Pamphlets (place, publisher, date, pages, annotations), Part III, Periodicals (date, volume, pages, annotations), Part IV, Dissertations (brief entries taken from *Dissertations Abstracts*); Keough, pp. 20-24, 36-41.

Clara A. Milliken. "Reading List of Modern Dramatists ... Shaw..." *Bulletin of Bibliography* 5 (October, 1907): 52-53.

Reviews and studies listed under title of the work criticized. Date; volume and page number, or place and publisher.

Earl Farley and Marvin Carlson. "George Bernard Shaw: A Selected Bibliography (1945-1955)." *Modern Drama* 2 (1959): 188-202, 295-325.

Books listed alphabetically by author: place, publisher, date, page references. Periodical contributions listed alphabetically by author under "General" or under title of appropriate play: date, volume and page numbers.

T. J. Spencer, "An Annotated Check-list of Criticism of the post- *Saint Joan* Plays." *Shaw Review* 2 (1959): 45-48.

Date, volume and page numbers, annotations. Selected.

Arthur O. Lewis, Jr., and Stanley Weintraub, "Bernard Shaw-- Aspects and Problems of Research." *Shaw Review* 3 (1960): 18-26.

An important survey of the secondary bibliographies.

GENERAL

Millett; Batho & Dobrée; Longaker & Bolles; Temple & Tucker; Coleman & Tyler; Adelman & Dworkin; Salem; Palmer & Dyson; NCBEL, III, 1169-1182.

SHEARING, JOSEPH: see LONG, MRS. GABRIELLE.

SHERRIFF, ROBERT CEDRIC   (1896-   )

Daiches; Temple & Tucker; Palmer & Dyson; Salem; WW 71.

SHERRINGTON, SIR CHARLES SCOTT   (1857-1952)

WWW 51-60.

SHIEL, MATTHEW PHIPPS   (1865-1947)

PRIMARY

John Gawsworth. *Ten Contemporaries. Notes Toward their Definitive Bibliography* [First Series]. London: Ernest Benn Ltd., 1932. Pp. 224.

Pp. 174-191, primary books, first editions, 1895-1930. Chronological arrangement. Transcribed TP, full collation, pagination, binding, date, bibliographical notes. (This information is reprinted in Morse, below).

A. Reynolds Morse. *The Works of M. P. Shiel. A Study in Bibliography*. Los Angeles: Fantasy Publishing Co., Inc., 1948. Pp. 170. 1000 copies.

Primary. Form arrangement. Pp. 24-28, checklist of book titles. Pp. 32-113, books: short essay about or précis of each title; for each edition, transcribed TP, full collation, pagination, binding, bibliographical notes. Pp. 114-124, list of shorter writings and periodical contributions; pp. 125-136, description of MSS; pp. 137-154, collaborations (described like primary books). Also includes biographical essay, list of books in Shiel's library, and index.

A very informative, if idiosyncratically arranged, work.

Harold W. Billings. "Matthew Phipps Shiel: A Collection and Comments." *Library Chronicle of the University of Texas* 6, ii (1958): 34-43.

A discursive essay mentioning many primary books with place, publisher, date, and bibliographical notes.

SHIELS, GEORGE (1886-1949)

Salem.

SHORTER, CLEMENT KING (1857-1926)

PRIMARY

John M. Bulloch, ed. *Clement King Shorter An Autobiography. A Fragment by Himself.* Edinburgh: Privately Printed, 1927. Pp. 176.

Pp. 153-168, bibliography. Primary books and regular columns in periodicals and newspapers. Chronological arrangement. Books: place, publisher, date, part collation, limitations of issue. A checklist mainly of books; other references to Shorter's editorial work and periodical contributions in text, *passim*.

SHUTE, NEVIL (1899-1960)

Pseudonym of N. S. Norway.

Temple & Tucker.

SIDGWICK, ETHEL (1877-1970)

Millett; Temple & Tucker; WW 70.

SIEVEKING, LANCELOT DE GHIBERNE   (1896-   )

WW 71; Hagen.

SIGERSON, DORA MARY   (1866-1918)

(Mrs. Clement Shorter).

PRIMARY

Edith Somerville. "Bibliography of Dora Sigerson [Shorter]."
Studies (Dublin) 7 (March, 1918): 144-145.

Not seen.

[Thomas James Wise]. *The Books of Dora Sigerson Shorter.
(Mrs. Clement Shorter)*. Edinburgh: Privately Printed, 1924.

Not seen.

GENERAL

NCBEL, III, 1911-1912.

SILKIN, JON   (1930-   )

Temple & Tucker.

SILLITOE, ALAN   (1928-   )

Temple & Tucker; WW 71.

SIMPSON, NORMAN FREDERICK   (1919-   )

Adelman & Dworkin; Salem.

SIMPSON, PERCY   (1865-1962)

PRIMARY

A List of the Published Writings of Percy Simpson. Oxford:
Clarendon Press, 1950. Pp. 29.

Pp. 5-11, appreciation and biography. Pp. 15-29, bibliography. Primary, including works edited by Simpson. Form
arrangement. Books: date, publisher. Periods: date, pages,
volume.

GENERAL

Daiches; WW 62.

SINCLAIR, MAY   (1865-1946)

Pseudonym of Mary Amelia St. Clair Sinclair.

PRIMARY

T. E. M. Boll. "May Sinclair: A Check List." *Bulletin of
the New York Public Library* 74 (1970): 454-467.

Pp. 454-458, introductory, biographical essay. Pp. 459-467,
primary writings. Arranged by genre, topic, and form in 24
sections. Books: place, publisher and date for all editions.
Periods: dates. Cross-references to show reprintings.

A complete list of Miss Sinclair's varied writings, the arrangement serving as annotation on the entries. Also see T. E. M.
Boll. "On the May Sinclair Collection." *Library Chronicle*
(University of Pennsylvania) 27 (1961): 1-15, for an important
description of the Sinclair primary and secondary materials in
the Pennsylvania Library, including many references to secondary criticism.

SECONDARY

Above, Boll, *Library Chronicle*.

GENERAL

Millett; Batho & Dobrée; Temple & Tucker.

SISSON, CHARLES JASPER   (1885-1966)

Daiches; WW 66.

SITWELL, DAME EDITH   (1887-1964)

PRIMARY

Richard Fifoot. *A Bibliography of Edith, Osbert and Sacheverell
Sitwell.* London: Rupert Hart-Davis (Soho Bibliography No.
11), 1963. Pp. 394.

Pp. 17-126, bibliography of Edith Sitwell. Primary first editions. Form arrangement. Books: transcribed TP, part collation, pagination, binding, date, price, contents, selected
later editions and issues (Fifoot's Preface, p. 9, explains
selection), number of copies, bibliographical and textual
notes. Periods: volume, pages, date; title and author of
books reviewed by Dame Edith. Lists of translations of
her writings (translator, place, publisher, date), of recordings by her, and of musical settings of works by her. Pp.
361-394, index for the entire volume indicates the inclusion
of individual pieces in later collections.

The standard bibliography.

SECONDARY

Lois D. Rosenberg. "Edith Sitwell: A Critical Bibliography,
1915-1950." *Bulletin of Bibliography* 21 (1953-1954): 40-43,
57-60.

Arranged: [Selected] Critical Writings by Sitwell [concern-
ing her own works]; Bibliography, Biography and Criticism;
Reviews (listed under title of book reviewed). Books: place,
publisher, date. Periods: volume, pages, date. Brief anno-

tations.

James D. Brophy. *Edith Sitwell. The Symbolist Order.* Carbondale: Southern Illinois University Press, 1968. Pp. [xviii],
170.

Pp. 162-164, selected primary bibliography. Alphabetically
arranged. Place, date. Pp. 161-162, selected secondary
bibliography. Alphabetical-by-author arrangement. Additional
entries in notes, pp. 153-160.

GENERAL

Millett; Longaker & Bolles; Daiches; Temple & Tucker.

SITWELL, SIR OSBERT   (1892-1969)

PRIMARY

Roger Fulford. *Osbert Sitwell.* London: Longmans, Green and
Co. (WTW 16), 1951. Pp. 44.

Pp. 37-40, selected primary and secondary bibliography.
Date, genre. Pp. 41-44, Index to Essays and Short Stories.
Alphabetical list of titles with title of volume in which col-
lected.

Richard Fifoot. *A Bibliography of Edith, Osbert and Sacheverell
Sitwell.* London: Rupert Hart-Davis (Soho Bibliography No.
11), 1963. Pp. 394.

Pp. 131-248, bibliography of Osbert Sitwell. Primary first
editions. Form arrangement. Books: transcribed TP, part
collation, pagination, binding, date, price, contents, selected later editions and issues (Fifoot's Preface, p. 9,
explains selection), number of copies, bibliographical and
textual notes. Periods: volume, pages, date; title and
author of books reviewed by Sir Osbert. Listings of translations of Sir Osbert (translator, place, publisher, date),
of recordings by him, and of musical settings of works by
him. Pp. 361-394, index for the entire volume indicates the

inclusion of individual pieces in later collections.

The standard bibliography.

SECONDARY

Above, Fulford, p. 39.

GENERAL

Millett; Longaker & Bolles; Temple & Tucker; WW 69.

SITWELL, SIR SACHEVERELL   (1897-   )

PRIMARY

Richard Fifoot. *A Bibliography of Edith, Osbert and Sacheverell Sitwell*. London: Rupert Hart-Davis (Soho Bibliography No. 11), 1963. Pp. 394.

Pp. 253-357, bibliography of Sacheverell Sitwell. Primary first editions. Form arrangement. Books: transcribed TP, part collation, pagination, binding, date, price, contents, selected later editions and issues (Fifoot's Preface, p. 9, explains selection), number of copies, bibliographical and textual notes. Periods: volume, pages, date; title and author of books reviewed by Sir Sacheverell. Lists of translations of his writings (translator, place, publisher, date), of recordings by him, and of musical settings of works by him. Pp. 361-394, index for the entire volume indicates the inclusion of individual pieces in later collections.

The standard bibliography.

SECONDARY

Rodolphe L. Mégroz. *The Three Sitwells*. London: Richards Press, 1927.

P. 333, bibliography.

GENERAL

Millett; Longaker & Bolles; Temple & Tucker; WW 71.

SKEFFINGTON, FRANCIS SHEEHY (- 1916)

PRIMARY

Patrick Sarsfield O'Hegarty. "Bibliographies of 1916 and the
Irish Revolution. XI. Francis Sheehy Skeffington." *Dublin
Magazine* 11 (October-December, 1936): 76-78.

Primary books. Chronological arrangement. Transcribed
TP, part collation, pagination, binding, bibliographical and
occasionally biographical notes.

SLADE, JULIAN PENKIVIL (1930-)

WW 71.

SLANEY, GEORGE WILSON (1884-)

Pseudonym used: George Woden.

WW 71; Hagen.

SMITH, DODIE [DOROTHY GLADYS] (1896-)

Pseudonym used to 1935: C. L. Anthony.

(Mrs. A. M. Beesley).

Salem; WW 71.

SMITH, VERY REV. SIR GEORGE ADAM (1856-1942)

Batho & Dobrée; WWW 41-50.

SMITH, GEORGE CHARLES MOORE   (1858-1940)

PRIMARY

A Bibliography of the Writings of George Charles Moore Smith.
Cambridge, 1928.

Not seen.

GENERAL

WWW 29-40.

SMITH, JANET BUCHANAN ADAM   (1905-   )

(Mrs. John Carleton).

WW 71.

SMITH, LOGAN PEARSALL   (1865-1946)

PRIMARY

"Bibliographies of Modern Authors. Logan Pearsall Smith."
London Mercury 4 (1921): 436.

Primary books, 1895-1920. Chronological arrangement. Publisher, year, notes.

Robert Gathorne-Hardy. *Recollections of Logan Pearsall Smith*.
London: Constable, 1949. Pp. 259.

No bibliography. Bibliographical information in text, *passim*,
especially for the post-1928 period.

GENERAL

Temple & Tucker.

SMITH, PAULINE URMSON   (1883-1959)

PRIMARY

Geoffrey Haresnape. *Pauline Smith.* New York: Twayne Publishers, Inc (TWAS 80), 1969. Pp. 198.

Pp. 189-192, "Selected Bibliography." Primary selected,
secondary selected. Form arrangement. Primary books:
place, publisher, date, all editions. Periods: volume, pages,
date. MSS: location. Includes four secondary articles, annotated.

SMITH, STEVIE [FLORENCE MARGARET]   (1902-1971)

Temple & Tucker; WW 71.

SMITH, SYDNEY GOODSIR   (1915-   )

Daiches; Temple & Tucker.

SMYTH, SIR JOHN GEORGE   (1893-   )

WW 71.

SNAITH, STANLEY   (1903-   )

WW 71.

SNOW, CHARLES PERCY, LORD SNOW   (1905-   )

PRIMARY

Robert Greacen. *The World of C. P. Snow.* Lowestoft: Scorpion Press, 1962. Pp. 64.

Pp. 41-64, bibliography compiled by Bernard Stone. Primary,

secondary selected. Form arrangement. Books: publisher, place, date, list of all editions and reprints, translations listed with name of translator; occasional notes. Pp. 51-59, periodical contributions and other writings: dates, occasionally volume and pages. Pp. 59-63, secondary bibliography.

A good checklist, although its value is decreased by various omissions (as of page numbers).

Jerome Thale. *C. P. Snow*. Edinburgh: Oliver and Boyd (Writers and Critics Series), 1964. Pp. 112.

Pp. 108-112, bibliography. Primary first editions, British and American; secondary selected. Form arrangement. Primary books: place, publisher, date. Periods: date, pages, volume. Pp. 110-112, secondary bibliography.

[For collaborations with Pamela Hansford Johnson, see above, JOHNSON, PAMELA HANSFORD.]

SECONDARY

Above, Greacen, pp. 59-63, and Thale, pp. 110-112.

GENERAL

Daiches; Temple & Tucker; WW 71.

SOMERVILLE, EDITH ANNA ŒNONE   (1858-1949)

Including collaborations with Martin Ross, pseudonym of Violet Florence Martin (1862-1915).

PRIMARY

Elizabeth Hudson. *A Bibliography of the First Editions of the Works of E. Œ. Somerville and Martin Ross*. New York: The Sporting Gallery and Bookshop, Inc., 1942. Pp. 79. 300 copies.

Primary first editions. Form arrangement. Books: transcribed

TP, full collation, pagination, price, binding, number of copies, British Museum Pressmark, extensive notes by Somerville. Periods: dates. Also sections on Collected Editions, Selected Criticism, Picture Books, Awards.

Geraldine Cummins. *Dr. E. Œ. Somerville: A Biography.* London: Andrew Dakers Ltd., 1952. Pp. 271.

Pp. 245-271, "The First Editions of Edith Œnone Somerville and Violet Florence Martin. A Bibliography compiled by Robert Vaughan." Primary books. Chronological arrangement. Transcribed TP, full collation, pagination, binding, price, number of copies, full bibliographical notes include information on American first editions.

Maurice Collis. *Somerville and Ross. A Biography.* London: Faber and Faber, 1968. Pp. 286.

Pp. 13-15, 279-280, location and description of manuscripts.

Hudson, Vaughan, and Collis together provide a fairly complete primary bibliography.

SECONDARY

Above, Hudson.

GENERAL

WWW 41-50; Batho & Dobrée.

SOMMERVILLE, FRANKFORT: see STORY, A. M. SOMMERVILLE.

SORLEY, CHARLES HAMILTON   (1895-1915)

PRIMARY

W. R. Sorley, ed. *The Letters of Charles Sorley.* Cambridge: Cambridge University Press, 1919. Pp. 320.

No bibliography, but much information about Sorley's writings, *passim.* Bound-in advertisement, pp. [321-322], for *Marl-borough* includes quotations from critical comments.

SECONDARY

Thomas Burnett Swann. *The Ungirt Runner: Charles Hamilton Sorley. Poet of World War I.* Hamden, Connecticut: Archon Books, 1965. Pp. 154.

Pp. 151-153, secondary bibliography. Form arrangement, including Unpublished Letters and Other Unpublished Materials. P. 154, primary books: place, publisher, dates of all editions. Additional information is given in the Acknowledgements, pp. 9-10.

GENERAL

Longaker & Bolles; Temple & Tucker.

SORLEY, WILLIAM RITCHIE   (1855-1935)

Batho & Dobrée; NCBEL, III, 1583.

SOUTAR, WILLIAM   (1898-1943)

PRIMARY

William Russell Aitken. "William Soutar. Biographical Notes and a Checklist." *Bibliotheck* (Glasgow), 1, ii (1957): 3-14.

Not seen.

Alexander Scott. *William Soutar. 1898-1943. Still Life.* London: Chambers, 1958. Pp. 218.

P. 210, primary books. Place, publisher, date. Pp. 211-212, Principal Manuscript Sources: Autobiographical Writings, Correspondence, Verses, Miscellaneous Prose.

GENERAL

SOU

Daiches; WWW 41-50.

SOWERBY, KATHERINE GITHA   (-1970)

(Mrs. John Kendall).

WW 70.

SPARK, MURIEL SARAH   (1918-   )

PRIMARY

Derek Stanford. *Muriel Spark: A Biographical and Critical
Study*. Fontwell: Centaur Press Ltd., 1963. Pp. 184.

Pp. 167-184, bibliography compiled by Bernard Stone. Primary, secondary selected. Form arrangement. Books: place,
publisher, date, later editions and reprints. Pp. 175-179,
selected contributions to periodicals (periodicals listed
alphabetically by title): title of contribution, volume, date
(see also pp. 167-169 for suggestion of other periodicals
containing primary writings). Pp. 180-182, selected secondary bibliography, including reviews.

A start toward a bibliography, although not at all complete.

SECONDARY

Above, Stanford, pp. 180-182.

GENERAL

Temple & Tucker; WW 71; Hagen.

SPARKE, ARCHIBALD   (1871-   )

WW 71.

SPARROW, JOHN HANBURY ANGUS   (1906-   )

WW 71.

SPEAIGHT, ROBERT WILLIAM   (1904-   )

WW 71.

SPENCER, BERNARD   (1909-1962)

Temple & Tucker.

SPENDER, STEPHEN HAROLD   (1909-   )

PRIMARY

Warren Roberts. *Stephen Spender, 1928-1959. Notes for an Account of His Writings.* Austin: University of Texas Humanities Research Center, 1959. Pp. 28. 200 copies.

Not seen.

A. Trevor Tolley. *The Early Published Poems of Stephen Spender.* Ottawa: Carleton University, 1967. Pp. [ii], [18]. Reproduced from typescript.

Pp. 1-6, general bibliographical information. Pp. [7]-[18], chronological list of poems, 1926-1934. Each entry provides title, first line, date of composition, and identifies first and subsequent publications. Books: place, publisher, date, pages. Periods: volume, date, pages.

GENERAL

Millett; Daiches; Longaker & Bolles; Temple & Tucker; WW 71.

SPRIGG, CHRISTOPHER ST. JOHN   (1907-1937)

Pseudonym used: Christopher Caudwell.

Temple & Tucker; Hagen.

SPRIGG, ELIZABETH MIRIAM SQUIRE   (1900-   )

WW 71; Hagen.

SPRING, HOWARD   (1889-1965)

WW 65.

SPURGEON, CAROLINE F. E.   (1869-1942)

Daiches.

SQUIRE, SIR JOHN COLLINGS   (1884-1958)

PRIMARY

Iolo A. Williams. *Bibliographies of Modern Authors. No. 4 . J. C. Squire and James Stephens.* London: Leslie Chaundy and Co., 1922. Pp. 13.

Pp. 1-9, bibliography of Squire. Primary books, English first editions. Genre arrangement. Part collation, publisher, date, binding, occasional notes. Includes checklist of books edited, selected, or introduced by Squire.

Patrick J. F. Howarth. *Squire: ' Most Generous of Men .'* London: Hutchinson, 1963. Pp. 308.

Pp. 289-297, "A Partial Bibliography of the Works of Sir John Collings Squire," by B. S. Benedikz. Part I, pp. 289-292, books partly or completely by Squire, arranged under type of authorship. Title, part collation, publisher, place, year, later editions. Part II, pp. 294-297, Squire's contributions to the *London Mercury*, arranged by genre. Volume, pages.

The text shows that much of Squire's journalism has been omitted: this is indeed a partial bibliography.

GENERAL

Millett; Longaker & Bolles; Batho & Dobrée; Daiches; Temple & Tucker.

STANDISH, ROBERT   (1898-   )

Pseudonym of Digby George Gerahty.

Temple & Tucker.

STANFORD, DEREK   (1918-   )

Temple & Tucker.

STANFORD, JOHN KEITH   (1892-   )

WW 71.

STARK, FREYA MADELINE   (1893-   )

(Mrs. Stewart Perowne).

Daiches; Temple & Tucker; WW 71.

STARKEY, JAMES SULLIVAN: see O'SULLIVAN, SEUMAS.

STARKIE, ENID MARY   (-1970)

WW 70.

STARKIE, WALTER FITZWILLIAM   (1894-   )

WW 71.

STEELE, HARWOOD ROBERT ELMES   (1897-   )

WW 71.

STEEN, MARGUERITE   (1894--   )

WW 71.

STEPHENS, JAMES   (1882-1950)

PRIMARY

Birgit Bramsbäck. *James Stephens A Literary and Bibliograph-ical Study.* Upsala: Irish Institute of Upsala University (Upsala Irish Studies, No. 4), 1959. Pp. 209.

Pp. 57-209, primary and secondary bibliography. Form and genre arrangement, with primary material divided Manuscript (pp. 57-112) and Printed Sources (pp. 115-169). MSS: complete identification, précis or abstract, description, location; includes letters written to or about Stephens. Primary books: date, publisher, place, occasionally format and binding, reprints; contents with page numbers and information concerning previous publication; occasionally number of copies; extensive notes. Other books: date, publisher, place. Periods: volume, pages, date, reprintings, notes. P. 199, list of BBC recordings by Stephens. Index.

The authoritative bibliography, although not complete.

Patricia McFate. "The Publication of James Stephen's Short Stories in 'The Nation.' " *Papers of the Bibliographical Society of America* 58 (1964): 476-477.

Corrections and additions to Bramsbäck.

"The James Stephens Papers [at Kent State University Library]:

A Catalogue." *Serif* 2, ii (1965): 29-32.

Not seen.

SECONDARY

Above, Bramsbäck, pp. 170-191.

Richard Cary. "James Stephens at Colby College." *Colby Library Quarterly* 5, ix (March, 1961): 242-252.

Important association material.

Hilary Pyle. *James Stephens. His Work and an Account of His Life.* London: Routledge and Kegan Paul, 1965. Pp. [xii], 196.

Pp. 190-191, general secondary bibliography. (Also. pp. 183-190, primary bibliography: inferior to that in Bramsbäck).

GENERAL

Millett; Longaker & Bolles; Batho & Dobrée; Daiches; Temple & Tucker.

STERN, GLADYS BERTHA   (1890-   )

(Mrs. Geoffrey L. Holdsworth).

Millett; Temple & Tucker; WW 71.

STEVENSON, D. E.   (1892-   )

(Mrs. J. R. Peploe).

WW 71.

STEVENSON, ROBERT LOUIS   (1850-1894)

PRIMARY

W. F. Prideaux. *A Bibliography of the Works of Robert Louis
Stevenson*, edited and supplemented by Mrs. Luther S. Livingston. London: Frank Hollings, 1917. Pp. 401.

Primary complete, secondary selected. Form and genre arrangement. Books: transcribed TP, part collation, pages,
price, binding, contents with details of previous publication,
subsequent editions, notes. Periods: volume, pages, date;
details of subsequent publication in book form. Includes details of the collected editions. Pp. 313-382, secondary bibliography. Index.

A lucid, easy-to-use, and authoritative account of the publications to 1917.

George L. McKay. *A Stevenson Library. Catalogue of a Collection of Writings by and about Robert Louis Stevenson
formed by Edwin J. Beinecke.* New Haven: Yale University
Press, 1951-1964. 6 volumes. 500 copies of each volume.

I (1951): 1-370; II (1952): 373-526, 793-802, primary published
writings, form arrangement. Books: transcribed TP, pagination,
full collation, binding, date, contents, extensive notes; includes translations. Periods: volume, date, pages, notes.
II: 529-762, secondary bibliography. Also includes: II: 765-
790, books from Stevenson's library; II: 805-859, indices; III
(1956): 861-1180, autograph letters by the Stevensons; IV
(1958): 1197-1694, letters to and about Stevenson; V (1961):
Manuscripts by Stevenson and others; VI (1964): 2221-2670,
addenda, corrigenda, indices.

McKay's account of Stevenson's literary work is so complete
as to be almost self-defeating. Thus Prideaux is the easy-
to-use, authoritative bibliography; McKay is the more com-
plicated final word; and all other bibliographical work is
derivative--or merely a supplement necessitated by the pas-
sage of time.

SECONDARY

Above, Prideaux, pp. 313-382; McKay, II, 529-762.

GENERAL

Batho & Dobrée; NCBEL, III, 1004-1014.

STEWART, DESMOND STIRLING   (1924-   )

WW 71.

STEWART, JOHN INNES MACKINTOSH   (1906-   )

Pseudonym used: Michael Innes.

Daiches; WW 71; Hagen.

STOKES, ADRIAN DURHAM   (1902-   )

Daiches; WW 71.

STONIER, GEORGE WALTER   (1903-   )

Daiches; WW 71.

STOPES, CHARLOTTE CARMICHAEL   (1841-1929)

PRIMARY

Gwendolen A. Murphy. "A Bibliographical List of the Writings of Charlotte Carmichael Stopes." *Essays by Divers Hands*, ed. Sir Francis Younghusband. Royal Society of Literature. 10 (1931): 95-107.

Primary. Divided: "Shakespeare and his Background" and "Miscellaneous Subjects." Chronological in each section. Books: publisher, date, pages, contents. Periods: date, pages. Many primary periodical contributions are listed only under title of volume in which they were collected.

STOPES, MARIE CHARLOTTE CARMICHAEL   (1880-1958)

(Mrs. Reginald R. Gates; later Mrs. Humphrey Roe).

PRIMARY

Keith Briant. *Passionate Paradox. The Life of Marie Stopes.*
New York: W. W. Norton and Co., 1962. Pp. [286].

Pp. 269-274, primary bibliography. Genre arrangement.
Books: date, publisher, pages; if book was in print in 1962,
publisher, date, and price; list of languages into which each
title translated. Periods: volume, date, pages.

STOPPARD, TOM   (1937-)

WW 71.

STORM, LESLEY   (-)

Née Margaret Cowie (Mrs. J. D. Clark).

WW 71.

STORRS, SIR RONALD   (1881-1955)

WWW 51-60.

STORY, A. M. SOMMERVILLE   (-)

Pseudonym used: Frankfort Sommerville.

WW 71.

STOUT, GEORGE FREDERICK   (1860-1944)

Batho & Dobrée; WWW 41-50; NCBEL, III, 1593-1595.

STOW, JULIAN RANDOLPH   (1935-   )

PRIMARY

Patricia Anne O'Brien. *Bibliography of Randolph Stow*.
Adelaide: Libraries Board of South Australia (Bibliographies
of Australian Writers), 1968. Pp. 29.

Not seen.

GENERAL

Hetherington; WW 71.

STRACHEY, EVELYN JOHN ST. LOE   (1901-1963)

WW 63.

STRACHEY, GILES LYTTON   (1880-1932)

PRIMARY

R. A. Scott-James. *Lytton Strachey*. London: Longmans, Green
and Co. (WTW 65), 1955. Pp. [40].

Pp. 33-34, primary books: date, genre. Pp. 35-39, alphabetical
by title list of primary essays with titles of the volumes in
which they are collected. A useful addition to Sanders' authoritative checklist (below).

Charles R. Sanders. *Lytton Strachey. His Mind and Art*. New
Haven: Yale University Press; London: Oxford University
Press, 1957. Pp. [xii], [382].

Pp. 355-366, primary bibliography. One chronological list.

Books: British and American first editions only: place, publisher, date, details if any of serial publication. Periods: volume, pages, date, details of reprinting in collections. Reviews by Strachey include author and title of book reviewed. Includes unsigned and pseudonymous writings, also unpublished writings. A complete list of Strachey's writings.

SECONDARY

Martin Kallich. "Lytton Strachey: An Annotated Bibliography of Writings about Him." *English Fiction in Transition* 5, iii (1962): 1-77.

Alphabetical by author. Books: place, publisher, date. Periods: volume, pages, dates. Annotations. Subsequent issues of *English Fiction* (later *English Literature*) *in Transition* provide additions to this basic list.

GENERAL

Millett; Longaker & Bolles; Daiches; Temple & Tucker.

STREATFEILD, NOEL   (?1899-   )

PRIMARY

Barbara Ker Wilson. *Noel Streatfeild.* London: Bodley Head (Bodley Head Monograph), 1961. Pp. 63.

P. 63, primary books. Chronological arrangement. Publisher, year, illustrator.

Noel Streatfeild. *A Vicarage Family. An Autobiographical Story.* New York: Franklin Watts, Inc., 1963. Pp. [xii], [249].

Pp. [248-249], primary books, British and American editions. Arranged by genre. Publisher.

GENERAL

WW 71.

STREET, ARTHUR GEORGE   (1892-1966)

WW 66.

STREETER, BURNETT HILLMAN   (1874-1937)

WWW 29-40.

STRONG, LEONARD ALFRED GEORGE   (1896-1958)

PRIMARY

John Gawsworth. *Ten Contemporaries. Notes Toward their
Definitive Bibliography. (Second Series)*. London: Joiner
and Steele Ltd., 1933. Pp. 240. 1000 copies.

Pp. 219-234, bibliography of Strong, 1919-1932. Primary
first editions, books. Chronological arrangement. Transcribed TP, full collation, pagination, binding, date,
bibliographical notes.

R. L. Mégroz. *Five Novelist Poets*. London: Joiner and
Steele Ltd., 1933.

Pp. 243-244, bibliography of Strong, 1921-1932. Primary
books. Chronological arrangement. Publisher, place, date,
pages.

GENERAL

Millett; Longaker & Bolles; Daiches; Temple & Tucker; Hagen.

STUART, FRANCIS   (1902-   )

Millett; Temple & Tucker; WW 71.

STURT, GEORGE   (1863-1927)

Pseudonym used: George Bourn.

PRIMARY

E. D. Mackerness. "George Sturt and the English Humanitarian Tradition" in *Essays and Studies 1969* (NS 22), ed. Francis Berry for The English Association. London: John Murray, 1969. Pp. 105-122.

A survey of Sturt's literary work providing many titles and dates.

GENERAL

Batho & Dobrée.

SUMMERS, MONTAGUE   (1880-1948)

PRIMARY

Timothy d'Arch Smith. *A Bibliography of the Works of Montague Summers*. London: Nicholas Vane Ltd., 1964. Pp. 164.

Primary. Form arrangement. Books: transcribed TP, full collation, pagination, binding, date, price, contents, illustrations, later editions and impressions described fully. Lengthy notes. Periods: volume, pages, date, notes. Includes section on untraced, unpublished, and projected works, and a list of programme notes written by Summers for theatrical societies. Pp. 137-148, chronological list of published writings. Index.

Cecil Woolf, *Book Collector* 14 (1965): 106: "in every way this is an excellent piece of bibliographical work."

Joseph Jerome. *Montague Summers. A Memoir*. London: Cecil and Amelia Woolf, 1965. Pp. 105.

Pp. 91-94, "Bibliographical Checklist," by T. d'A. Smith. Primary. Form and subject arrangement. Publisher, date, place, reprints.

Drawn from Smith's work above, this checklist is particularly complete, while its arrangement helps to guide one through Summer's writings.

SUMMERSON, SIR JOHN NEWENHAM   (1904-   )

WW 71.

SUTCLIFF, ROSEMARY   (1920-   )

WW 71.

SUTHERLAND, JAMES RUNCIEMAN   (1900-   )

Daiches; WW 71.

SUTHERLAND, ROBERT GARIOCH: see GARIOCH, ROBERT.

SUTRO, ALFRED   (1863-1933)

Millett; Temple & Tucker.

SUTTON, DENYS   (1917-   )

WW 71.

SWANTON, ERNEST WILLIAM   (1907-   )
WWW 71.

SWEET, HENRY   (1845-1912)
NCBEL, III, 1663-1664.

SWINNERTON, FRANK ARTHUR   (1884-   )

Millett; Longaker & Bolles; Batho & Dobrée; Daiches; Temple
& Tucker; WW 71.

SYKES, CHRISTOPHER HUGH   (1907-   )

WW 71.

SYMONDS, JOHN ADDINGTON   (1840-1893)

PRIMARY

Percy L. Babington. *Bibliography of the Writings of John
Addington Symonds*. London: John Castle, 1925. Pp. [xi],
244. 500 copies.

Primary, secondary selected. Form arrangement. Books:
transcribed TP, part collation, brief pagination, binding,
contents, textual variants, bibliographical notes. Periodical
contributions listed chronologically under name of particular
periodical (pp. 131-204): volume, date, pages. Pp. 207-224,
the following sections give for each title the publisher, place,
date, and bibliographical notes: Later Editions and Reprints,
American Issues; European Translations and Reprints. Index .

Phyllis Grosskurth. *John Addington Symonds. A Biography*.
London: Longmans, Green and Co., 1964. Pp. 370.

Pp. 329-355, a useful listing and identification of the primary
MSS.

SECONDARY

Above, Babington, pp. 227-237, "Some Biographical and Critical
Books and Notices."

GENERAL

NCBEL, III, 1501-1503.

SYMONS, ALPHONSE JAMES ALBERT   (1900-1941)

PRIMARY

Julian Symons. *A. J. A. Symons. His Life and Speculations.* London: Eyre and Spottiswoode, 1950. Pp. 283.

This biography by Symon's brother is the beginning point of any bibliographical investigation, although it does not provide an actual bibliography.

GENERAL

WWW 41-50.

SYMONS, ARTHUR   (1865-1945)

PRIMARY

Henry Danielson. *Bibliographies of Modern Authors.* London: Bookman's Journal, 1921. Pp. [xii], [212].

Pp. 175-194, primary books and pamphlets, 1886-1920. Chronological arrangement. Transcribed TP, part collation, pagination, binding, variants, miscellaneous bibliographical notes.

Thomas Earle Welby. *Arthur Symons. A Critical Study.* London: Philpot, 1925. Pp. 148.

Pp. 141-148, bibliography. Primary books, secondary selected. Arrangement according to Symon's part in the book, including translations by, works edited or introduced by, and anthologies edited by. Titles and dates, only.

Roger Llombreaud. *Arthur Symons. A Critical Biography.*

London: Unicorn Press, 1963. Pp. 333.

Pp. 325-326, checklist of primary books, British and American first editions. Chronological arrangement. Date, place, publisher.

SECONDARY

Above, Welby, pp. 147-148.

GENERAL

Millett; Longaker & Bolles; Batho & Dobrée; Temple & Tucker; NCBEL, III, 649-651.

SYMONS, JULIAN GUSTAVE   (1912-   )

Longaker & Bolles; Temple & Tucker; WW 71; Hagen.

SYNGE, JOHN MILLINGTON   (1871-1909)

PRIMARY

Maurice Bourgeois. *John Millington Synge and the Irish Theatre.* London: Constable and Co., 1913. Photographic reprint, New York: Blom, 1965. Pp. xiv, [338].

Pp. 251-314, bibliography. Primary, secondary. Form arrangement. Books: place, publisher, date, part collation, price, annotations, reprints and subsequent editions (information not consistently given). Translations of Synge listed separately. Periodicals arranged alphabetically by title: date, pages, annotations. Secondary bibliography, pp. 265-296. Annotated. Appendices: List of the best-known portraits of Synge; Bibliographical note on the exegesis and the non-dramatic versions of the Deirdre Saga; First performances of Synge's plays in various countries and places.

The earliest bibliography which gives information not elsewhere available.

Ian MacPhail and M. Pollard. *John Millington Synge 1871-1909: A Catalogue of an Exhibition Held at Trinity College Library Dublin on the Occasion of the Fiftieth Anniversary of his Death*. Dublin: Dolmen Press, 1959. Pp. 38.

Primary. Form arrangement. Books: transcribed TP, part collation, bibliographical notes, reprints and subsequent editions. Pp. 30-32, annotated list of periodical contributions: volume, pages, date. Pp. 32-34, list of MSS.

In "John Millington Synge: Some Bibliographical Notes," *Irish Book*, I (1960), 3-10, MacPhail reports his work on the above *Catalogue* and surveys the bibliographical problems connected with Synge.

David H. Greene and E. M. Stephens. *John Millington Synge*. New York: Macmillan and Co., 1959. Pp. 321.

Pp. 308-310, "A List of the Published Writings of Synge": place, publisher, date, brief notes. Pp. 309-310, Synge's contributions to periodicals: alphabetical list of periodicals with dates and page numbers.

A convenient checklist in an important critical study.

Donna Gerstenberger. *John Millington Synge*. New York: Twayne Publishers, Inc. (TEAS 12), 1964. Pp. 157.

Pp. 142-147, primary bibliography. Form and genre arrangement. Books, first editions: place, publisher, date, bibliographical notes. Periods: dates, pages. Contents of collected editions. Pp. 147-152, secondary bibliography. Annotated.

There is no single, complete primary bibliography; one must refer to the four volumes listed above and to the bibliographies listed in them.

SECONDARY

Above, Bourgeois, pp. 265-296; Gerstenberger, pp. 147-152.

Alice Thurston McGirr. "Reading List on John Millington Synge." *Bulletin of Bibliography* 7 (1913): 114-115.

Useful list of the first reviews, listed under the primary titles: volume, pages, date, quotations and annotations.

Alan Price. *Synge and Anglo-Irish Drama*. London: Methuen and Co., Ltd., 1961. Pp. 236.

Pp. 229-231, general secondary bibliography.

Edward Halim Mikhail. "Sixty Years of Synge Criticism, 1907-1967. A Selective Bibliography." *Bulletin of Bibliography* 27 (1970): 11-13, 53-56.

Arranged: Bibliographies; General Studies; Individual Plays; Introductions to editions; Unpublished material; Recordings; Background. Books: place, publisher, date. Periods: volume, pages, date.

A very helpful bibliography, especially in its listings of earlier bibliographies, to which reference must be made.

GENERAL

Longaker & Bolles; Batho & Dobrée; Temple & Tucker; Coleman & Tyler; Adelman & Dworkin; Salem; Palmer & Dyson; NCBEL, III, 1934-1938.

TABORI, GEORGE   (1914-   )

Salem.

TAGORE, RABINDRANATH   (1861-1941)

[Ravindranatha Thakura].

PRIMARY

Virgil Cândea. *Tagore en Roumanie*. Bucharest: UNESCO,

1961. Pp. 38.

List of primary writings translated into Roumanian; also
includes secondary bibliography, especially relating to
Tagore's visit to Roumania in 1926. Publisher, date,
place. Index. (In French).

Odette Aslan, ed. *Rabindranath Tagore.* Paris: Editions
Pierre Seghers (Poètes d'Aujourd'hui No. 80), 1961. Pp.
207.

Pp. 202-204, list of primary books published in French: title,
translator, publisher (no dates). Arranged by genre.

Rabindranath Tagore, 1861-1961. Paris: Bibliothèque Nationale,
1961. Pp. 152.

Catalogue of an exhibition arranged to illustrate Tagore's
life and career. Includes much peripheral material, but
amplifies details given by Sen and Bhaumik (below). Ar-
ranged: Chronologie de la Vie et des Œuvres de Tagore;
Le Cadre Familial et Social; La Pensée et la Religion du
Poète; L'Œuvre Littéraire; L'Œuvre Musicale; L'Œuvre
Pédagogique; Apôtre du Rapprochement Orient-Occident;
Artisan de la Libération de L'Inde--Tagore et Ghandi;
L'Œuvre Picturale; Hommages à Tagore. Usually title,
publisher, place, date, part collation, annotations.

A Centenary Volume. Rabindranath Tagore, 1861-1961.
New Delhi: Sahitya Akademi, 1961. Pp. 531.

Pulinbihari Sen and Jagadindra Bhaumik, "Works of Tagore.
A Bibliography," pp. 504-519. Pp. 504-511, writings in
Bengali: title, date, genre. Pp. 512-518, writings in English:
title, place, publisher, date, translator, genre.

This checklist, along with the Bibliothèque Nationale catalogue (above), provides a fairly complete list of the primary
writings.

SECONDARY

Above, Cåndea, pp. 20-24, and Bibliothèque Nationale Catalogue.

Ethel M. Kitch. "Rabindranath Tagore--A Bibliography." *Bulletin of Bibliography* 11 (1921): 80-84.

Pp. 81-84, secondary selected bibliography. Topic arrangement; includes reviews of primary writings. Books: place, publisher, date. Periods: dates.

GENERAL

Adelman & Dworkin.

TATE, ELLALICE: see HIBBERT, ELEANOR.

TAWNEY, RICHARD HENRY   (1880-1962)

Daiches; WW 62.

TAYLOR, ALAN JOHN PERCIVALE   (1906-   )

Daiches; WW 71.

TAYLOR, ALFRED EDWARD   (1869-1945)

Batho & Dobrée; WWW 41-50.

TAYLOR, ELIZABETH   (1912-   )

(Mrs. J. W. K. Taylor).

Bufkin; WW 71.

TAYLOR, RACHEL ANNAND   (1876-1960)

WWW 51-60.

TEMPEST, MARGARET MARY   (-   )

    (Lady Mears).

WW 71.

TEMPLE, WILLIAM   (1881-1944)

    WWW 41-50.

TENNANT, KYLIE   (1912-   )

    (Mrs. Lewis Rodd).

Hetherington.

TENNYSON, SIR CHARLES BRUCE LOCKER   (1879-   )

WW 71.

THIRKELL, ANGELA MARGARET   (1890-1961)

    (Mrs. G. L. Thirkell).

Longaker & Bolles; Temple & Tucker.

THOMAS, DYLAN MARLAIS   (1914-1953)

PRIMARY

Elder Olson. *The Poetry of Dylan Thomas*. Chicago: University of Chicago Press, 1954. Pp. 164.

Pp. 102-146, "Bibliography" by William H. Huff. Primary, secondary. Chronological arrangement, subdivided by genre. Books: place, publisher, date, reprints, reviews. Periods: volume, date, pages. Reviews by Thomas include title and author of book reviewed. Includes BBC broadcasts by Thomas. Pp. 127-146, secondary bibliography.

J. Alexander Rolph. *Dylan Thomas. A Bibliography.* London: Dent and Co.; New York: New Directions, 1956. Pp. 108.

Primary. Genre and form arrangement. Books: transcribed TP, part collation, pagination, binding, price, number of copies, contents, extensive notes. Periods: volume, date, pages. Pp. 1-38, chronological list of Thomas's poems: for each, details of its publication and of textual variants. Includes translations and recordings. Indexed.

The authoritative bibliography: additions and corrections to it are made by: William B. Todd. "The Bibliography of Dylan Thomas." *Book Collector* 6 (1957): 71-73; Timothy d'Arch Smith. "Note 227. The Second Edition of Dylan Thomas's *18 Poems.*" *Book Collector* 13 (1964): 351-352; William White. "Dylan Thomas, Mr. Rolph, and 'John O'London's Weekly'." *Papers of the Bibliographical Society of America* 60 (1966): 370-372.

Hélène Bokanowski and Marc Alyn. *Dylan Thomas.* Paris: Editions Pierre Seghers (Poètes d'Aujourd'hui 92), 1962. Pp. 222.

Pp. 216-217, French translations of Thomas. Title, publisher, place, date, translator.

Roberto Sanesi. *Dylan Thomas.* Milan: Lerici Editori, 1960. Pp. 200.

Pp. 185-186, list of translations of Thomas into Italian, French, German, Swedish, and Danish.

Ralph Maud, assisted by Albert Glover. *Dylan Thomas in Print. A Bibliographical History.* Pittsburgh: University of Pittsburgh Press, 1970. Pp. [xii], 261.

Primary complete, secondary complete (to 1968-1969). Five sections: Books, anthologies, theses (arranged chronologically); Welsh periodicals and newspapers; London, etc., periodicals and newspapers; United States and Canadian periodicals and newspapers (entries listed under title of publication); Foreign-language publications (arranged according to language). Books: place, publisher, date, relevant pages, contents of new primary editions, extensive textual and bibliographical notes. Periods: volume, pages, date, notes and quotations. Pp. 229-261, index.

While Rolph remains the standard bibliography, Maud offers a wealth of supplementary information about the primary writings, and his annotations to them and the secondary bibliography make this book an indispensable aid to the student, who should always begin with the Index in order to overcome the idiosyncrasies of the presentation.

SECONDARY

Above, Olson, pp. 127-146; Maud, *passim.*

Sister Lois Theisen. "Dylan Thomas. A Bibliography of Secondary Criticism." *Bulletin of Bibliography* 26 (1969): 9-28, 32, 36, 59-60.

Topic and form arrangement. Includes list of previous bibliographies. Books: place, publisher, date, pages. Periods: volume, date, pages. Each entry numbered. Although providing less information than Maud, the simpler arrangement makes this an easier starting point for work with the secondary bibliography.

GENERAL

Longaker & Bolles; Daiches; Temple & Tucker; Coleman & Tyler; Adelman & Dworkin; Salem; Palmer & Dyson.

THOMAS, GILBERT OLIVER   (1891-   )

WW 71.

THOMAS, GWYNN   (1913-   )

WW 71.

THOMAS, PHILLIP EDWARD   (1878-1917)

PRIMARY

Gwendolen Murphy. "Bibliographies of Modern Authors, No.
2. Edward Thomas." *London Mercury* 16 (1927): 71-75, 193-
198, 525-530; 17 (1928): 76.

Primary books and periodical contributions other than reviews.
Form and genre arrangement. Books: transcribed TP, full
collation, pagination, binding, price. Pp. 529-530, periodical
contributions listed under title of period: date, pages.

One of the 1920 bibliographies aimed at the collector of
"firsts"--less complete than Eckert (below), but still useful.

Robert P. Eckert. *Edward Thomas: A Biography and a Bibliography.* London: J. M. Dent and Sons, 1937. Pp. 328.

Pp. 185-289, bibliography. Primary, secondary selected.
Form arrangement. Books: transcribed TP, partial collation,
binding, date, previous publication of contents noted, bibliographical notes. Periods: volume, date, pages; notes on the
reprinting of individual items; reviews by Thomas include
title and author of book reviewed. Pp. 278-289, secondary
bibliography: alphabetical by author, annotated. The standard bibliography.

Vernon Scannell. *Edward Thomas.* London: Longmans, Green
and Co. (WTW 163), 1963. Pp. 36.

Pp. 34-35, selected primary books: date, place, genre. Pp.
35-36, selected secondary bibliography.

SECONDARY

Above, Eckert, pp. 278-289; Scannell, pp. 35-36.

GENERAL

Longaker & Bolles; Batho & Dobrée; Temple & Tucker.

THOMAS, RONALD STUART   (1913-   )

PRIMARY

R. G. Thomas. *Ronald Stuart Thomas.* London: Longmans,
Green and Co. (WTW 166), 1964. Pp. 43.

P. 43, bibliography. Primary books. Chronological arrangement. Place, date. Also names periodicals to which Thomas
contributed.

GENERAL

Temple & Tucker; WW 71.

THOMPSON, ALEXANDER HAMILTON   (1873-1952)

PRIMARY

*An Address Presented to Alexander Hamilton Thompson with a
Bibliography of his Writings.* Oxford: Privately Printed at
the University Press, 1948. Pp. [50].

Pp. 19-49, primary writings. Chronological arrangement.
Books: publisher, date, pages. Periods: volume, date, pages.

GENERAL

WWW 51-60.

THOMPSON, EDWARD JOHN   (-1946)

WWW 41-50.

THOMPSON, FRANCIS JOSEPH   (1859-1907)

PRIMARY

C. A. and H. W. Stonehill. *Bibliographies of Modern Authors* (Second Series). London: John Castle, 1925. Pp. [xiv], 162. 750 copies.

> Pp. 143-162, primary books; also incomplete other writings. Form arrangement. Transcribed TP, full collation, pagination, binding, price, number of copies, variants, bibliographical notes.

> A collector's bibliography, concentrating upon the physical form of the book, rather than upon its contents.

Myrtle Pihlman Pope. "A Critical Bibliography of Works by and about Francis Thompson." *Bulletin of the New York Public Library* 62 (1958): 571-576; 63 (1959): 40-49, 155-161, 195-204.

> P. 157, critical essays by Thompson; pp. 157-160, chronological list of Thompson's literary criticism; pp. 160-161, 195-196, other primary writings; pp. 196-203, chronological list of Thompson's poems; pp. 203-204, separate printings of "The Hound of Heaven." Pp. 48-49, list of 13 primary and secondary bibliographies; pp. 155-156, secondary bibliography.

> A useful checklist of titles; the list of Thompson's unreprinted journalism is supplemented by Terence L. Connolly, "A Revised Essay toward a Bibliography of Francis Thompson's Book Reviews and Literary Criticism Contributed to Periodicals" in Francis Thompson, *The Real Robert Louis Stevenson and Other Critical Essays*. New York: University Publishers, Inc., for Boston College, 1959. Pp. xiv, 409. Pp. 353-398, primary, unsigned writings. Alphabetical list of periodicals with contributions listed chronologically under each. Dates. Author and title of books reviewed. For an account of MSS collections, see below, Danchin.

Peter Butter. *Francis Thompson*. London: Longmans, Green and Co. (WTW 141), 1961. Pp. 38.

Pp. 37-38, primary books: place, date, with notes on editors and revisions. Note also the list of bibliographies.

SECONDARY

Above, Pope, pp. 48-49, 155-156; Butter, p. 38.

Pierre Danchin. *Francis Thompson. La Vie et L'Œuvre d'un Poète.* Paris: A.-G. Nizet, 1959. Pp. 554.

Pp. 524-544, secondary bibliography. Form and genre arrangement. Annotations. Pp. 526-527, list of MSS collections and descriptions of catalogues of them. (In French).

The most comprehensive study of Thompson, with an important secondary bibliography.

J. C. Reid. *Francis Thompson. Man and Poet.* London: Routledge and Kegan Paul, 1959. Pp. [xii], 232.

Pp. 218-219, primary books. Pp. 219-224, secondary bibliography.

GENERAL

Longaker & Bolles; Batho & Dobrée; NCBEL, III, 597-601.

THOMPSON, SYLVIA ELIZABETH (1902-1968)

(Mrs. Peter Luling).

Millett; Temple & Tucker; WW 68.

THOMSON, HUGH (1860-1920)

PRIMARY

Marion H. Spielmann and Walter Jerrold. *Hugh Thomson: His Art, His Letters, His Humour and His Charm.* London: A. and C. Black, Ltd., 1931. Pp. 269.

THO

Pp. 237-254, bibliography of printed work. Primary, secondary selected. Form arrangement. Books: author, title, publisher, date. Periods: date, title of work illustrated. Pp. 251-252, index of authors illustrated by Thomson.

SECONDARY

Above, Spielmann and Jerrold, pp. 250-251.

TIBBLE, JOHN WILLIAM   (1901-   )

WW 71.

TILLER, TERENCE   (1916-   )

Daiches; Temple & Tucker.

TILLOTSON, GEOFFREY   (1905-1969)

Daiches; WW 69.

TILLOTSON, KATHLEEN MARY   (1906-   )

(Mrs. Geoffrey Tillotson).

WW 71.

TILLYARD, EUSTACE MANDEVILLE WETENHALL (1889-1962)

Daiches; WW 62.

TODD, RUTHVEN   (1914-   )

Temple & Tucker.

382

TOLKIEN, JOHN RONALD REUEL   (1892-   )

PRIMARY

Richard C. West. *Tolkien Criticism. An Annotated Checklist.*
Kent: Kent State University Press (Serif Series, 11), 1970.
Pp. [xvi], 73.

Pp. 1-8, primary bibliography. Chronological arrangement.
Books: place, publisher, date, selected subsequent editions.
Periods: volume, date, pages, reprintings. Annotations. Pp.
9-64, secondary bibliography, annotated. Reviews of Tolkien's
books listed under title of book. Index of secondary titles.
Pp. viii-xi, list of periodicals devoted to or largely concerned
with Tolkien.

Bonniejean McGuire Christensen. "J. R. R. Tolkien: A Bibliography." *Bulletin of Bibliography* 27 (1970): 61-67.

Primary, secondary. Genre and topic arrangement with
particular emphasis on separation of scholarly and popular
writings. Books: place, publisher, date, all editions, reprints, occasionally textual notes. Periods: volume, pages,
date. Reviews of Tolkien listed under title of primary work
being reviewed.

West and Christensen together provide quite as much information as one should ever need about Tolkien.

SECONDARY

Above, West, pp. 9-64; Christensen, pp. 62-67.

GENERAL

Temple & Tucker; WW 71.

TOMLIN, ERIC WALTER FREDERICK   (1913-   )

WW 71.

TOMLINSON, CHARLES   (1927-   )

Temple & Tucker.

TOMLINSON, HENRY MAJOR   (1873-1958)

PRIMARY

Howard S. Mott, Jr. "H. M. Tomlinson. A Checklist Bibliography." *Reading and Collecting* 1, iii (February, 1937): 25.

Primary books, including books with contributions by Tomlinson. Chronological arrangement. Place, date, binding,
bibliographical notes usually concerned with "points,"
all editions.

Apparently this is the only available bibliography, although
in the *Book Collector* 11 (Summer, 1962): 219, Peter R. Haack
asked for information for a bibliography he was preparing.

GENERAL

Millett; Daiches; Longaker & Bolles; Temple & Tucker.

TOUT, THOMAS FREDERICK   (1855-1929)

Batho & Dobrée; WWW 29-40.

TOYNBEE, ARNOLD JOSEPH   (1889-   )

PRIMARY

Monica Popper. *A Bibliography of the Works in English of
Arnold Toynbee, 1910-1954*. London and New York: Royal
Institute of International Affairs, 1955. Pp. 59, mimeo-
graphed one side.

Primary. Chronological arrangement. Books: place, publisher, date, pages, subsequent editions and reprints, textual

notes. Periods: volume, pages, date.

Rush Greenslade. "Arnold J. Toynbee: A Checklist." *Twentieth-Century Literature* 2 (1956): 92-104.

Primary. Arranged: books by Toynbee; translations of Toynbee's books; works edited by Toynbee; translations by Toynbee; joint author; miscellaneous (including lectures, essays, parts of books; periodical contributions (arranged alphabetically by title). Books: place, publisher, date, pages. Periods: volume, pages, date.

GENERAL

Daiches; WW 71.

TOYNBEE, THEODORE PHILIP   (1916-   )

Daiches; Temple & Tucker; WW 71.

TRAVERS, BEN   (1886-   )

WW 71.

TREECE, HENRY   (1911-1966)

Daiches; Longaker & Bolles; Temple & Tucker.

TRENCH, FREDERICK HERBERT   (1865-1923)

PRIMARY

"Bibliographies of Modern Authors. Frederick Herbert Trench." *London Mercury* 4 (1921): 87.

Primary books, 1901-1919. Chronological arrangement. Publisher, year, brief notes.

GENERAL

Batho & Dobrée; Temple & Tucker; NCBEL, III, 1911.

TREVELYAN, GEORGE MACAULAY   (1876-1962)

PRIMARY

J. H. Plumb. *G. M. Trevelyan*. London: Longmans, Green and
Co. (WTW 17), 1951. Pp. 39.

Pp. 35-39, primary books, selected. Arranged: Collected Editions and Separate Works. Place, date, genre, contents, miscellaneous notes.

One of the most complete of the WTW bibliographies.

GENERAL

Batho & Dobrée; Temple & Tucker.

TREVELYAN, ROBERT CALVERLEY   (1872-1951)

WWW 51-60.

TREVOR, ELLESTON   (1920-   )

WW 71; Hagen.

TREVOR, MERIOL   (1919-   )

WW 71.

TREVOR, WILLIAM   (1928-   )

Pseudonym of William Trevor Cox.

WW 71.

TREVOR-ROPER, HUGH REDWALD   (1914-   )

Daiches; WW 71.

TREWIN, JOHN COURTENAY   (1908-   )

WW 71.

TUOHY, JOHN FRANCIS [FRANK]   (1925-   )

WW 71.

TURNER, JAMES ERNEST   (1909-   )

Temple & Tucker; Hagen.

TURNER, REGINALD   (1867?-1938)

PRIMARY

Stanley Weintraub. *Reggie. A Portrait of Reginald Turner.*
New York: George Braziller, 1965. Pp. [x], 293.

Bibliographical information, both primary and secondary,
in text, *passim*, and in notes, pp. [281]-288. Index.

TURNER, WALTER JAMES REDFERN   (1889-1946)

Millett; Longaker & Bolles; Daiches; Temple & Tucker.

TWEEDSMUIR, SUSAN, LADY TWEEDSMUIR   (-   )

WW 71.

TYNAN, KATHERINE   (1861-1931)
(Mrs. Henry Albert Hinkson).

Millett; Longaker & Bolles; Temple & Tucker; Dictionary of
National Biography, 1931-1940; NCBEL, III, 1910-1911.

TYNAN, KENNETH PEACOCK   (1927-   )

Temple & Tucker; WW 71.

UNDERHILL, EVELYN   (1875-1941)

(Mrs. Hubert Stuart Moore).

PRIMARY

Evelyn Underhill. London: Ernest Benn Ltd. (Augustan Books
of Poetry), 1932. Pp. 32.

P. [31], primary books. Publisher, price.

Margaret Cropper. *Evelyn Underhill*. London: Longmans, Green
and Co., 1958. Pp. 244.

While there is no bibliography, this authorized biography
gives a full account of Underhill's literary work.

GENERAL

Millett.

UNSTEAD, ROBERT JOHN   (1915-   )

WW 71.

UNWIN, DAVID STORR   (1918-   )

WW 71.

UNWIN, SIR STANLEY   (1884-1968)

WW 68.

UPFIELD, ARTHUR   (1891-   )

Hetherington; Hagen.

USTINOV, PETER ALEXANDER   (1921-   )

PRIMARY

Geoffrey Williams. *Peter Ustinov*. London: Peter Owens Ltd.,
1957. Pp. 180.

P. 180, "Summary." Plays by Ustinov (theatre and date of
production); films by Ustinov, and also those in which he
appeared; books by Ustinov (publisher, date). Other works
by Ustinov mentioned in text, *passim*.

GENERAL

Daiches; Temple & Tucker; Coleman & Tyler; Adelman & Dworkin; Salem; Palmer & Dyson; WW 71.

UTTLEY, ALISON   (-   )

WW 71.

VACHELL, HORACE ANNESLEY   (1861-1955)

Temple & Tucker; WWW 51-60.

VAN DRUTEN, JOHN WILLIAM   (1901-1957)

Daiches; Temple & Tucker; Adelman & Dworkin; WWW 51-60.

VAN

VANE, SUTTON   (1891?-1963)

Coleman & Tyler; Salem; Palmer & Dyson.

VAUGHAN, CHARLES EDWYN   (1854-1922)

PRIMARY

H. B. Charlton. "A List of the Writings of Professor C. E.
Vaughan." *Bulletin of the John Rylands Library* 7 (1922-
1923): 494-506.

Pp. 494-498, introductory essay. Pp. 498-506, primary bibliography. Form arrangement. Books: publisher, date, pages,
date of reprints. Periods: volume, date, pages. Extensive
bibliographical and textual annotations. P. 506, list of
obituary notices.

VAUGHAN, HILDA   (1892-   )

(Mrs. Charles Morgan).

PRIMARY

G. F. Adam. *Three Contemporary Anglo-Welsh Novelists: Jack
Jones, Rhys Davies, and Hilda Vaughan.* Bern: A. Francke
A. G. (University of Bern Monograph), [1950]. Pp. 109.

P. 108, bibliography. Primary books. Genre arrangement.
Publisher, date.

GENERAL

WW 71.

VERNEY, SIR JOHN   (1913-   )

WW 71.

VERSCHOYLE, DEREK HUGO   (1911-   )

WW 71.

VESEY-FITZGERALD, BRIAN SEYMOUR   (-   )

WW 71.

VIDLER, ALEXANDER ROPER   (1899-   )

WW 71.

VILLIERS, ALAN JOHN   (1903-   )

WW 71.

VINES, WALTER SHERARD   (1890?-1965)

WW 65.

VINOGRADOFF, SIR PAUL   (1854-1925)

Batho & Dobrée; WWW 16-28.

VULLIAMY, COLWYN EDWARD   (1886-   )

Temple & Tucker; WW 71; Hagen.

WADDELL, HELEN JANE   (1889-1965)

Daiches; Longaker & Bolles; WW 65.

WADDELL, SAMUEL: see MAYNE, RUTHERFORD.

WAD

WADE, ROSALIND HERSCHEL   (-   )

(Mrs. William Kean Seymour).

WW 71.

WAIN, JOHN BARRINGTON   (1925-   )

Temple & Tucker; WW 71.

WALEY, ARTHUR DAVID   (1889-1966)

PRIMARY

Francis A. Johns. *A Bibliography of Arthur Waley* [English
title: *The Strategist: A Bibliography of Arthur Waley*].
New Brunswick, New Jersey: Rutgers University Press;
London: George Allen and Unwin, 1968. Pp. xii, 188.

Primary, secondary selected. Form and genre arrangement.
Books: transcribed TP, part collation, binding, date, price,
number of copies, printer, contents with cross-references to
previous publications, subsequent impressions and editions,
translations (date, publisher, number of copies). Extensive
bibliographical and textual notes. Periods: date, pages, occasionally volume; reviews by Waley include title and author
of book reviewed. Index.

Lawrence S. Thompson, *Papers of the Bibliographical Society of America* 63 (1969): 354: "a carefully detailed
record of Waley's work."

SECONDARY

Above, Johns, pp. 173-174.

GENERAL

Daiches.

WALKLEY, ARTHUR BINGHAM   (1855-1926)

Temple & Tucker; NCBEL, III, 1455.

WALLACE, DOREEN   (1897-   )

(Mrs. D. E. A. Rash).

WW 71.

WALLACE, RICHARD HORATIO EDGAR   (1875-1932)

PRIMARY

William Oliver Guillemont Lofts and Derek Adley. *The British Bibliography of Edgar Wallace*. London: Howard Baker, 1969. Pp. [xvi], 246.

Primary. Form and genre arrangement. Variously arranged lists of titles with cross-references, the most important being an alphabetical by title list of primary books: publisher, date, format, pages, dedication (pp. 15-35); the same list with contents of each book listed with place of first publication (pp. 36-143); alphabetical by title list of periodicals, Wallace's contributions listed under each title: date, occasionally volume or pages, cross-reference to primary book in which collected (pp. 155-246). Many notes and miscellaneous bibliographical information.

Not an easy book to use, but immensely informative about the British publications (no others are considered).

GENERAL

Temple & Tucker; Hagen.

WALLER, SIR JOHN STANIER   (1917-   )

WW 71.

WALPOLE, SIR HUGH SEYMOUR   (1884-1941)

PRIMARY

Henry Danielson. *Bibliographies of Modern Authors.* London: Bookman's Journal, 1921. Pp. [xii], [212].

Pp. 201-208, primary books, 1909-1921. Chronological arrangement. Transcribed TP, part collation, pagination, binding, variants, miscellaneous bibliographical notes.

Jean Marty. "Hugh Walpole Bibliography." *Reading and Collecting* 2 (February-March, 1938): 26.

Primary books. Chronological arrangement. Place, date, occasionally collector's "points," subsequent editions. Includes books with contributions by Walpole and books about Walpole.

A Note by Hugh Walpole on the Origins of the Herries Chronicle. New York: Doubleday, Doran and Co., Inc., 1940. Pp. 27.

An advertisement brochure listing (pp. 26-27) the American editions of Walpole's books: place, publisher, date (44 titles).

Rupert Hart-Davis. *Hugh Walpole A Biography.* New York: Harcourt, Brace and World, Inc., 1952. Pp. xii, [468].

Pp. 445-447, primary books. Chronological arrangement. Date. Contents listed for collections.

SECONDARY

Above, Marty.

GENERAL

Millett; Daiches; Batho & Dobrée; Temple & Tucker; Bufkin.

WALTON, JOHN: see CONWAY, OLIVE.

WARD, JAMES   (1843-1925)

PRIMARY

E. B. Titchener, W. S. Foster, *et al.* "A List of the Writings of James Ward." *Monist* 36 (1926): 170-176.

Primary. Chronological arrangement. Books: place, publisher, date, pages, format. Periods: volume, pages, date. Annotated. Reviews by Ward include title and author of book reviewed.

GENERAL

Batho & Dobrée; NCBEL, III, 1597-1598.

WARD, MARY AUGUSTA   (1851-1920)

(Mrs. Humphrey Ward).

Batho & Dobrée; Longaker & Bolles; NCBEL, III, 1081-1082.

WARLOCK, PETER: see HESELTINE, PHILIP.

WARNER, OLIVER   (1903-   )

WW 71; Hagen.

WARNER, REGINALD (REX) ERNEST   (1905-   )

PRIMARY

A. L. McLeod. *Rex Warner: Writer. An Introductory Essay.* Sydney, N. S. W.: Wentworth Press, 1964. Pp. vi, 50.

Pp. 46-50, "A Select Bibliography." Primary. Genre and form arrangement. Books: place, publisher, date. Periods: date, pages. Includes list of unpublished radio and TV talks.

WAR

Pp. 49-50, selected secondary bibliography.

SECONDARY

Above, McLeod, pp. 49-50.

GENERAL

Daiches; Temple & Tucker; WW 71.

WARNER, SYLVIA TOWNSEND   (1893-   )

Millett; Longaker & Bolles; Daiches; Temple & Tucker; WW 71.

WATERHOUSE, KEITH SPENCER   (1929-   )

WW 71.

WATKINS, VERNON PHILLIPS   (1906-1967)

PRIMARY

Brynmor James. *Vernon Watkins 1906-1967*. Welsh Arts Council
(Bibliographies of Anglo-Welsh Literature, 5), 1968.

Not seen.

Jane McCormick. "Vernon Watkins: A Bibliography." *West
Coast Review* 4, i (Spring, 1969): 42-48.

Primary, secondary selected. Form arrangement. Books:
place, publisher, date, subsequent editions. Periods: volume, pages, date. Includes selected translations by Watkins
and selected anthologies in which his poems appear; also
recordings by Watkins. Pp. 46-48, secondary bibliography.
Alphabetical-by-author arrangement; annotated.

GENERAL

Longaker & Bolles; Temple & Tucker; WW 67.

WATSON, SIR WILLIAM   (1858-1935)

PRIMARY

Cecil Woolf. "Some Uncollected Authors. XII: Sir William
Watson." *Book Collector* 5 (Winter, 1956): 375-380.

Primary books. Chronological arrangement. Place, publisher, date, format, binding and variants, limitations of
edition, miscellaneous notes.

Norman Colbeck. "Sir William Watson: Additions and Cor-
rections." *Book Collector* 6 (Spring, 1957): 66-67. Walter
E. Swayze. "Sir William Watson: Additions and Corrections."
Book Collector 6 (Autumn, 1957): 285-286 (Winter, 1957): 402.

These several entries together provide a fairly complete list
of Watson's books.

GENERAL

Millett; Longaker & Bolles; Temple & Tucker; NCBEL, III,
653-654.

WAUGH, ALEXANDER [ALEC] RABAN   (1898-   )

Millett; Daiches; Longaker & Bolles; Temple & Tucker; WW 71.

WAUGH, EVELYN ARTHUR ST. JOHN   (1903-1966)

PRIMARY

Paul A. Doyle. "Evelyn Waugh: A Bibliography (1926-1956)."
Bulletin of Bibliography 22 (1957): 57-62.

Primary first editions, secondary selected. Form and genre
arrangement. Books: date, place, publisher (both British and

American first editions). Periods: volume, pages, date.

Charles E. Linck, Jr. "Works of Evelyn Waugh, 1910 to 1930."
Twentieth Century Literature 10 (April, 1964): 19-25.

Primary. Chronological arrangement, subdivided by genre.
Books: place, publisher, date. Periods: volume, date, pages.
Reviews by Waugh include title and author of book reviewed.

Robert Murray Davis. "Textual Problems in the Novels of
Evelyn Waugh." *Papers of the Bibliographical Society of
America* 62 (1968): 259-263.

Important criticism of and additions to Doyle and Linck;
also references to other bibliographical-textual studies of
Waugh, including those by Anthony Newnham and Jackson R.
Bryer.

D. Paul Farr. "Evelyn Waugh. A Supplemental Bibliography."
Bulletin of Bibliography 26 (1969): 67-68, 87.

Primary. Genre arrangement. Books: place, publisher, date.
Periods: volume, pages, date. Reviews by Waugh include
author and title of book reviewed.

These several entries provide much information, although
even collectively not a complete bibliography. *TLS* (18
June 1970), p. 669: "Mr. Anthony Newnham...is at work on
'what promises to be the definitive bibliography of Evelyn
Waugh.'"

SECONDARY

Above, Doyle, pp. 60.62.

Heinz Kosok. "Evelyn Waugh. A Checklist of Criticism."
Twentieth Century Literature 12 (1966): 211-215.

Selected secondary. Arranged: General Studies, Studies of
Individual Works. Books: place, date. Periods: volume,
pages, date.

Paul A. Doyle, ed. *The Evelyn Waugh News Letter* 1 (1967)--
to date.

By volume 5 (1971) this journal had published too many primary and secondary bibliographical items for them to be listed here; it is the most important and the most up-to-date supplement to the bibliographies described above and is indispensable for the student concerned with Waugh.

GENERAL

Millett; Daiches; Longaker & Bolles; Temple & Tucker.

WEBB, BEATRICE POTTER   (1858-1943)
    (Lady Passfield).
WEBB, SYDNEY JAMES, LORD PASSFIELD   (1859-1947)

PRIMARY

R. H. Tawney. "Beatrice Webb, 1858-1943." *Proceedings of
the British Academy* 29 (1943): 25-27.

Primary books. Arranged according to authorship: pp. 25-
26, by Beatrice Webb; pp. 26-27, by Beatrice and Sydney
Webb; p. 27, by Sydney Webb. Dates, pages.

See above, FABIAN SOCIETY.

GENERAL

Batho & Dobrée; WWW 41-50.

WEBB, MARY GLADYS MEREDITH   (1881-1927)

PRIMARY

Charles Sanders. "Mary Webb: An Introduction." *English*

Literature in Transition 9 (1966): 115-118.

An essay in which the primary books are mentioned with date and genre.

SECONDARY

Charles Sanders. "Mary Webb: An Annotated Bibliography of Works about Her." *English Literature in Transition* 9 (1966): 119-136.

Alphabetical by author. Books: place, publisher, date. Periods: volume, pages, date. Annotations. Continued in subsequent issues, especially 11 (1968): 56.

GENERAL

Millett; Temple & Tucker.

WEBB, SYDNEY JAMES, LORD PASSFIELD: *see* WEBB, BEATRIX POTTER, and FABIAN SOCIETY.

WEDGEWOOD, DAME CICELY VERONICA   (1910-   )

PRIMARY

Richard Curle. *The Richard Curle Collection of the Works of Cicely Veronica Wedgewood.* Beaminster: J. Stevens Cox, Toucan Press, 1961. Pp. 19. 65 copies.

Pp. 5-19, primary books and pamphlets. For each title, publisher, date, bibliographical notes.

Idiosyncratic, perhaps, but a useful checklist.

GENERAL

Daiches; Temple & Tucker; WW 71.

WELCH, MAURICE DENTON   (1917-1948)

PRIMARY

Jocelyn Brooke, ed. *Denton Welch. Extracts from his Published Works*. London: Chapman and Hall, Ltd., 1963. Pp. xxvi, 261.

Pp. vii-xxvi, "Introduction" by Brooke; provides many bibliographical details, although no lists.

GENERAL

Temple & Tucker.

WELLESLEY, DOROTHY VIOLET ASHTON   (1889-1956)

(Duchess of Wellington).

Longaker & Bolles; Daiches; Temple & Tucker.

WELLS, HERBERT GEORGE   (1866-1946)

PRIMARY

Geoffrey H. Wells. *The Works of H. G. Wells, 1887-1925, A Bibliography, Dictionary and Subject Index*. London: George Routledge and Sons, Ltd.; New York: H. W. Wilson Co., 1926. Pp. [xxvi], 274.

Primary. Form arrangement: books and pamphlets, pp. xxiii-xxiv, 1-65; books with contributions by Wells, pp. 66-72; unreprinted primary writings, pp. 73-79; letters to the press, pp. 80-81. Books: transcribed TP, full collation, pagination, printer, binding, variants, brief account of previous serial publication, occasional textual or bibliographical notes. Periods: date. [Pp. 89-251, the dictionary; pp. 255-274, subject index].

Costa (below), p. 168: "no Wells scholar should be without it." The authoritative bibliography for the years covered.

Gordon N. Ray. "H. G. Wells' Contributions to the *Saturday Review." Library* (5th Series) 16 (1961): 29-36.

Pp. 29-32, introductory essay; pp. 32-36, primary writings, signed and unsigned. Chronological arrangement. Volume, date, pages. Reviews by Wells include author and title of books reviewed.

Ingvald Raknem. *H. G. Wells and his Critics.* Oslo and Bergen, Universitatsforlaget (Scandinavian University Books), 1962. Pp. [iv], 475.

Pp. 432-434, unreprinted primary writings. Chronological arrangement. Volume, pages, date. Pp. 435-440, general secondary books and books about Wells: place, publisher, date. Pp. 446-459, reviews of primary books listed under title of book reviewed: volume, pages, date. Pp. 460-471, general studies in periodicals. P. 472, obituary notices.

[H. G. Wells Society]. *H. G. Wells. A Comprehensive Bibliography.* London: H. G. Wells Society, 1968. Pp. vi, 70.

Pp. 1-45, primary books. Chronological arrangement. Place, publisher, date, pages, annotations, brief bibliographical notes. Pp. 46-50, short stories listed with periodical and date in which originally published. Pp. 51-57, other primary writings. Pp. 57-63, secondary bibliography. Chronological arrangement. Pp. 64-66, stage and film adaptations of Wells' writings.

The inaccurately-named *"Comprehensive Bibliography"* supplements the 1926 bibliography list of books but does not provide full information about these books. It, along with Ray and Raknem (above), lists a small part of Wells' unreprinted journalism. Lacking any complete bibliography of Wells' writings, the student may turn with relief to the simple checklist in Montgomery Belgion. *H. G. Wells.* London: Longmans, Green and Co. (WTW 40), 1955. Pp. 43. Selected primary books, pp. 37-42: date and genre; or to Costa (below).

SECONDARY

Above, Raknem and [H. G. Wells Society].

Robert P. Weeks. "H. G. Wells." *English Fiction* (later *English Literature*) *in Transition* 1 (Fall-Winter, 1957): 37-42.

Annotated secondary bibliography. Note references to previous compilations, the contents of which are not here relisted. This bibliography is continued by various writers in subsequent issues, particularly 1, ii, 35; 4, ii (1961): 59-64; 5, ii (1962): 36-43; 6, ii (1963): 119-123; etc.

Richard Hauer Costa. *H. G. Wells*. New York: Twayne Publishers Inc. (TEAS 43), 1967. Pp. 181.

Pp. 165-167, primary books (fiction complete, other genres selected). Chronological arrangement. Place, publisher, and date of either English or American first edition. Pp. 167-173, secondary bibliography. Annotated. Additional items in notes, pp. 151-164.

By examining the bibliographies in each of the books listed in the books above, one begins to locate some of the references to Wells: there is no single, comprehensive listing, although Raknem (above) probably provides the most representative list.

GENERAL

Millett; Longaker & Bolles; Batho & Dobrée; Temple & Tucker.

WESKER, ARNOLD   (1932-   )

PRIMARY

Harold U. Ribalow. *Arnold Wesker*. New York: Twayne Publishers, Inc. (TEAS 28), 1965. Pp. 154.

Pp. 137-138, primary bibliography. Chronological arrangement. Books: place, publisher, date, British and American editions, revisions and reprints. Periods: date, pages. Pp.

138-150, secondary bibliography. Alphabetical by author under divisions Criticism and Background Material. Information as for primary writings, with extensive annotations. Additional secondary material on pp. [11] - [13] and 123-136. One of the better bibliographies in this series.

SECONDARY

Above, Ribalow, pp. [11] - [13], 123-136, 138-150.

Glenda Leeming and Simon Trussler. *The Plays of Arnold Wesker*. London: Gollancz, 1971.

Not seen.

GENERAL

Temple & Tucker; Coleman & Tyler; Adelman & Dworkin; Salem; WW 71.

WEST, ANTHONY PANTHER   (1914-   )

Temple & Tucker; Who's Who in America, 1970-1971.

WEST, MORRIS LANGLO   (1916-   )

Pseudonym used: Michael East.

Temple & Tucker; Hetherington; WW 71; Hagen.

WEST, DAME REBECCA   (1892-   )

Pseudonym of Cicily Isabel Fairfield.

(Mrs. Henry M. Andrews).

PRIMARY

G. Evelyn Hutchinson. *A Preliminary List of the Writings of*

Rebecca West. New Haven: Yale University Library, 1957. Pp. 102.

Primary first editions, British and American. Form and genre arrangement. Books: transcribed TP, part collation, binding, date, price, contents and cross-references to earlier publication, occasional notes on limitations of issue, reprints, presence of advertisements, and variants. Periods: volume, pages, date, reviews by West include title and author of book reviewed. Separate list of translations of primary books with information as for first editions. Also lists of dramatisations, of works announced but not published, and of spurious titles.

The author disclaims completeness, but lists 671 periodical contributions for the 1912-1951 period.

GENERAL

Millett; Daiches; Temple & Tucker; WW 71.

WESTRUP, SIR JACK ALLAN   (1904-   )

WW 71.

WEYMAN, STANLEY JOHN   (1855-1928)

Batho & Dobrée; NCBEL, III, 1082.

WHEATLEY, DENNIS YATES   (1897-   )

WW 71; Hagen.

WHEELER, HUGH   (1916-   )

Salem.

WHIBLEY, CHARLES   (1859-1930)

PRIMARY

T. S. Eliot. *Charles Whibley, A Memoir*. London: The English
Association (Pamphlet No. 80), December, 1931. Pp. 13.

While there is no bibliography, the most important sources to
consult are referred to, *passim*.

GENERAL

Longaker & Bolles; Batho & Dobrée; NCBEL, III, 1458.

WHISTLER, LAURENCE   (1912-   )

WW 71.

WHISTLER, REGINALD JOHN [REX]   (1905-1944)

PRIMARY

Laurence Whistler and Ronald Fuller. *The Work of Rex Whistler*.
London: Batsford, 1960. Pp. [lxxxvi], 122.

Pp. 1-113, Catalogue. Arranged by topic and genre. "A Note,"
p. [lxxv] explains details provided. Index, pp. 115-122.

SECONDARY

Whistler and Fuller, above, p. 114, "Bibliography of the principal books and articles on Rex Whistler, and printed references
to him."

Includes more specialized bibliographies.

WHITE, ANTONIA   (1899-   )

Daiches; WW 71.

WHITE, ELIZABETH EVELYNE MCINTOSH   (-   )

   (Mrs. Ernest James Battey).

WW 71.

WHITE, PATRICK VICTOR MARTINDALE   (1912-   )

PRIMARY

Janette Helen Finch. *Bibliography of Patrick White*. Adelaide: Libraries Board of South Australia, [1965]. Pp. 47.

   Not seen.   Referred to by all authorities as providing necessary bibliographical information.

R. F. Brissenden. *Patrick White*. London: Longmans, Green and Co., Ltd. (WTW 190), 1966. Pp. 48.

   P. 47, primary books. Year, genre. Pp. 47-48, selected secondary bibliography.

   Less informative than Argyle, below.

Barry Argyle. *Patrick White*. New York: Barnes and Noble, Inc; Edinburgh: Oliver and Boyd, 1967. Pp. [viii], 109.

   P. 108, primary books. Chronological arrangement. Place and year for all English and foreign language editions. Pp. 108-109, secondary bibliography. Alphabetical by author. Books: place, date. Periods: volume, date, pages.

SECONDARY

Above, Brissenden, pp. 47-48; Argyle, pp. 108-109.

GENERAL

Hetherington; Coleman & Tyler; WW 71.

WHITE, TERENCE HANBURY   (1906-1964)

PRIMARY

Sylvia Townsend Warner. *T. H. White*. New York: Viking Press;
London: Jonathan Cape, 1968. Pp. 352.

Pp. 346-348, bibliography. Primary books. Chronological
arrangement. Place, publisher, date. Also list of unpublished writings and titles of short stories. See text for
references to primary periodical contributions.

GENERAL

Temple & Tucker.

WHITEHEAD, ALFRED NORTH   (1861-1947)

PRIMARY

Paul Arthur Schilp, ed. *The Philosophy of Alfred North Whitehead*. New York: Tudor Publishing Co. (Library of Living
Philosophers, Vol. III; 2nd edition), 1951.

Pp. 745-778, "Bibliography of the Writings of Alfred North
Whitehead Published through January 3, 1951 (with Selected
Reviews [of Whitehead's writings])" by Victor Lowe and
Robert C. Baldwin. Primary, secondary selected. Chronological arrangement. Books: place, publisher, date, pages,
contents, textual notes, reviews. Periodicals: volume, pages,
date, reprints, brief annotations. Reviews of Whitehead: author,
periodical, date, volume and page numbers.

See pp. 747-749 for the limitations of this bibliography.

Franklin Parker. "Alfred North Whitehead (1861-1947): A Partial Bibliography," *Bulletin of Bibliography* 23 (1961): 90-
93.

Primary books, first editions. Secondary, arranged: Dissertations, Books, Articles, Obituaries. Each section alpha-

betical by author. Books: place, publisher, date. Periodicals: volume, pages, date.

William L. Reese and Eugene Freeman, eds. *Process and Divinity. The Hartshorne Festschrift.* LaSalle, Illinois: Open Court Publishing Co., 1964.

Pp. 593-609, ''Bibliography of Writings by and about Alfred North Whitehead in Languages other than English,'' by George L. Kline. Primary selected; secondary selected. Arrangement: Translations of Whitehead, chronologically listed; Works by Whitehead originally published in French; Studies of Whitehead. Books: date, place, publisher, pages, language. Periodicals: volume, pages, date, language.

SECONDARY

Above, Parker, Schilp, Reese and Freeman.

GENERAL

Daiches; Batho & Dobrée.

WHITEING, RICHARD   (1840-1928)

PRIMARY

Vincent Brome. *Four Realist Novelists.* London: Longmans, Green and Co. (WTW 183), 1965. Pp. 36.

P. 34, bibliography. Primary books. Chronological arrangement. Place, date, genre.

SECONDARY

Wendell V. Harris. ''A Selective Annotated Bibliography of Writings about Richard Whiteing.'' *English Literature in Transition* 8 (1965): 44-48.

GENERAL

Batho & Dobrée.

WHITING, JOHN   (1917-1963)

PRIMARY

Ronald Hayman, ed. *The Collected Plays of John Whiting*.
London: Heinemann, 1969. Two volumes.

This edition includes all of the primary plays, while the
Introductory Note to each play gives selected secondary
references. I, vi: acknowledgement of bibliographical aid
to G. S. Robinson's unpublished London Ph. D. thesis. II,
273-275: Bibliography of Whiting's Other Writings. Genre arrangement. Films (date, producer); Translations by Whiting;
Interviews; Periodical Contributions (dates; not complete, but
names periodicals for which Whiting wrote).

GENERAL

Adelman & Dworkin.

WICKHAM, ANNA   (1884-1947)

Millett; Longaker & Bolles; Daiches.

WIGHTMAN, RALPH   (1901-   )

WW 71.

WILDE, OSCAR FINGAL O'FLAHERTIE WILLS   (1856-1900)

PRIMARY

Stuart Mason [pseudonym of Christopher Millard]. *Bibliography
of Oscar Wilde*. London: T. W. Laurie, 1914. Reprinted with
introduction by Timothy d'Arch Smith, London: Bertram Rota,
1967. [3 unnumbered leaves], xxxix, 605.

Primary bibliography, arranged: Periodical contributions listed under title of periodical; books; collected editions; pirated
editions; selections. Transcribed TP, full collation, bibliographical and textual notes. Information is not consistently
given, but this is the single most important source of bibliographical information. It incorporates much of the information
in Stuart Mason. *A Bibliography of the Poems of Oscar
Wilde*. London: E. Grant Richards, 1907. Pp. [xii], 148.
475 copies, although this volume is still valuable for its account of textual variants. Mason is the standard bibliography
for Wilde up to 1914.

Owen Dudley Evans, *Book Collector* 16 (1967): 530-534: lists
errors in this unchanged reprint of the 1914 edition, pointing
out that it is not to be used without the cautions he has put
forward; "a totally new bibliography is overdue."

Robert Ernest Cowan, William Andrews Clark, Jr., Cora Edger-
ton Sanders, Harrison Post. *The Library of William Andrews
Clark, Jr. Wilde and Wildeiana*. San Francisco: John Henry
Nash, 1922-1931. 5 volumes. 100 copies of each, privately
circulated.

Primary and secondary bibliography. Generally genre arrangement, with exceptions. Description of unique copies in the
Clarke collection. Transcribed TP, binding, pagination, full
collation, date, extensive historical, bibliographical and
textual notes. Includes translations of Wilde. Annotations.
Exclusively secondary bibliographies are found in I (1922):
67-93; II (1922): 85-99; III (1924): 107-144; V (1931): 39-112.
Other secondary references, *passim*.

Although Mason (1914) is the presiding genius, this catalogue
of an important collection (since 1934 in the Clark Memorial
Library, Los Angeles) supplements and corrects Mason; it contains numerous indices; and it should be used in conjunction
with Mason.

John Charles Finzi. *Oscar Wilde and his Literary Circle. A
Catalogue of manuscripts and letters in the William Andrews
Clark Memorial Library*. Berkeley: University of California
Press, 1957. Pp. [xviii]; unnumbered pages containing

reproductions of 2892 file cards; indices on pp. xix-xxxiv.

Preface, pp. [vii-viii], describes the unique collection, including sections of it not herein catalogued. Cards arranged alphabetically by writer of manuscript or letter: each gives brief physical description, place of publication if published, and Clark pressmark. No details of contents of manuscripts.

James Laver. *Oscar Wilde*. London: Longmans, Green and Co. (WTW 53, revised edition), 1963. Pp. 32.

Pp. 27-30, primary books. Chronologically arranged. Genre, date. Pp. 30-32, secondary books and periodical articles. Chronologically arranged. Author, title, date.

The student who wants only a list of the primary titles may find Laver easier to use than the preceding works, while the secondary bibliography in Laver is particularly complete within its limits.

SECONDARY

Above, Mason, pp. 565-582, and *passim;* Cowan (as noted above); Laver, pp. 30-32. Many of the books described in these lists (as well as those named below) themselves contain secondary bibliographies which should be consulted.

Peter Funke. *Oscar Wilde in Selbstzeugnissen und Bilddokumenten.* Hamburg: Rowohlt Taschenbuch Verlag (Rowohlt Monographien Series), 1969. Pp. [186].

Pp. 177-[186], secondary bibliography by Helmut Riege. Books and periodicals, including many Continental writings.

Karl Beckson, ed. *Oscar Wilde. The Critical Heritage.* London: Routledge and Kegan Paul, 1970. Pp. xiv, 434.

Chronological list (1881-1927) of secondary criticism with extensive quotations and bibliographical annotations; additional references are given in Introduction, pp. 1-32, *passim.*

GENERAL

Longaker & Bolles; Coleman & Tyler; Adelman & Dworkin;
Salem; Palmer & Dyson; NCBEL, III, 1182-1188.

WILDSMITH, BRIAN LAWRENCE   (1930-   )

WW 71.

WILKINSON, LOUIS UMFREVILLE: see MARLOW, LOUIS.

WILLEY, BASIL   (1897-   )

PRIMARY

Hugh Sykes Davies and George Watson, eds. *The English
Mind. Studies in the English Moralists Presented to Basil
Willey.* Cambridge: Cambridge University Press, 1964. Pp.
302.

Pp. 1-6, "Basil Willey, A Tribute," by Herbert Butterfield.
No bibliography, but many references to primary writings.

GENERAL

Daiches; WW 71.

WILLIAMS, CHARLES WALTER STANSBY   (1886-1945)

PRIMARY

John Heath-Stubbs. *Charles Williams.* London: Longmans,
Green and Co. (WTW 63), 1955. Pp. 44.

Pp. 40-44, "Bibliography" by Linden Huddlestone. Primary,
secondary selected. Genre and subject arrangement. Books:
date, publisher. Periods: dates.

Charles Williams. *The Image of the City and Other Essays.* Selected by Anne Ridler with a Critical Introduction. London: Oxford University Press, 1958. Pp. lxxii, [200].

Pp. 196-199, bibliography. Primary selected. Genre and form arrangement. Books: publisher, date. Periods: date. Annotations here and in the Critical Introduction suggest the limitations of this bibliography.

Dawson (below), p. 100: "the best easily available bibliography."

Lawrence R. Dawson, Jr. "Checklist of Reviews by Charles Williams." *Papers of the Bibliographical Society of America* 55 (1961): 100-117.

Pp. 100-112, reviews by Williams, chronologically arranged. Periods: volume, pages, date; title and author of book reviewed. P. 112, index of periodicals; pp. 113-117, index of authors reviewed.

SECONDARY

Above, Heath-Stubbs.

GENERAL

Daiches; Temple & Tucker; Coleman & Tyler.

WILLIAMS, EMLYN   (1905-   )

Longaker & Bolles; Temple & Tucker; Coleman & Tyler; Adelman & Dworkin; Salem; Palmer & Dyson; WW 71.

WILLIAMS, ERIC   (1911-   )

WW 71; Hagen.

WILLIAMS, SIR HAROLD HERBERT   (1880-1964)

PRIMARY

Geoffrey Tillotson. "Harold Herbert Williams, 1880-1964."
Proceedings of the British Academy 51 (1965): 455-466.

An obituary notice mentioning many of the primary writings.

GENERAL

WW 64.

WILLIAMS, ORLANDO [ORLO] CYPRIAN   (1883-1967)

WW 66.

WILLIAMS, RAYMOND HENRY   (1921-   )

Temple & Tucker; WW 71.

WILLIAMSON, HENRY   (1895-   )

PRIMARY

I. Waveney Girvan. *A Bibliography and a Critical Survey of
the Works of Henry Williamson.* Chipping Campden, Glos.:
Alcuin Press, 1931. Pp. 56. 420 copies.

Pp. 17-56, primary books. Chronological arrangement.
Transcribed TP, part collation, pagination, binding, date,
price, number of copies in limited editions, contents, extensive textual notes.

Book Collector's Quarterly, No. 5 (March, 1932), p. 111:
"the bibliographer...has made the most (in two senses of the
word) of Mr. Williamson's not very extensive output."

GENERAL

Millett; Longaker & Bolles; Temple & Tucker; WW 71.

WIL

WILLIAMSON, HUGH ROSS (1901-   )

Temple & Tucker; WW 71; Hagen.

WILLIS, ANTHONY ARMSTRONG (1897-   )

WW 71; Hagen.

WILSON, ANGUS FRANK JOHNSTONE (1913-   )

PRIMARY

Jay L. Halio. *Angus Wilson*. Edinburgh: Oliver and Boyd (Writers and Critics Series), 1964. Pp. [viii], 120.

Pp. 117-120, bibliography. Primary selected, secondary selected. Genre arrangement. Books: place, publisher, date (English editions only). Periods: volume, date, pages. Includes selected periodical contributions by Wilson, 1951-1963.

K. W. Gransden. *Angus Wilson*. London: Longmans, Green and Co. (WW 208), 1969. Pp. 31.

P. 31, "A Select Bibliography." Primary books, 1949-1967, plus four primary periodical contributions. Date, place, genre. Three secondary items from periodicals: volume, date.

While Halio and Gransden provide lists of book titles to 1967, there is no complete record of Wilson's extensive journalism or of his periodical contributions.

SECONDARY

Above, Halio and Gransden.

GENERAL

Daiches; Temple & Tucker; WW 71.

WILSON, COLIN   (1931-   )

PRIMARY

R. H. W. Dillard, "Books by Colin Wilson," *Hollins Critic*
4 (October, 1967): 6-7.

Primary books, all English-language editions. Chronological
arrangement. Place, publisher, date, price; gives English
and American titles.

GENERAL

Temple & Tucker; WW 71; Hagen.

WILSON, JOHN BURGESS: see BURGESS, ANTHONY.

WILSON, JOHN DOVER   (1881-1969)

PRIMARY

[John Butt and J. C. Maxwell], *A List of his Published Writings, Presented to John Dover Wilson.* Cambridge: Cambridge
University Press, 1961. Pp. 31. Reprinted "With Later Additions by the Author" in John Dover Wilson, *Milestones on
the Dover Road.* London: Faber and Faber, 1969. Pp. 320.

Pp. 290-309, primary bibliography. Chronological arrangement within topical divisions. Books: publisher, date,
place. Periods: volume and pages, or date. Reviews by
Wilson include author and title of book reviewed. Descriptive annotations.

GENERAL
Daiches.

WILSON, ROMER

Pseudonym of Flora Roma Muir Wilson.   (1891-1930)
Millett.

WILSON, SANDY   (1924-   )

  WW 71.

WINCH, JOHN: see LONG, MRS. GABRIELLE.

WINGFIELD-STRATFORD, ESMÉ CECIL   (1882-   )

  WW 71.

WINTER, KEITH   (1906-   )

  Salem; WW 71.

WISE, THOMAS JAMES   (1859-1937)

PRIMARY

Wilfred Partington. *Thomas James Wise in the Original Cloth.
The Life and Record of the Forger of the Nineteenth-Century
Pamphlets*. London: Robert Hale, Ltd., 1946. Pp. 372.

  Pp. 323-346, bibliography. Primary. Form and genre arrangement. Part collation, date, number of copies. Bibliographical notes. Includes identification of the Wise forgeries.

  Easier to use than Todd (below), but less complete.

William B. Todd, ed. *Thomas James Wise. Centenary Studies*.
Austin: University of Texas Press, 1959. Pp. [x], [129].

  Pp. 80-122, William B. Todd, "A Handlist of Thomas James
  Wise." Primary. Arranged alphabetically by author of the

works edited, printed, or listed by Wise. Place, publisher, date, number of copies. Extensive bibliographical notes; numerous statistical tables and other information; also references to all previous bibliographical studies of Wise.

A difficult-to-use gathering of all the available information.

G. E. Haslam, ed. *Wise After the Event: A Catalogue of Books, Pamphlets, Manuscripts and Letters Relating to T. J. Wise Displayed in an Exhibition in Manchester Central Library, September, 1964.* Manchester: Manchester Libraries Committee, 1964. Pp. xii, 86.

Not seen.

SECONDARY

Above, Todd and Haslam.

WODEHOUSE, PELHAM GREVILLE (1881-   )

PRIMARY

Richard J. Voorhees. *P. G. Wodehouse.* New York: Twayne Publishers, Inc. (TEAS 44), 1966. Pp. 205.

Pp. 191-197, bibliography. Primary books, secondary selected (10 items). Books: place, publisher, date. Periodicals: volume, pages, dates. Secondary items annotated.

Robert Butler Digby French. *P. G. Wodehouse.* Edinburgh and London: Oliver and Boyd (Writers and Critics Series), 1966. Pp. [viii] , 120.

Pp. 118-120, bibliography. Primary books, secondary selected (10 items). Genre arrangement. Books: place, date. Periods: date.

David A. Jasen. *A Bibliography and Reader's Guide to the First Editions of P. G. Wodehouse.* Hamden, Connecticut: Archon Books, 1970. Pp. [x] , 290.

Primary books. Chronological arrangement. Date, place, publisher, pages, binding, and contents for both British and American first editions. Also list of places and of characters with descriptions for each title. Various indices, including one of publishers of the primary books.

The most complete list of primary books, 1901-1970.

[NB. At the time of his death, John Hayward was compiling a bibliography of Wodehouse. His papers on this project are now at King's College Cambridge.]

SECONDARY

Above, Voorhees, and French.

GENERAL

Daiches; Temple & Tucker; WW 71.

WODEN, GEORGE: see SLANEY, GEORGE WILSON.

WOLFE, HUMBERT   (1885-1940)

Millett; Daiches; Temple & Tucker.

WOODCOCK, GEORGE   (1912-   )

Temple & Tucker.

WOODHOUSE, HON. CHRISTOPHER MONTAGUE   (1917-   )

Temple & Tucker; WW 71.

WOODS, MARGARET LOUISA BRADLEY   (1856-1945)

(Mrs. H. G. Woods).

NCBEL, III, 1083.

WOOLF, LEONARD SIDNEY   (1880-1969)

PRIMARY

There is no bibliography of primary writings, but Woolf refers
to many of his journalistic and other writings and all of his
books in his autobiographies, published in London by the
Hogarth Press, and in New York by Harcourt, Brace, Inc.

Sowing: An Autobiography of the Years 1880-1904. 1960.
Pp. 206. Growing: An Autobiography of the Years 1904-1911.
1961. Pp. 256. Beginning Again: An Autobiography of the
Years 1911-1918. 1963. Pp. 263. Downhill All the Way: An
Autobiography of the Years 1919-1939. 1967. Pp. 259. The
Journey Not the Arrival Matters: An Autobiography of the
Years 1939-1969. 1969. Pp. 217.

GENERAL

Millett; Daiches; Temple & Tucker; WW 69.

WOOLF, VIRGINIA STEPHEN   (1882-1941)

(Mrs. Leonard Sidney Woolf).

PRIMARY

Brownlee Jean Kirkpatrick. A Bibliography of Virginia Woolf.
London: Rupert Hart-Davis (Soho Bibliography 9, Revised
Edition), 1967. Pp. xii, 212.

Primary. Arrangement: Books and Pamphlets; Contributions
to Books and Translations by Woolf; Contributions to Periodicals and Newspapers by Woolf; Translations of Woolf; Foreign Editions of Woolf; Books and Articles containing letters
by Woolf; MSS and Autograph letters; Index. First editions
of books: transcribed TP, part collation, pagination, binding,
date, number of copies, price, contents, bibliographical notes ;

reprints and later editions (information about these editions is less complete). Periods: date, pages. Reviews by Woolf include title and author of book reviewed. Includes unsigned pieces and information about reprinting of periodical contributions.

The authoritative bibliography.

SECONDARY

Maurice Beebe. "Criticism of Virginia Woolf: A Selected Check-list with an Index to Studies of Separate Works." *Modern Fiction Studies* 2 (February, 1956): 36-45.

General criticism listed alphabetically by author. Studies of specific titles listed under those titles.

The beginning point for study of the criticism of Woolf.

Jean Guiget. *Virginia Woolf and Her Works*, translated by Jean Stewart. London: Hogarth Press, 1965. Pp. 488.

Pp. 466-482, secondary bibliography, arranged: Books on Woolf; Articles on Woolf; General studies.

This bibliography is more complete and more accurate than that in the original French edition (Paris: Didier, 1962).

GENERAL

Millett; Daiches; Longaker & Bolles; Temple & Tucker.

WRIGHT, SIR ALMROTH EDWARD   (1861-1947)

PRIMARY

Leonard Colebrook. *Bibliography of the Published Writings of Sir Almroth E. Wright*. London: William Heinemann, 1952.

Not seen.

GENERAL

WWW 41-50.

WRIGHT, JUDITH   (1915-   )

(Mrs. J. P. McKinney).

PRIMARY

Patricia A. O'Brien. *Bibliography of Judith Wright*. Adelaide: Libraries Board of South Australia (Bibliographies of Austalian Writers), 1968.

Not seen.

GENERAL

WW 71.

YATES, DORNFORD   (1885-1960)

Pseudonym of Major Cecil William Mercer.

PRIMARY

Richard Usborne. *Clubland Heroes*. London: Constable, 1953. Pp. 217.

Although there is no bibliography, details of the primary writings can be gathered from pp. 21-79.

GENERAL

WWW 51-60; Hagen.

YEATS, JACK BUTLER   (1871-1957)

PRIMARY

E. MacC [arvill]. "Jack B. Yeats. His Books." *Dublin Magazine* NS 20 (July-September, 1945): 47-52.

Primary books and broadsheets, 1901-1944, written and illustrated by Yeats. Chronological arrangement. Transcribed TP, full collation, pagination, illustrations, binding, notes.

Hilary Pyle. *Jack B. Yeats. A Biography.* London: Routledge and Kegan Paul, 1970. Pp. xii, 228.

Pp. [175]-180, primary bibliography. Arranged: Books written and illustrated by Yeats; Contributions to periodicals; Books illustrated by Yeats; Magazine articles and stories illustrated by Yeats; Prints for Cuala Press. Books: place, publisher, date. Periods: date. Pp. 181-185, secondary bibliography. Pp. 187-201: portraits by Yeats; public collections of his works; his contributions to illustrated papers. Pp. 203-219, chronological list of Yeats' exhibitions.

An all-inclusive list without bibliographical details.

GENERAL

WWW 51-60.

YEATS, WILLIAM BUTLER (1865-1939)

PRIMARY

Allan Wade. *A Bibliography of the Writings of W. B. Yeats.* London: Rupert Hart-Davis (Soho Bibliographies No. 1, Third Edition, Revised and Edited by Russell K. Alspach), 1968. Pp. 514.

Primary, secondary books. Form arrangement. Books: transcribed TP, part collation, pagination, binding, date, contents including details of earlier publication, limitations of edition, bibliographical and textual notes. Complete descriptions of later editions follow that of the first edition. Periods: date, brief bibliographical note includes titles of volumes in which later collected; reviews by Yeats include author and title of book reviewed. Translations of Yeats listed separately. Appendices include: pp. 451-457, list of books published by the Cuala (previously Dun Emer) Press, 1903-1938; pp. 458-466, short-title list of books about Yeats; pp. 467-477, details and descriptions of radio broadcasts by Yeats (by George Whalley). Pp. 479-514, Index.

The definitive primary bibliography. See pp. 9-10 for descriptions of earlier bibliographies, and pp. 9-15 for the history of this volume.

SECONDARY

Above, Wade-Alspach, pp. 458-466.

Alice Thurston McGirr. "Reading List on William Butler Yeats." *Bulletin of Bibliography* 7 (1913): 82-83.

Valuable list of early reviews arranged under title of book reviewed. Annotated; other information.

(The following entries are cumulative: that is, items listed in these entries themselves include extensive secondary bibliographies).

George B. Saul. "Thread to a Labyrinth: A Selective Bibliography in Yeats." *Bulletin of the New York Public Library* 58 (1954): 344-347.

A severely restricted list of books selected for their "helpfulness."

-- *Prolegomena to the Study of Yeats's Poems*. Philadelphia: University of Pennsylvania Press, 1957. Pp. 196. *Prolegomena to the Study of Yeats's Plays*. Philadelphia: University of Pennsylvania Press, 1958. Both reprinted, 1971.

Particularly useful because the critical writings are listed under the title of the Yeats work being studied.

Hazard Adams. "Yeats Scholarship and Criticism: A Review of

425

Research.'' *Texas Studies in Literature and Language* 3 (Winter, 1962): 439-451.

An important essay-survey, with subject headings, of primary material and of secondary writings.

K. G. W. Cross. ''The Fascination of What's Difficult: A Survey of Yeats Criticism and Research'' in *In Excited Reverie: A Centenary Tribute to William Butler Yeats, 1865-1939*, ed. by A. Norman Jeffares and K. G. W. Cross. New York; London: Macmillan Co., 1965. Pp. viii, [354].

Pp. 315-337, an essay on the history of Yeats scholarship.

K. P. S. Jochum. *W. B. Yeats's Plays. An Annotated Check-list of Criticism*. Saarbrücken: Anglistisches Institut der Universitat des Saarlandes, 1966. Pp. 180.

Subject arrangement, including on pp. 35-38, bibliographies, reviews of research and concordances, and on pp. 113-156, chronological list of the plays, with criticism arranged under the appropriate title. Pp. 161-180, Index.

John E. Stoll. *The Great Deluge: A Yeats Bibliography*. Troy, New York: Whitston Publishing Co., 1971. Pp. ii, 100.

Not seen. Described as containing approximately 1000 titles of works by and about Yeats, arranged under subject headings.

[Announced for publication in 1971: K. G. W. Cross and R. T. Dunlop. *A Bibliography of Yeats Criticism, 1887-1965*. London: Macmillan.]

GENERAL

Millett; Longaker & Bolles; Temple & Tucker; Coleman & Tyler; Adelman & Dworkin; Salem; Palmer & Dyson; NCBEL, III, 1915-1934.

YORKE, HENRY: see GREEN, HENRY.

YOUNG, ANDREW JOHN   (1885-   )

PRIMARY

Andrew Young. _Collected Poems_. London: Rupert Hart-Davis, 1960. Pp. 219.

Pp. 13-22, bibliographical essay by Leonard Clark. Titles, publisher, date; complete information about contents and many references to textual changes between editions.

Leonard Clark. _Andrew Young_. London: Longmans, Green and Co., Ltd. (WTW 166), 1964. Pp. 43.

Pp. 25-26, primary books. Place, date, genre.

GENERAL

Daiches; WW 71.

YOUNG, CHARLES KENNETH   (1916-   )

WW 71.

YOUNG, DOUGLAS   (1913-   )

Daiches.

YOUNG, EMILY HILDA   (1880-1949)

(Mrs. J. A. H. Daniell).

Millett; WWW 41-50.

YOUNG, FRANCIS ERIC BRETT   (1884-1954)

PRIMARY

Jessica Brett Young. *Francis Brett Young, A Biography*. London: Heinemann, 1962. Pp. 360.

No bibliography, but details concerning almost all the novels and references to much of the secondary criticism are given in the text, *passim*. Indexed, with titles of primary novels italicized.

SECONDARY

Above, Young.

GENERAL

Millett; Longaker & Bolles; Temple & Tucker; WWW 51-60; Hagen.

YOUNG, GEORGE MALCOLM   (1882-1959)

Daiches; Temple & Tucker.

YOUNG, WAYLAND, LORD KENNET   (1923-   )

WW 71.

ZANGWILL, ISRAEL   (1864-1926)

PRIMARY

Annamarie Peterson. "Israel Zangwill (1864-1926): A Selected Bibliography." *Bulletin of Bibliography* 23 (1961): 136-140.

Primary selected. Form arrangement, principal divisions being Books and pamphlets; Published writings apparently not gathered into Zangwill's books; Unpublished plays. Books: place, publisher, date, British and American editions but no translations. Miscellaneous notes. Periods: volume, pages, date, genre, occasional notes. Important introductory note concerning Zangwill's periodical contributions.

A very comprehensive checklist.

Maurice Wohlgelernter. *Israel Zangwill A Study*. New York: Columbia University Press, 1964. Pp. 344.

Pp. 321-334, primary selected, secondary selected bibliography. Form arrangement. Books: place, publisher, date, translations. Periods: volume, pages, date.

Although a checklist of only the works referred to in the text, it gives additions to Peterson.

SECONDARY

Above, Wohlgelernter, pp. 327-334.

Elsie B. Adams. "Israel Zangwill: An Annotated Bibliography of Writings about Him." *English Literature in Transition* 13 (1970): 209-244.

Secondary selected. Books: place, publisher, date. Periods: volume, pages, date. Complete annotations for each entry.

The beginning point for study of the criticism of Zangwill.

GENERAL

NCBEL, III, 1084; Hagen.

INDEX OF NAMES

excluding

the names of principal entries and the
names of authors of the general bibliographies listed on pp. viii-xi.